DATE DUE

FROM SLAVE TO STATE LEGISLATOR

FROM SLAVE TO STATE LEGISLATOR

JOHN W. E. THOMAS, ILLINOIS' FIRST AFRICAN AMERICAN LAWMAKER

DAVID A. JOENS

Southern Illinois University Press
Carbondale and Edwardsville

Frontispiece: The earliest known photograph of John
W. E. Thomas, taken in 1877 in Springfield during his first
term as a state representative. Courtesy of Virginia State
University Archives, Luther P. Jackson Papers, box 75.

Library of Congress Cataloging-in-Publication Data
Joens, David A., 1961–
From slave to state legislator : John W. E. Thomas, Illinois'
first African American lawmaker / David A. Joens.
    p. cm.
Includes bibliographical references and index.
ISBN-13: 978-0-8093-3058-4 (cloth : alk. paper)
ISBN-10: 0-8093-3058-X (cloth : alk. paper)
ISBN-13: 978-0-8093-3060-7 (ebook)
ISBN-10: 0-8093-3060-1 (ebook)
1. Thomas, John W. E. (John William Edinburgh),
1847–1899. 2. African American legislators—Illinois—
Biography. 3. Legislators—Illinois—Biography.
4. Illinois—Politics and government—1865–1950.
5. Illinois—Race relations—History—19th century.
I. Title.
F546.T45J64 2012
328.73'092—dc23
[B]   2011017313

To my wife, Mona, and my son, Benjamin.
Without their patience, understanding, and
support, this would never have been done.

Contents

Acknowledgments

No one can write a book such as this without the help and assistance of many people. Generous historians hear of such a project and kindly offer their expertise or, when contacted, give it freely. Certainly librarians and special collections curators have been essential to this project by giving their time and sharing their knowledge. Friends offered moral support and encouragement. Even strangers came to me at times to offer their help and advice.

In thanking those who assisted me in my efforts, I would like to start with Cheryl Pence, Jennifer Ericson, Jan Perone, Debbie Hamm, and Debbie Ross of the Abraham Lincoln Presidential Library Newspaper Microfilm Collection. Their assistance, starting from the times when they made newspaper copies for me in the basement of the Old State Capitol and extending to the many hurried lunch hours I spent conducting research in their brightly lit new facility, will always be appreciated. The help of Jane Ehrenhart, Mary Michals, Gwen Podeschi, Cheryl Schnirring, and Kathryn Harris, also of the Abraham Lincoln Presidential Library, was also important. John Reinhardt, Elaine Evans, Barb Heflin, and the staff at the Illinois State Archives provided their always friendly and courteous service. Other institutions that provided great assistance include the Chicago History Museum, the Richard J. Daley Library at the University of Illinois at Chicago, the Archives of the Clerk of the Circuit Court of Cook County, the Newberry Library, the Vivian G. Harsh Research Collection at the Carter G. Woodson Library in Chicago, the Kiplinger Research Library of the Historical Society of Washington, D.C., the Library of Congress, the Illinois State Library, and the Grand Rapids, Michigan, Public Library.

Several persons came out of the blue to offer their help. These include John McMuir, Bob Cavanaugh, Lisa Oppenheim, Steve Dyer, Jim Donelan, Roger Bridges, and Christopher Reed. Members of the Thomas family itself who helped me include Celeste Holmes, Jackie Rhodes, Roma Stewart Jones, and Asa Hilliard III. Phil Blackman, an honorary member of the family, also helped.

Friends who helped me get started in this project or who offered advice and encouragement include Lisa Guinan, who taught me about genealogical work, Jack Van Der Slik, Wayne C. Temple, Mark Sorensen, Alice Palmer, Becky Gibson, Jeff Stauter, and State Senator Margaret Smith, No list of friends, however, would be complete without mentioning my best friend, my wife Mona, whose support I received throughout this project.

This book never would have happened without Randy Witter and Bruce Kinnett from Cook-Witter, Inc. It was while writing for their newsletter that I first became interested in this topic. Deborah McGregor, Robert McGregor, and Hugh Harris from the University of Illinois at Springfield helped me refine my topic. I owe a large debt of gratitude to my dissertation committee at Southern Illinois University, especially chairman Michael Batinski, as well as Kay Carr, Peter Argersinger, Pamela Smoot, and Charles Fanning, for their insightful critiques of my research.

I would be remiss if I didn't mention my friend and adviser John Y. Simon, who passed away before this project could be finished. His thoughtful advice made this book possible and made every three-hour drive to meet with him worthwhile. I miss him greatly.

Finally, I would like to thank Karl Kageff and everyone at SIU Press who worked on bringing this book to publication. Their professionalism and expertise has been greatly appreciated. After all the help I received in this project, any mistakes or omissions are, of course, solely my own. It is hoped, however, that this study will assist others in researching the African American community in post–Civil War Chicago and finding new information that will help bring a more complete picture of this era to the public.

Chronology: John William Edinburgh Thomas

1847   Born a slave in Alabama. His father was a free black man and his mother was a slave.

1847–65   Owned by Dr. L. A. McCleskey, who provides him with a good education.

1864   Marries Maria Reynolds.

1869   Daughter Hester is born. Moves to Chicago. Opens a school for African Americans and a grocery.

1874   Home burns down in the fire of 1874.

1876   Elected state representative from the Second Legislative District.

1877   Serves in legislature.

1878   Wife Maria dies. Fails to be renominated for the legislature.

1880   Passes bar. Marries Justine Latcher. Loses nomination for the legislature.

1881   Moves to Washington, D.C., and works for the Treasury Department. Daughter Blanche is born.

1882   Moves back to Chicago. Elected to a second term in the Illinois House. Blanche dies.

1883   Serves in legislature. Wife Justine and infant daughter die. Chairs state colored convention.

1884   Reelected to Illinois House. Loses bid for delegate to the GOP National Convention.

1885   Serves in legislature. Passes state's first civil rights bill. Chairs state colored convention.

1886   Fails to be renominated for the legislature.

1887   Elected South Town clerk. Marries Crittie Marshall.

1888   Loses bid for county board nomination. Daughter Ethel born.

1890   Loses bid for state senate nomination. Attends founding of the
        Afro-American League. Daughter Martha born and dies at age
        six months.

1891   Son John W. E. born.

1892   Becomes the first African American in Illinois selected to run as
        a presidential elector. Son John W. E. dies. Son Joseph born.

1893   Moves to 3308 S. Indiana.

1894   Son Logan born.

1898   Birth of his daughter Grace.

1899   Dies December 18. Thought to be the wealthiest African Ameri-
        can in Chicago at the time.

FROM SLAVE TO STATE LEGISLATOR

Introduction: "A Representative of Its Colored Citizens"

Tuesday, January 3, 1877, was a historic day in the Illinois General Assembly. At exactly 12:15 P.M., fifteen minutes after its scheduled start, the Thirtieth Session of the House of Representatives convened for the first time.[1] This marked the first gathering of the legislature in the new state capitol, which would not be completely finished for another nine years. The next day, after being elected Speaker of the House, Irish-born representative James Shaw (R-Mt. Carroll) noted the occasion in his acceptance speech. "It is the first time the General Assembly ever convened in this grand and noble State House—a structure so magnificent that he who walks its pillared halls and gazes upon its granite and marbled stairways, must feel himself lifted into a broader appreciation of our loved Prairie State, and the great resources garnered from its rich and virgin soil."[2]

The gathering was also historic for another reason. Numbered among the 153 legislators was Republican John William Edinburgh Thomas of the Second Legislative District in Chicago—the first African American to serve in the Illinois legislature. Speaker Shaw, in his opening speech, noted the significance of Thomas's presence in the chamber: "It is the first General Assembly in all the legislative history of the State in which a representative of its colored citizens ever took his seat among honorable colleagues and associates."[3]

Both the building of the new capitol and the election of Thomas were significant events that marked the end of one era and the beginning of another. With sectionalism and the divisive issue of slavery past, the young nation was entering the Industrial Age. Illinois was a settled state and soon to become a leader in the nation's transportation, livestock, manufacturing, coal, and agriculture industries and the home to its largest inland city.[4] The new capitol in Springfield served as a symbol of the state's growth, prosperity, and confidence in the future.[5]

The participation of Thomas in the legislature also signified a new era. The Civil War that ended in 1865 had abolished slavery in the South. While Illinois had been a "free" state before the war, its infamous Black Laws during the antebellum period severely restricted the freedoms of African Americans. These laws, the first of which was passed just after Illinois became a state in 1818, became null and void in 1865. Yet African Americans were not given the right to vote in Illinois until 1870, with the passage of both the Fifteenth Amendment to the U.S. Constitution and the 1870 Illinois state constitution. The career of John W. E. Thomas reflects the first steps of a distinct ethnic community that no longer fought for emancipation, suffrage, and equality but rather collaborated and competed with other interest groups in the political, social, and economic spheres.[6]

If Thomas's career had ended with his being the first African American in the Illinois legislature, his life would be worth examining only as a footnote in Illinois history. However, Thomas's life and career were much more than that. For almost two decades, he was the recognized leader of the state's African American community, and his actions showed a commitment to improving that community worth remembering. Perhaps just as important, his life exemplifies the way that many newly freed African Americans who migrated North immediately took advantage of the opportunities presented them.

Born a slave in Alabama in the 1840s, Thomas moved to Chicago around 1869, at a time when African Americans accounted for less than 1.5 percent of that city's total population. From the time of his move to Chicago until his death in 1899, he served as a political leader of the city's often divided African American community. In an era when African Americans did not have the numbers to secure their fair share of the political pie and when ethnic considerations often determined the candidates for office, Thomas was able, through example and hard work, to ensure that African Americans were able to compete with other ethnic groups and had a voice in the legislature to defend their new rights.

Thomas served three terms in the Illinois legislature and succeeded in passing the state's first civil rights bill. While at times he was hampered as much by the schisms within the African American community as he was by racial discrimination from the white community, he continually pushed the limits of African American progress in the political arena. In doing so, he laid the groundwork for future African American leaders to succeed in Chicago's local politics. When the Great Migration during the 1910s and 1920s greatly increased its numbers, the African American community already had in place a political tradition and leadership that could trace its roots directly to Thomas.[7]

Thomas's life serves as an example of the opportunities afforded some African Americans in Chicago in the post–Civil War era. As the slave of a doctor's family in Mobile, Alabama, Thomas received a good education. After Emancipation, he went to Chicago, where he opened a grocery store, founded a private school for African Americans, attended a small business college, participated in church activities, and entered politics. He later became an attorney, real estate investor, and one of the wealthiest African Americans in the city. Despite his accomplishments, Thomas's life also demonstrates the limits that constrained African Americans. As historians St. Clair Drake and Horace R. Cayton note, "the badge of color marked [African Americans] as socially different. Also, the fact that no Negroes rose to the highest positions in the commercial and public life of early Chicago suggests that in a vague but nevertheless decisive sense they were thought of as having a subordinate place."[8]

This was clearly seen in the political sphere. African Americans were largely loyal Republicans after the Civil War, and the white Republican Party leaders often saw this loyalty less as an ideological decision than as a debt owed to the party that freed the slaves. This view often affected the way many whites perceived African Americans' demands and, at times, meant a relationship that was more paternalistic and patronizing than egalitarian. Such a situation was frustrating to African American political leaders in Chicago and the North, especially when combined with their lack of power due to their small number. The ideological issue for many African Americans in the North during Thomas's lifetime was whether or not to remain loyal to the Republican Party. On this issue, Thomas was committed to staying within the party.

African Americans' economic and political success also did not translate into elevation into the upper echelons of Chicago's social circles. The elite clubs in Chicago, such as the Hamilton, Marquette, and Union League, all excluded African Americans. Although Lloyd G. Wheeler became the first African American lawyer in Chicago in 1869 and Thomas entered the law profession in 1880, African Americans were not allowed to join the Chicago Bar Association until 1944.[9] When major nonpolitical events occurred in the city, such as the 1893 World's Fair or the 1899 Chicago Day celebration, African Americans were not involved in the planning of these events.

In response, the African American community, like other ethnic groups in the city, formed its own social subculture. African American attorneys formed the separate Cook County Bar Association in 1914.[10] African American elites formed the Prudence Crandall Study Club, and African American women founded the Ida B. Wells Woman's Club. African

Americans formed their own chapters of Masons and Knights of Pythias. And, of course, there were always the African American churches that, since before the Civil War, had, as historian St. Clair Drake has written, helped give African Americans a sense of "place" in society and served as the mechanism by which they could change their "place." Thomas was a major player in working with or helping develop these separate institutions. In 1898, for example, he founded the Sumner Club for African Americans, a social and political equivalent to the Hamilton Club.[11]

Although certainly not rich, Thomas had enough money when he came to Chicago to quickly establish a home and business on the near South Side, where a majority of the city's African American population lived, and within four years of his arrival, he and four others founded a building and loan company, with Thomas investing the large sum of $700 in the company's initial $50,000 stock offering.[12] He remained in that near South Side neighborhood for most of his life, despite the fires in 1871 and 1874 that devastated the area, transforming it into a vice district known as "the levee" and driving many middle- and upper-class African Americans further south to "better" parts of the city. In 1880, Thomas received his law license, which became the basis for his later wealth. He worked as a police court lawyer, and most of his clients were petty offenders from "the levee." Although police court lawyers were frowned upon by many because of their clientele, Thomas made a good living in his law practice and as a bondsman, even if it caused him to be shunned by some in the African American community. When Thomas and his family did finally move, in 1893, they became one of the first African American families in a neighborhood that, thirty years later, would be the heart of an African American residential district known as the "black belt."[13]

Thomas would not live to see the African American migration of the World War I era and the transformation of the South Side into one of the largest African American neighborhoods in the country. By not being a part of that transformation, his name has largely been forgotten in Illinois history, for the migration and the resulting large-scale African American community has proven more fascinating to historians, political scientists, and sociologists than the immediate post–Civil War Chicago in which Thomas lived.[14]

Indeed, with the exception of John Jones, none of the leading African American politicians of Chicago in that era have had their biographies made.[15] Such biographies are difficult to write because sources are scarce. None of Chicago's African American leaders of the era, including Thomas, left behind their papers, letters, or other writings.[16] Although Chicago's first African American newspaper, the *Chicago Conservator*, began publishing in 1878, almost no copies of that paper or any other African American newspapers from Chicago or the rest of Illinois published before the late 1890s have been preserved. Copies of two African American weekly newspapers, the *Cleveland Gazette*, started in 1883, and the *St. Paul Western Appeal*, later the *Appeal*, started in 1885, do exist, and while neither paper was based in Chicago, both covered the city as part of their efforts to be national in scope.

Faced with these limited sources, I have relied on Chicago's many daily newspapers for information, despite the fact that their coverage of the African American community ranged from inconsistent at best to racist and discriminatory at worst. For the most part, journalists in the late nineteenth century did not receive bylines, and their articles reflected the biases and partisanships of their employers. For the purposes of this book, the opinions and views expressed in those "news" articles and editorials are cited as those of the newspaper in which they appeared. Official government documents also served as a major source of information. These documents included census records, birth, death, and marriage certificates, Illinois House and Senate Journals, bills and public acts from the Illinois General Assembly, the correspondence files of Illinois governors, court documents, and land records.

What historian Lawrence Grossman observed back in 1976, that the role of African Americans in Northern politics in the late nineteenth century has not been told, remains largely true today.[17] John W. E. Thomas is a prime example. He played an important role in the political history of the state of Illinois and the city of Chicago. He was the most successful Chicago African American politician of his time. He made sure that issues of concern to African Americans were addressed, and his crowning achievement, the passage of the 1885 Illinois Civil Rights Act, remains a testament to his legislative abilities and his political skills. This biography of Thomas is intended to raise awareness of African American politics and the African American community in post–Civil War Chicago.

[1]

"Let Us Come Out Like Men": The Historic Election of 1876

John W. E. Thomas came to Chicago as a young man around 1869 and, taking advantage of the opportunities afforded African Americans in the North in the immediate post–Civil War era, he became financially successful and socially prominent. Within eight years of arriving, he was a leading figure in the African American community and had demonstrated a commitment to helping that community. He also became active in politics and learned the nuts and bolts of big-city, ethnic-based politics that would enable him to lead the African American community politically for the next two decades.

The Early Years

Thomas was born a slave in Montgomery, Alabama, sometime in the 1840s. The official birth date listed on his gravestone is May 1, 1847, but he probably was born anywhere from two to five years before then.[1] Although his father, Edinboro (or "Edinburgh," as it was sometimes spelled) Thomas, was a free black man, his mother, Martha Morgan, was a slave. Little is known about how they met or when they were married, but apparently Edinboro was the steward of a steamboat when Thomas was born, and Martha was owned by Dr. and Mrs. Lawrence McCleskey.[2] A native of Virginia born around 1817, Edinboro Thomas ended up in Chicago in the late 1850s, where he worked as a waiter and bellboy at the Sherman House, one of the most prestigious hotels in the city. Martha Morgan was also from Virginia, born around 1828. It appears that Martha and Edinboro had just one child, John.[3]

There is not much information about either Edinboro or Martha Thomas. During the Civil War, Edinboro earned enough money to attempt to buy his son's freedom, but to no avail. Immediately after the war, in December 1865, he bought a home on Chicago's near South Side for $1,250.[4] That house, located at 198 Fourth Avenue, now Federal Street, eventually became the home that John Thomas lived in after moving to Chicago.

John Thomas appears to have been close to his parents, judging from the deed and the living arrangements of the house at 198 Fourth Avenue. Although John lived in the home from 1869 to 1881 and then for a few years after that, Edinboro legally owned it until right before his death, when he sold it to his son for one dollar. When the house burned down in 1874, it was Edinboro who borrowed the money to rebuild.[5]

John W. E. Thomas was raised in Mobile, Alabama, in the home of Dr. Lawrence A. McCleskey, and his wife Emily, who owned his mother.[6] According to the 1860 U.S. Census, McCleskey owned twelve slaves. Although no names are given in the slave schedule of the census, one of the twelve slaves is listed as a seventeen-year-old male mulatto, and that probably would have been John Thomas.[7] Despite his unenviable position as a slave, Thomas received a good education from the McCleskey family. One of Dr. McCleskey's sisters helped tutor Thomas, and he was allowed to go to school and to read books from Dr. McCleskey's office. Impressed with Thomas's abilities, the doctor sent him to collect fees and run other errands and lent him out to other doctors for similar purposes. Thomas also occupied his time by teaching other slaves. His 1876 campaign biography stated, "He used for two years, while in Mobile, as his school a horse stall. During the War he had about forty pupils and came near losing his eye-sight in teaching by lightwood knot fires." According to that biography, Thomas started teaching at the age of eight.[8]

In 1864, Thomas married Maria Reynolds, of Camden, South Carolina, who was a Native American from the Catawba tribe, according to Thomas's descendants. John and Maria Thomas had one child, a daughter named Heather, who in later years went by the name of Hester. The June 1870 census lists Hester as being one year old and her place of birth as South Carolina, meaning Thomas and his wife must have spent time there before migrating to Chicago.[9]

Sometime after the Civil War, Thomas visited his father in Chicago and, impressed with the bustling city, he moved his family there around 1869. The house at 198 Fourth Avenue was a three-story frame building located just south of the downtown area. Immediately upon their arrival, the family opened a grocery store on the first floor of the house. To the rear of the building was the entrance to the family rooms.[10]

The house was located in the Cheyenne district, which had a reputation as the worst part of an infamous area of Chicago known as "the levee." The levee was the city's main red-light district and featured saloons, gambling dens, prostitution, cockfights, and dog races.[11] It was so notorious that following the large fire in 1874 that destroyed several blocks of the levee, the *Chicago Tribune* unsympathetically wrote, "as things turned out, it was more of a blessing than a curse. It knocked the air out of the Cheyenne District—a place infested by human vagrants for the most part." An 1892 guide to Chicago revealed, "So desperate are many of 'Cheyenne's known characters that no policeman who patrols a beat in that locality is permitted to do so alone." In 1893, one Chicago policeman declared there was no place in the country that could compare with the levee in depravity.[12]

Despite its location in the levee area, the block Thomas lived on appears to have been a middle-class, integrated neighborhood of African Americans, whites, and immigrants. Most of the wives kept house and many took in boarders. The immigrants were usually from Austria or Germany. For the 1870 census, Thomas listed the value of the real estate that he owned as $5,000 and the value of his personal estate at $400, which made him the wealthiest resident of his street. Robert Gray, a mulatto who worked as a hotel waiter, listed his assets as $4,000 in real estate and $500 as the value of his personal estate. Lewis (Louis) White, another neighbor, was a rising African American political activist and ally of Thomas who worked as a clerk in the post office. He owned real estate valued at $3,000 and had a personal estate valued at $200. Other occupations listed on this middle-class neighborhood were grain inspector, shoemaker, store clerk, and retired grocer.[13]

In 1870, 22 percent of Chicago residents were property owners, and the median property value was $2,500, placing Thomas at double the median for the city. The Thomases lived in the Third Ward, which, along with the low-income levee, also included the wealthiest neighborhoods in the city near the lakefront. Because of the wealthy areas in the ward, the median land value for the ward was $10,000, twice the value of the Thomas home. However, only 12 percent of the residents of the Third Ward owned their own property, well below the city average.[14]

Located just across Fourth Avenue from the Thomas house was Olivet Baptist Church, perhaps the most influential African American church in the city. John Jones, the leading African American political activist in Chicago, had co-founded the church. The congregation had opened a new building in 1868, under the dynamic leadership of Reverend Richard DeBaptiste, a nationally known African American minister and civil rights leader. Thomas became a member of the church and a friend of DeBaptiste. From 1871 to 1873 and again in 1876, Thomas served as Olivet's clerk. In 1873, he served as Sunday school superintendent, and in 1884 he was elected to serve as one of Olivet's seven trustees.

Membership in Olivet helped Thomas politically because, like other churches, Olivet often served as an arena for political action in the African American community. Under the direction of Reverend DeBaptiste, the church would host many meetings important to Thomas's career.[15] Thomas's longtime friend and political ally William C. Phillips was very active in both the church and in local ward politics and helped Thomas get started in local politics. Through Reverend DeBaptiste, Thomas became active in the Wood River Baptist Association, an organization comprised of African American Baptist churches, mostly from Illinois. Thomas attended at least one of the association's annual meetings, where he served as an assistant clerk and as a member of the Temperance Committee. This helped provide Thomas with a network of acquaintances throughout the state, such as the Rev. L. A. Coleman, who Thomas would stay with while in Springfield as a legislator.[16]

Thomas pursued several other activities in Chicago. Shortly after arriving, he enrolled at Bryant and Chase's Business College, located at the corner of Clark and Washington Streets. Thomas also opened a private school for African Americans in his home while his wife Maria ran the grocery. In Chicago's city directories, Thomas's occupation was listed as a teacher and a grocer from various times between 1871 and 1880.[17] The *Inter-Ocean* described Thomas's teaching activities this way: "Mr. Thomas established the first school for colored people in Chicago being himself a teacher. The child and the gray-haired freedman, side by side, learned their letters in his home." The *Chronicle* stated that Thomas would teach African American children during the day and their fathers at night.[18]

The Great Chicago Fire on October 8, 1871, passed two blocks to the west and two blocks to the north of the city block that contained both Olivet and the Thomas home. The fire destroyed more than 18,000 buildings and 2,000 acres of the city.[19] Chicago rebuilt itself after the fire, and Thomas participated in the rebuilding process. A year after the fire, he helped form a building and loan company. Incorporated on December 5, 1872, the Cook County Building Loan and Homestead Association began with a $50,000 capital stock and a mandate to raise funds to be lent to its members for the purposes of building construction and purchasing and selling real estate. Shares cost $100 each.

The association operated out of Olivet Baptist Church and directed its business toward African Americans. Among the initial subscribers were John Jones, who purchased two shares of stock; Reverend DeBaptiste, who bought three shares; and W. C. Phillips, who purchased two shares. Thomas purchased five shares of stock in his name and an additional two shares of stock in his daughter Hester's name. Thomas also was elected as one of the original members of the board of directors, as were all five of the corporation's founders. The corporation lasted until 1903.[20]

Three years after the 1871 Great Chicago Fire, another large fire burned through Chicago. The area affected was south of the area burned by the 1871 fire, although there was some overlap. This fire burned down 18 city blocks (47 acres) on the near South Side. Approximately 812 structures were burned, including the Thomas home and Olivet Baptist Church.[21] Thomas rebuilt his home on the same lot, this time building a three-story house of stone and brick.[22] Edinboro Thomas borrowed $1,500 for the rebuilding of the house, using the property as collateral. However, he repaid the bank into an account that listed him as "Thomas Edinboro," rather than Edinboro Thomas. John Thomas had assisted in drawing up the papers for the loan and did not catch the error. When the bank failed, the bank's creditors sought to take the property at 198 Fourth Avenue, stating that Edinboro Thomas had never repaid the loan. The case went to court in 1877 and the judge ruled in favor of the elder Thomas.[23] That Edinboro and John Thomas were able to repay the loan within three years, despite having suffered the loss of the house and business at 198 Fourth Avenue, demonstrates their early financial successes.

During his early years in Chicago, John Thomas appears to have stayed largely within the African American community. His school, loan company, and grocery catered mainly to African Americans. He was active in the influential Olivet Baptist Church and his early church associates were African Americans who would become friends and, eventually, political allies. He also was involved in African American fraternal organizations. By 1875, he was president of the Brothers of Union, a benevolent and social organization founded in 1869 and comprised of African American men. The organization had a membership of about one hundred, and its general fund was used to assist the sick and bury the dead.[24]

While Thomas limited his social and economic contacts mainly to the African American community during his early years in Chicago, as he became increasingly successful, his horizons expanded. His interests turned to politics, where he would work with and compete against Chicago whites.

African Americans received the vote in Illinois in 1870, with the passage of both the Fifteenth Amendment to the United States Constitution and the 1870 state constitution. African Americans in Chicago quickly took advantage of the franchise. By the fall of 1870, the *Chicago Tribune* could report that a meeting of the Third Ward Republican Club was largely composed of African Americans, "who seemed to take a lively interest in the coming contest."[25] In 1871, tailor John Jones became the first African American to be elected to office at the county level when he was elected to a one year term on the Cook County Board. Jones ran on a bipartisan "Fire-Proof" ticket put together by *Chicago Tribune* publisher Joseph Medill in the immediate aftermath of the 1871 fire. Jones was reelected to a three-year term in 1872, running as a Republican candidate. During that election campaign, Jones and 111 other Chicago African Americans signed an open letter to all African Americans, urging them to support Ulysses S. Grant and the Republicans in the November election.[26]

There certainly was room for African Americans to participate in the political system. Politics of the time consisted of a seemingly endless number of elections and political conventions. In 1876, for example, there was an April 4 township election, an April 6 Republican primary election to elect delegates to a city convention, an April 18 city election, and a May 18 Republican primary to select delegates to a county convention where delegates were selected to attend the state Republican convention, which was held May 24. There was also a July election for mayor, Republican primaries and conventions in the fall, and the November national and state elections. Robert Ingersoll, a nationally known orator from Illinois, once said that Chicago always seemed to be in a state of boil over an election and that, whenever he came to Chicago, it was in the midst of a contest that its participants all swore was the most important election ever.[27]

For an overwhelming majority of African Americans, participation in politics meant supporting the Republican Party. Thomas summed up the view of most African Americans in 1875: "What we are, the Republican Party made us. And the success of the Republican Party is our success and the downfall of it will be our downfall." It was a view Thomas would keep his entire career.[28]

Thomas lived in Chicago's Third Ward, one of the city's twenty wards and the one containing the largest number of African Americans, although they were still a decided minority. The City of Chicago had just under 300,000 residents at the time of redistricting, of whom fewer than 4,000 were African Americans.[29]

By 1874, several African Americans were active and successful in the Republican Party. As previously mentioned, Jones served as a Cook County commissioner. William Baker, a whitewasher, and Robert M. Mitchell, a waiter, were active in the Third Ward Republican Club, as were W. C. Phillips, a carpenter, and Thomas.[30] In June 1874 Thomas was elected to serve as one of ten delegates to the county Republican convention.[31] In October of this same year, Thomas and Phillips were elected as two of eight Third Ward delegates to another county Republican convention.[32] Although there were no African Americans competing for office and Phillips and Thomas did not play large roles at the convention, their election demonstrates both an acceptance of African Americans into the Republican Party and a level of African American participation in the political process above the grassroots level. Phillips further demonstrated this when he was selected the Third Ward member of the county Republican central committee, the decision-making arm of the party.[33] Despite the efforts of Phillips and Thomas on behalf of the Republicans, 1874 turned out to be a Democratic year in both the nation and the state.[34]

The following year, African American leaders started to work to open the process to elective office for themselves. Although few in number, African Americans provided a loyal bloc of votes for the Republican Party, and their leaders felt that they deserved the opportunity to run for political office. However, the first office some of them focused on was the only one already held by an African American, that of Cook County commissioner, as certain leaders felt that the community itself should decide which African American the Republicans should nominate for the position.

At an August 31 meeting, several African Americans vied for the support of the community for the commissionership position held by John Jones. They complained that Jones was not serving the needs of his African American constituents. Although the meeting was split between pro- and anti-Jones forces, it ended with a resolution of endorsement for Jones. Undeterred, the anti-Jones forces coalesced around S. W. Scott, a former bailiff with the Cook County Sheriff's office, as their choice for commissioner. At a riotous September 21 meeting of about 125 African American voters, Scott was able to secure an endorsement over Jones for the commissionership.[35]

The *Tribune* was stunned by the actions of the African American voters. In an editorial following the September 21 meeting, it noted that any candidate would need the support of the white community to be elected and it wondered why the African American community would select an unknown such as Scott over the well-respected and well-known Jones. In a later editorial, it also questioned why the African American community felt entitled to have a commissionership position.[36] The split between Jones and Scott went all the way to the Republican county nominating convention, where it took Jones three ballots to fend off Scott's challenge. Thomas was one of two African American delegates at the nominating convention, although it is not known if he voted for Jones or Scott.[37]

The opposition to Jones appeared to be more about the lack of opportunities for ambitious young African American politicians than because of any strong feelings against Jones himself. As Thomas noted at the August 31 meeting, African Americans needed more representation in government. Although he was mentioned as a possible candidate for commissioner, it appears that Thomas was actually angling for support for the Third Ward aldermanic nomination. Still, with the possibility of receiving support for the commissionership, he took the opportunity to speak out against Jones. His ally Louis White also opposed Jones, and W. C. Phillips may have as well.[38]

But again, it appears that the county commissionership was not what Thomas aspired to. On October 2, he announced to the Third Ward Republican Club that he would be a candidate for alderman. This led the Democratic *Chicago Times* to write sarcastically, "Thomas is a candidate for alderman and is evidently quite confident that he is the best man."[39]

The aldermanic campaign would not begin until the spring, so Thomas and his fellow Republicans were still concerned about the fall election. For Thomas, it was a busy election season. In October, he was elected secretary of the Third Ward Republican Party. He also served as an election judge in the October 19 Republican primary, held to elect delegates to the county nominating convention, and was elected one of the Third Ward's eight delegates to that convention. The party's central committee named him as one of almost 500 members of the Republican Party Campaign Committee for the city. On October 30, Thomas and Phillips served as two of the fifty vice presidents of a large preelection Republican meeting that was addressed by U.S. Senator Richard Oglesby.[40]

Thomas ended the 1875 campaign with a written appeal to the African American voters in which he encouraged them to vote for the Republican ticket. His appeal appeared on the front page of the *Tribune* and in other Republican newspapers. He wrote, "Let us come out like men on Tuesday and cast our votes for the party that has always defended our rights and is still defending them." It was an appeal that would reflect his lifelong belief that Chicago's small African American community was best served by loyally supporting the Republican Party. Thomas also was making his move to become the recognized leader of that community. Using language unusually flowery for him, he addressed his constituency: "Hear the voice of one who loves you and desires to see you grow in to strength and importance, both in this county and in this country."[41]

The fall election was generally a success for the Republican Party in Cook County. The only losses it took were its two county commissioner candidates running in the city district. John Jones was one of those two candidates who lost, meaning that despite five years of enthusiastic participation in the electoral process, there was not one African American who held public office in Cook County.

With his various businesses, his social contacts within the community, his membership in the politically influential Olivet Baptist Church and his participation in the political arena, Thomas was poised to change that. Although in the economic and social spheres he largely had stayed within the African American community, in the political world he now frequently interacted with whites. In doing so, he began a career that would test how far the commitment went in the North for giving full rights to African Americans and he laid the groundwork for how African Americans, although a small minority in the city and the state, could achieve individual and community success in politics.

The Election of 1876

Chicago had been a center of the abolitionist movement before the Civil War, and in 1876 the tradition of white support for African American rights still existed, at least in the Republican Party, and African Americans were overwhelmingly loyal to that party. Thomas was able to combine support of a united African American community with white Republican concern for African American rights to secure a nomination and subsequent election as a state representative. While white Republican commitment to African American rights would wane in future years, Thomas's success in this election secured in him the belief that the African American community had to be united and loyal to the Republican Party if it was to succeed politically in Chicago.

In the spring of 1876, Chicago was redistricted and the number of wards was reduced from twenty to eighteen, with each ward electing two aldermen. That spring, all thirty-six aldermanic positions were up for election, with half the winners receiving two-year terms and half receiving one-year terms. Beginning in 1877, eighteen aldermen a year, one per ward, were elected to two-year terms. The boundaries for the Third Ward did not change with the redistricting: Harrison Street on the north, Sixteenth Street on the south, Lake Michigan on the east, and the Chicago River on the west.[42] Although the borders did not change, the ward number did. The Third Ward became the Second Ward under the new plan, and on March 10 the Third Ward Republican Club, of which Thomas was secretary, officially changed its name to the Second Ward Republican Club.[43]

The new Second Ward remained very diverse, stretching from rich homes near the lake on the east side of the ward to the tough river wharfs on the west. The population of the ward in 1870 was 17,681. It was home to part of the downtown business district, the largest concentration of African American voters in the city, the levee vice district, and the wealthiest neighborhoods of Chicago. The African American voters and the wealthy residents made the ward predominantly Republican.[44]

Thomas did not run for alderman that spring. The Second Ward Republican Club nominated Jacob Rosenberg and F. C. Vierling, two white candidates, to run for the position. Although there was little to no dissent over the two nominees, Thomas did give a speech at the meeting where he asked the club to consider African Americans for public office in the future. Vierling, who was strongly supported in the African American community, would later have to decline the nomination. The club would replace him with another white candidate, Addison Ballard. Rosenberg and Ballard both won their races during the April election.[45]

Also to be elected that spring were the town offices. Chicago at the time consisted of three township-like units of government, known as towns. Divided by the Chicago River, they were known as the North, South and West Towns. Each town elected a supervisor, assessor, clerk, and collector to a one-year term. At the town level, taxes were assessed and collected for the other units of government in Cook County, including the city. It was an antiquated and unnecessary level of government rife with corruption. Both Republican and Democratic papers of the time advocated abolishing the town form of government, something that would not occur until the early twentieth century. In South Town, where Thomas lived, the 1876 election was so corrupt that public outcry forced the officials elected to resign. They were replaced by appointed officials, including Robert Todd Lincoln, Abraham Lincoln's son, as supervisor.[46]

Although he did not run for alderman, Thomas was extremely active in party politics that election cycle. He served as one of two representatives from his ward on the Grand Council of the Central Republican Club of Cook County. The Central Republican Club was the umbrella organization for all the auxiliary Republican clubs in the county. The Grand Council, the policy-making arm of the club, made recommendations on what the party's position should be on the issues of the day. It was hoped that the various ward and township clubs would select candidates who agreed with those policies. Of immediate concern to the council was excessive taxation and the sky-rocketing costs of rebuilding the city hall and county courthouse following the Chicago Fire.[47] Thomas echoed this concern at a ward Republican club meeting, stating that he favored honest and competent men for the upcoming municipal elections because although he was not a large taxpayer, he nevertheless felt his share of the burden of taxation.[48]

With Thomas on the Grand Council and Phillips still serving on the County Central Committee, African Americans had membership on two of the leading Republican campaign committees of the county. Thomas also continued to act as secretary of the Second Ward Republican Club. He served as an election judge in the April Republican primary for city offices and in the May Republican primary for the county convention. Thomas was also one of eleven delegates elected to represent the ward at the April 5 city nominating convention. Among the other Second Ward delegates was Richard Hancock, a machine shop foreman and the only other African American to serve as a delegate to the convention.[49]

On April 15, three days before the city election, Thomas called a meeting of the African American Republicans of the Second Ward to endorse the nominations of both Ballard and Rosenberg.[50] Thomas did not serve as a delegate to the county Republican convention, held May 20, and he also was not selected to serve as a delegate to the May 24 state Republican convention, although Phillips was selected as one of three alternate delegates from the Second Ward. John J. Bird, an African American politician from Cairo in deep southern Illinois, also served as a delegate to the state convention.[51]

Despite not attending the two May conventions, Thomas was recognized in Republican circles as a promising leader. This could be seen most vividly in the bipartisan response to the frauds conducted during the April South Town election. Republican and Democratic leaders met to plan a mass rally designed to bring pressure on those elected to resign. The meeting organizers created a list from each party of potential vice presidents who would lend credibility to the proposed meeting. Thomas was one of twenty-three names suggested by the Republicans. Others on the list were wealthy hotel magnate Potter Palmer, meatpacking tycoon George Armour, and politicians Abner Taylor, Elliott Anthony, and Murry Nelson. John Jones was also one of the names suggested.[52]

For all the success that Thomas and Phillips had working within the Republican Party and that other African Americans had working within the Second Ward Republican Club, the one undeniable fact coming into the fall 1876 election was that there were no African Americans holding elective office in Cook County. That fall, Thomas would change this situation.

Illinois in its 1870 constitution had adopted a unique system of electing its representatives, called cumulative voting. Under this system, three representatives per legislative district were elected to two-year terms. A voter had three votes he could cast for the office. He could give all three votes to one candidate, one and one-half votes each to two candidates, two votes to one candidate and one vote to another, or one vote to each of three candidates. The purpose of the system was to ensure minority party representation in areas where one party was weak. In such an area, the minority party would nominate one candidate and its partisans would each cast three votes for that candidate in an act called "plumping" or "bullet voting." The majority party would nominate two candidates and its partisans would cast one and one-half votes for each of the candidates. In super-majority districts, the dominant party would nominate three candidates, but such occurrences were rare. In swing districts, both parties would nominate two candidates and hope for the best. Third parties, independent candidates, disgruntled party members, and back-room political deals often upset the political equation.[53]

Cumulative voting was designed to ensure that both major parties could represent a legislative district, even in an area where one of the parties was in a decided minority. However, cumulative voting also made seeking a legislative seat an inviting goal for minority groups. The African American community recognized this. Cumulative voting eliminated the straight head-to-head competition of most elective offices, meaning that the majority white voters were not choosing strictly between a white candidate and an African American candidate. If an African American were elected, there would still be two white legislators elected as well. Also, with the use of plumping, a candidate with a small but unified base could win one of the seats. As such, this made the idea of an African American candidate running for the legislature attractive to the African American community.

Almost immediately after the implementation of the 1870 state constitution that created cumulative voting and granted African Americans the right to vote, the community began advocating John Jones be nominated for election to the legislature. In early October 1870, Phillips, Rev. Richard DeBaptiste, and fifty-seven other African Americans wrote a letter to Republican newspapers calling for the Republicans to nominate Jones to the legislature. The papers only printed the first five names on the petition but, given the presence of Phillips and DeBaptiste as signatories, Thomas more than likely also signed the letter. Despite this request and a strong endorsement from the *Tribune,* Jones declined to become a candidate.[54] In 1872, Jones noted that schools in Illinois were closing their doors to African American children, and he urged that an African American representative be elected to the legislature to help combat this problem. He recommended Louis White for the position. The Third Ward Colored Republican Club passed a resolution calling for the nomination of an African American to the legislature, but nothing came of it or of White's potential candidacy.[55]

In 1876, African American Republicans began to demand the nomination of one of their own to the state legislature. In July, Thomas chaired an African American Republican Club meeting where the two hundred attendees passed a resolution that endorsed Republican candidates at the national level as the best way to protect African Americans in the South and asked the local party to help put African Americans in both elected and appointed positions in local government. Although the resolution asked for an office, rather than demanded one, it also pointedly complained that, "We, the colored people of this city always have, and do now, give our votes and influence to the Republican party and have only been treated as haulers of wood and drawers of water."[56]

On August 8, the African American voters of the Second Ward met at Bethel Church to discuss both building united community support of an African American candidate for office and helping the poor in the city and the county. The meeting appointed a committee of five, including Thomas, Jones, and William Baker, to look in to the latter issue. In a follow-up meeting held at Olivet Baptist Church on August 14, the club discussed the need to elect an African American state representative. Thomas addressed the club and gave a strong Republican partisan speech. Whether Thomas at this point was publicly seeking the nomination cannot be determined from newspaper articles, but the meeting concluded with the club passing a resolution asking the Republican Party to nominate an African American for the legislature.[57]

Despite the activities of the Second Ward African American voters, none of the major Chicago newspapers mentioned Thomas or any African American as one of the potential Republican nominees for the legislature. On September 15, 1876, the Democratic-leaning *Chicago Times* listed potential Republican candidates as incumbent Sol Hopkins, Captain D. N. Bash and former alderman R. R. Stone. On September 17 the *Chicago Tribune* listed A. L. Rockwell as a potential candidate.[58] Thomas addressed audiences of African American Republicans on September 23 and again on October 7, but the reporters covering the events did not report that he discussed a potential candidacy.[59]

At the end of September, Thomas was selected to serve as one of nine delegates from the Second Ward at the Republican nominating convention for the First Congressional District. The selection consisted of being nominated by the Ward Club and then being elected the following day in a primary. Thomas received 243 votes, the most of any of the candidates for delegate.[60] Thomas probably supported Kirk Hawes for congressman. At the congressional nominating convention, Hawes received seven of the nine votes from the delegates of the Second Ward on the first ballot, but found himself in third place. On the ninth ballot, the nomination went to William Aldrich. During this time frame, Thomas also served as an election judge for the October 10 Second Ward County Convention primary. At that primary, Republicans nominated delegates for the October 12 county convention.[61]

The Second Senate District Republican convention also met on October 12. Its purpose was to nominate a candidate for Senate and two candidates for the Illinois House. Hawes chaired the meeting and W. C. Phillips served as a member of the credentials committee. Phillips for certain was a Thomas ally and Hawes probably was. The delegates at the convention decided to nominate two candidates for representative, as it was assumed that the Democrats would nominate just one in the Republican majority district. However, Hawes made it clear that if the Democrats nominated two candidates, the Republicans would nominate a third candidate and try to sweep the district. The *Inter-Ocean* newspaper reported, "It was decided to nominate just two candidates. The third Representative will be left to the minority party, provided the Democrats have the modesty to restrict themselves to one candidate. Should they put two men in the field, it was decided this impudence would be met by the immediate nomination of a third Republican."[62]

At the Second District Republican convention, each area of the district sent delegates. The district included all of Chicago's Second, Third, and Fourth Wards, which were located along Lake Michigan on Chicago's near South Side. The South Side townships of Lake and Hyde Park also were in the district. On the fourth ballot, delegates nominated D. N. Bash of the Fourth Ward for Senate. The convention then chose two candidates to run for the House. Four candidates, including Thomas, were nominated, with twenty-one votes needed for selection. Generally, geographic balance was sought for the ticket. On the first ballot, Sol Hopkins received twenty-two votes, Thomas received four, A. L. Rockwell received six, and W. O. Cole received nine. Hopkins, the incumbent from Lake Town on the southern end of the district, won the nomination.

Three more ballots were taken to choose the second nominee. Added as candidates were D. E. Smith and C. W. Colehour, bringing the total number of candidates up to five. Rockwell led the five remaining candidates on the first, informal ballot with fourteen votes. Cole had ten, Thomas eight, Smith five, and Colehour four. The number of nominees dropped to four on the second ballot, and Rockwell's total moved to seventeen votes. Smith went up to thirteen, Thomas stayed steady at eight, and Colehour dropped to three. With the number of candidates reduced to three on the third and final ballot, Thomas received the nomination. According to the *Inter-Ocean*, he received twenty-two votes, one more than necessary. The *Tribune*, however, reported that "the third ballot settled it—Mr. Thomas receiving 39 out of 41 votes, the delegations, when perceiving that their pet stood 'no show,' turning over solidly for Thomas." The *Times* reported the convention this way: "After several ballots, in which Mr. Rockwell, who was heartily indorsed by most of the whites, came near being nominated, there was a sudden 'flop over' to the dark-complexioned candidate, and Mr. Thomas was nominated." In his acceptance speech, Thomas thanked the convention and said his nomination was an honor to both him and the African American community.[63]

The Thomas nomination caused an immediate stir in Chicago. The large African American crowd at the convention erupted into cheers when Thomas won. At the July meeting of the Colored Republican Club, the members had passed a resolution asking that the party select an African American candidate for an office but also demanding that the community have the right to select who that candidate should be.[64] As such, it appears as if Thomas was the choice for state representative of a united African American community. The African American voters of the Second Ward later held at least one, if not two, ratification meetings at Olivet Church.[65]

The Republican press of the day took pains to describe Thomas as qualified for the position. The *Evening Journal* described him as "a colored man of talent and respectability" and as a "young colored gentleman of great promise." The *Inter-Ocean* noted that Thomas's acceptance speech "confirmed the high opinion in which he is held by all who know him as an able man and a sound Republican." The *Tribune* called him "a bright, intelligent colored man."[66]

However, not everyone had as high an opinion of Thomas. The *Chicago Times* ridiculed the nomination of Thomas, editorializing, "Mr. Thomas was nominated merely on the ground that he was a colored man and could command a number of votes for the general ticket and not particularly on account of his qualifications as a legislator, for so far as anybody knows he has none." Describing Thomas as an "Ethiopian," it wrote, "excepting the Ethiopian (who may be a skilled white washer), the candidates for the house are first class." It added, "the Ethiopian should be dropped, not on account of his race, color or previous condition, but because he is wholly unfit for any legislative function."

But, the *Chicago Times* was only the beginning of Thomas's worries. He needed to shore up his support among Republicans. The Saturday after the convention, he gave a speech at the Third Ward Republican Club, whose members had been grumbling about nominating an African American candidate. According to the *Inter Ocean*, the speech Thomas gave demonstrated a thorough familiarity with the current political situation. "In a word, he made it very clear that the conclusions of those who had condemned his nomination were the result of misapprehension, or prejudice, or both. Mr. Thomas will receive the solid support of the Republicans of the Third Ward." How solid the support was for Thomas from his own party would remain a question throughout the race. The *Times* reported that there were factions in the Republican Party that wanted Thomas knocked off the ticket because they felt an African American could not be elected in the Second District.[67]

While some Republicans sniped, Democrats debated the propriety of adding a second legislative candidate in light of the Thomas nomination. At a central committee meeting held October 21, Democrats decided that many Republicans would desert the African American candidate, enabling

Democrats to squeeze in a second nominee. As such, they nominated a second candidate, attorney Thomas A. Moran. However, Moran subsequently refused the nomination.[68]

Also in the legislative race was a third party (Greenback) candidate named W. D. Flavin. Along with the Greenback nomination, Flavin also was endorsed by the Workingmen's Protective Political League and an organization known as the Citizens Reform League, a Democrat-leaning organization that claimed to be nonpartisan. Just two nights after the Second District Republicans made their legislative nominations, the Citizens Reform League endorsed Hopkins, Smith, and Flavin as its choices for the three representative positions.[69] The Democrats considered endorsing Flavin but in the end stayed with their one candidate, Joseph Smith.

But the real problem for Thomas would come from a surprising source. Thomas was opposed by Robert Todd Lincoln, a leading member of what was known as the Municipal Reform Club. That club, made up of the "better elements" of the city, had formed in February of 1875 to protest corruption in government and work for the election of "the most proper men."[70] The Municipal Reform Club claimed to be nonpartisan but, in fact, leaned Republican, making its endorsement important. The club was reviewing the Republican candidates for the various offices and publicly debating whether to endorse the Republican candidates, endorse Democrats, or place on the ballot their own candidates.

At an October 24 meeting, the club expressed dissatisfaction with some of the South Side legislative candidates, including Thomas. The next day, the executive committee of the club met and decided not to endorse Thomas. The *Chicago Evening Journal* charged racism, writing, "Those Municipal reformers don't like a man because his skin is black." The Republican Central Committee ignored the Reform Club's actions and on October 27 allowed Thomas to pay his $200 candidate assessment fee, which the Republican Party required of its nominated candidates and used to fund campaign expenses. The other endorsed candidates had already paid the fee. Even the *Times* wrote that this meant it would be "out of order" for the club not to support Thomas."[71]

Still, the Reform Club persisted and events came to a head on October 30 when it met. Club member John G. Shortall stated that Thomas should not be endorsed, not because of his character or intelligence, but because of his lack of experience. He suggested nominating Huntington Jackson, an attorney, for the representative position. However, it was noted that Jackson had served as a delegate from the Second Ward to the Second District Legislative Convention and had, in fact, placed Thomas's name in nomination. Reform Club members decided that Jackson would probably decline their club's nomination.[72] Simeon W. King spoke in favor of Thomas, noting that he "was a rising colored man, who stood well among his people." After further discussion, Shortall moved that the issue of the endorsement in the Second District be referred to the executive committee for its consideration. With the election only eight days away, the club gave the executive committee the power to serve as the campaign committee for the full club.

At a Second Ward Republican Club meeting that night, President D. S. Smith denounced the Municipal Reform Club's actions. He said Reform Club members never attended Republican ward meetings or did any work for the party yet felt they should be the ones to decide who the Republican candidates should be. He added that there had been ward meetings for months and that every issue and every candidate had been discussed and should be supported by all true Republicans.

Meanwhile, Robert Todd Lincoln attended a large gathering of African American voters, many of whom were from Thomas's Second Ward. Lincoln attempted to persuade the voters that the Municipal Reform Club was working for the best interests of the Republican Party. He said the club was attempting to do this by working to have some of the more unqualified candidates removed from the ticket and replaced with more qualified candidates. Lincoln was followed by William Baker, an African American and Thomas supporter. On October 23, he had addressed a similar meeting of African Americans and praised them for ratifying the nomination of Thomas for the legislature. Now, he criticized both the Municipal Reform Club and Lincoln. He said he did not think that any body of men, however good they might be, had the power or right to say what should be done with the nominees of the Republican conventions. Then, in words similar to Smith's, Baker said it was the duty of all Republicans to vote for the men who had been selected.[73]

The Executive Committee of the Municipal Reform Club met almost daily as the election approached. Although it eventually supported most of the Republicans on the ticket with whom it had a problem, the club struggled with endorsing Thomas. On October 31, Republicans of the Fourth Ward passed a resolution that endorsed the entire Republican ticket and criticized the Municipal Reform Club and any Republicans who associated with it. A *Chicago Evening Journal* editorial that day stated, "The Municipal Reform League cannot defeat J. W. E. Thomas for the Legislature and, what's more, they ought not to try, for he is honest, faithful and capable." The next day it added, "Mr. J. W. E. Thomas will be as honest and intelligent Representative as will be sent to the Legislature. We know him."[74]

The criticism the club received from Republican circles for not endorsing Thomas only increased Thomas's confidence. On November 2, the club sent

Thomas a note, asking him to go to its headquarters for a meeting. The purpose of the meeting was to find out who Thomas would support for the U.S. Senate if he were elected to the legislature. At the time, senators were chosen by state legislators, not by direct election of the people. Thomas sent word to the club that if club members desired to meet with him, they could find him at his place of business. Even the *Times* was impressed by Thomas's actions, noting that he was "not the least confused or obfuscated by the opposition manifested to him in certain quarters." It wrote admirably of Thomas that, "The municipal reformers turned up their noses at him and he as promptly elevated his own proboscis."[75]

That same day, the last effort to have the club endorse Thomas failed. The club as a whole adopted a motion by Simeon King to endorse Thomas. However, the motion had to be passed by the executive committee, which it failed to do. The club endorsed only two candidates, Hopkins and Smith, for the three legislative positions.[76] Endorsement or no endorsement, Thomas campaigned hard. Two nights before the November 7 election, he went to his base, the African American voters of the Second Ward. There, he addressed the issue of the Municipal Reform Club's nonendorsement. Although his words were not recorded, he obviously was seeking to rally his supporters.[77] He was successful in his efforts.

On election day, Thomas came in second in the voting. The winners for the three House seats were Democrat Joseph Smith, with 15,709 votes, Thomas with 11,532 votes, and Hopkins with 11,237 votes. Because Smith was the only Democrat nominated for the office, it was only natural that he received the most votes, as most of the Democrats voting for him gave him three votes, while many of the Republican voters were giving Thomas and Hopkins one and one-half votes each. Flavin received 2,742½ votes. A last minute entry, J. E. Cassiday, received 404 votes. Cassiday may have been a last-minute attempt by some Democrats to elect a second Democrat. Although he is not mentioned in any of the postelection papers, other than his vote totals, he had been mentioned as a possible aspirant for a Democratic nomination for representative in September.[78]

Thomas was probably the beneficiary of some "plumping" by the African American community, meaning that these voters cast all three of their votes for Thomas, but by receiving as many votes as he did, he obviously also received the support of many white voters. Combining united African American community support with white support had been crucial to Thomas' nomination and election, and he would remember this lesson throughout his political career.

Thomas's election made Illinois the first state in the Midwest and only the second northern state to elect an African American to the state legislature.[79]

Thomas later wrote, "The majority which I received on election day demonstrated at the polls that the people approved my nomination. Without egotism, I may be permitted to say that it was a proud day for me and for the colored people of the great Republican State of Illinois, when, for the first time, and that in the Centennial year, a colored man took his seat in the Legislature of that state which gave to the world the emancipator of my race, the martyred Lincoln."[80]

"An Able, Attentive, and Sensible Representative": The First Term and a Failed Reelection Bid

As the first African American to serve in the Illinois General Assembly, Thomas knew that he would be judged by different standards than other incoming freshmen legislators. During his term, he quickly established himself as a loyal Republican although he demonstrated admirable streaks of independence when it came to good-government issues. He also was a strong supporter for the interests of Chicago. He did not, however, work on any issues or bills designed specifically to assist the African American community. Despite this, he always was made aware that he was not just a state legislator but was an "African American" state legislator and while serving he saw discrimination in many forms, especially from the state's southern Democrats.

The 1877 Legislative Session

The Thirtieth Session of the Illinois General Assembly convened on January 3, 1877, in the new state capitol in Springfield. Work on the building had begun in 1868. By 1869, the first rumors of fraud surfaced. The legislature began a full scale investigation into the building costs in 1871.[1] Such was the way of government in the post–Civil War era.

People had good reason to distrust government in the 1870s. At the federal level, the Credit Mobilier scandal tarnished the reputations of several congressmen, while the Whiskey Ring scandal, the Indian Trading scandal, and the Sanborn Contracts scandal reflected poorly on President Grant and his administration.[2] Closer to home, Thomas voted for a measure in the Thirtieth General Assembly calling for an investigation into alleged corruption in the South Parks Board, the governing agency for all the parks on Chicago's South Side. The General Assembly also voted on legislation designed to break up a corrupt ring of Cook County commissioners, whose kickback schemes in relation to the building of the new county courthouse had led to several indictments and the naming of the building "a thief's monument."[3]

The state legislature was part and parcel of the government of the era. Newspapers regularly reported on the members' chronic absenteeism, carousing in the evenings and drinking in the coat rooms behind the House and Senate chambers. Accusations would fly about legislators being bribed, going on all-expenses-paid junkets and receiving free railroad passes to go to and from their districts to the capital. The floor of the House was a loud, rowdy place, where fights were not uncommon, exploding cigars provided entertainment, paper balls were thrown to signal disapproval and, when measured debate would not do, the singing of songs, especially "John Brown's Body," was seen as a way for one side or another to prove their point or claim victory. The capitol had two janitors employed full-time to clean the 350 spittoons located in the halls, committee rooms, galleries, and rotunda of the building.[4]

Consisting of a 153-member House of Representatives and a 51-member Senate, the Illinois General Assembly was similar to the legislatures of other Midwestern states. Most of the members of the House were serving their first term of office and, at the age of twenty-nine, Thomas was one of the younger members. Wealthy farmers and lawyers dominated the membership, with 27 farmers and 27 lawyers serving as representatives. Only 30 of the 153 members of the House had been born in Illinois, and 21 members had been born in a foreign country. The youngest member of the House was twenty-eight years old. Sixty-eight-year-old Starkey Powell of Scott County, who had fought in the Black Hawk War with Abraham Lincoln, was the oldest member. Women were not allowed to vote or hold office, and Thomas was the only African American in the General Assembly.[5] During the 1877 session, William Baker, an African American from Chicago's First Ward, served as a First Assistant Doorkeeper of the House.[6]

The post–Civil War period was generally a golden era for Republicans in Illinois. The party controlled the governor's mansion for all but four years between 1857 and 1913. During Thomas's three terms in the House, he would serve under four governors, all of them Republican. From 1865 to 1913, Illinois always had at least one Republican United States Senator and it would have two Republicans serving at the same time for all but twelve of those forty-eight years. In the fourteen General Assembly sessions between 1873 and 1900, Republicans elected a Speaker of the House ten times and a president of the Senate twelve times. The rise of third parties and independent candidacies during these years, however, sometimes meant that independents held a balance of power in one or both of the chambers. For the thirtieth session of the General Assembly, Republicans had a 79 to 67 majority over the Democrats in the House, with 7 independents. In the Senate, although Democrats had a 22 to 21 majority over the Republicans, there were 8 independents.[7]

At the January 3 opening day of the General Assembly, Thomas cast his first vote: voting for Flavel F. Granger of McHenry County for temporary Speaker. Granger, a Republican, defeated George W. Armstrong of LaSalle County 77 to 75. On his second vote, Thomas cast one of 81 votes to make John M. Adair of Carroll County the temporary clerk. The House had convened just after noon and by 1:15 P.M. adjourned. That evening, legislators attended an 8 P.M. reception sponsored by the State Board of Agriculture in the Agriculture Room of the new capitol. The meeting, which featured "native but harmless wines," was addressed by retiring governor John Beveridge and U.S. Senator John A. Logan.[8]

January 4 was the day of inauguration ceremonies for House members and for the election of a permanent Speaker. Benjamin R. Sheldon, chief justice of the Illinois Supreme Court, swore in Thomas and the members of the House at about noon. The House then proceeded to elect a permanent Speaker. Republican James Shaw, an Irish-born lawyer from Carroll County, defeated Andrew Ashton of Winnebago County, Samuel Buckmaster of Madison County, and Richard Rowett of Macoupin County for Speaker of the House. The vote tally was 78 for Shaw, 65 for Ashton, 8 for Buckmaster and 1, Ashton's vote, for Rowett. Thomas, of course, voted for the Republican Shaw.[9] On January 5, the drawing was held for the members to choose their seats. Looking at the chamber from the Speaker's rostrum, the Republicans sat on the left side of the chamber and the Democrats on the right. As each name was drawn, that representative chose his seat. Thomas sat in seat number nine, which was located in the second of the seven rows, third seat in from the center aisle, on the Republican side of the chamber.[10]

Of the 153 members of the House, only 29 had previously served in the legislature, a low number consistent with Midwestern legislatures in the late nineteenth century.[11] Still, as befitting a freshman legislator, Thomas served on three fairly unimportant committees: Warehouses, Education, and Enrolled and Engrossed Bills.[12] The Education Committee was appropriate, given that Thomas was a teacher. The other two committees had little business, although the subject of regulating warehouses, which directly affected storage for farmers, was an important issue throughout the decade. The issue also was important to Chicago because it was a major transportation and shipping center. The most important committee in the legislature was the Judiciary Committee.[13] In his third term, after he had passed the bar, Thomas became a member of this committee.

One of the most important votes Thomas cast as a representative was actually several votes. Illinois, like the rest of the nation in 1877, did not have direct election of its U.S. senators. Instead, the members of the General Assembly elected them. On January 5, the Republicans of the House and the Senate held a joint caucus at Springfield's Leland Hotel. They voted to support General John A. Logan for Senate. Logan, a Civil War hero from southern Illinois, was the incumbent U.S. senator and a staunch defender of the rights of African Americans. Eighteen Republicans seconded the nomination and gave short speeches, including Thomas, who was given the honor "as a representative of the colored people of Illinois and the nation."[14] Thomas understood his role in seconding the nomination, stating that he was happy to do so because, "as the representative of many millions—the colored people—he knew that General Logan was their unanimous choice."[15] Thomas later named his son Logan after the general.

The procedure to elect a senator was governed by Article 1 of the Constitution, as interpreted by Congress. Each chamber was required to meet separately on the second Tuesday following its organization and the members were then to cast their ballots for senator. If a majority of both chambers voted for the same candidate, that person was elected. If not, the members of the two chambers would meet in joint session and vote. In a joint session a majority vote of those voting was needed for election. This meant that a Senate candidate needed at least 103 votes to win if all of the 204 members of the General Assembly were present. If fewer than 204 members were present, the number needed to achieve a majority was reduced accordingly. In the House, Logan received 77 votes. General John Palmer, who served as a Republican governor of Illinois from 1869 to 1873 and was now the endorsed candidate of the Democrats, received 67 votes. Supreme Court Justice David Davis, the choice of the independents in the House, received 7 votes and William Lathrop received 1 vote. In the Senate, Palmer received 22 votes to Logan's 20. Three other candidates split 9 votes.

The separate House and Senate votes occurred January 16. The next day, the two chambers met jointly in a session that would take forty ballots and more than a week to elect a senator. Thomas proved to be a loyal Republican throughout the voting. Although Republicans entered the contest confident of victory, it soon became apparent that the 7 independents in the House and the 8 in the Senate controlled the balance of power. Neither Logan, the choice of the Republicans, nor Palmer, the choice of the Democrats, received the 103 votes needed to be elected. Andrew Ashton, leader of the independents in the House, wanted to support Davis for the Senate. The independents in the Senate were supporting General William B. Anderson, a downstate congressman.

During the balloting, Logan received as many as 100 votes, just three shy of the majority. Palmer peaked at 88 votes, and at no point did he ever lead in the voting. Other candidates also received a few votes. Davis was never close. From the seventeenth to the thirty-fourth ballot, he did not receive any votes. Generally, five or six ballots were taken each day, beginning January 17. On January 22, Palmer withdrew as a candidate and the Democrats switched to supporting Anderson. On the thirty-second ballot, Anderson caught Logan, who had led on every ballot up until then, and both received 89 votes, with former Illinois congressman and current minister to France E. B. Washburne receiving 13 votes. Seven other candidates also received some votes. On the next ballot, Anderson actually outpolled Logan, and on January 24 Logan withdrew from the contest. On the first ballot taken that day, the thirty-fifth, Davis, who had not received a vote since the sixteenth ballot, jumped to a 97–86 lead over C. B. Lawrence, the new choice for the Republicans.

Thomas had voted for Logan on all thirty-four ballots, until the former general withdrew. On the thirty-fifth ballot, he switched to Lawrence. He stuck with Lawrence on the thirty-sixth ballot, but cast the only vote for Washburne on the thirty-seventh ballot. Thomas went back to Lawrence on the thirty-eighth ballot, but Lawrence's vote total declined to 39, placing him behind Davis, with 98, and state senator J. C. Haines, with 56. Republican support for Haines grew on the thirty-ninth ballot, with the votes being 82 for Davis, 69 for Haines, and 42 for Lawrence. This time, Thomas voted for Haines. On the fortieth ballot, taken on January 25, Republicans, including Thomas, again went to Lawrence, but Davis captured the majority and received the nomination. Davis went on to pursue an independent course in his one term in the Senate and frequently sided with the Republicans.[16]

Thomas voted for the same candidate as the Republican Speaker of the House on every ballot but the thirty-seventh, when Thomas cast the one vote for Washburne. On that ballot, Speaker Shaw was one of six house members who did not vote. It was a demonstration of party loyalty by Thomas that would be a hallmark of his political career.

There would be repercussions in the Republican Party following Logan's failure to be selected. At a February 27 Republican caucus, some leaders questioned the loyalty of certain party members and demanded that a committee be formed to issue a report explaining how Logan could have lost. Thomas spoke forcefully against it, stating that the issue was finished. He called for the resolution to be tabled, which, after more discussion, it finally was.[17]

Following the election in November 1876, numerous civic groups, private citizens, and members of the media offered suggestions for legislation to the new members. In Chicago, a bipartisan organization known as the Citizens'

Association convened a series of meetings that brought the newly elected Republican and Democrat legislators from Cook County together to discuss issues of concern to the city and county. Thomas attended these meetings. It was hoped that common ground could be reached on these issues, so that the Cook County delegation would be able to present a united front in Springfield. The main issue discussed during these December meetings was modifying the state's revenue laws to allow the City of Chicago to collect back taxes it felt it was owed.[18]

The *Tribune* endorsed the activities of the Citizens' Association and offered up numerous suggestions for legislation that it felt could be supported by both Cook County Republicans and Democrats. Among the issues advocated by the *Tribune* were revenue reform, changing the way the Cook County Board was elected, legislation to protect the public from overpayment in cases of property condemnation for public use, and allowing the private sector to inspect grain warehouses instead of state grain inspectors.[19]

Thomas apparently took these suggestions to heart and worked hard for the interests of Chicago and Cook County. He strongly supported House Bill 536, which would have instituted the changes to the state's revenue law that were advocated by the Citizens' Association. Thomas voted for the bill on final passage in the House and on every procedural vote needed to help it pass. Ultimately, the bill passed the Senate also, but with amendments. A committee of members from both chambers met to work out the differences between the House and Senate versions of the bill, but the two sides could not reach agreement before the end of session, and the bill never reached the governor's desk.[20] Thomas sponsored three bills during the session, two of which echoed the sentiments expressed by the *Tribune* and the Citizens' Association. The first bill, House Bill 544, sought to protect the city from losing money when it condemned property for public use. According to the *Tribune*, under existing law, damages and benefits were decided at different hearings, so inequities could be created between the two. The *Tribune* advocated, and Thomas proposed, combining the hearings, so that benefits and damages would offset each other. Thomas's bill never made it out of committee.[21]

Thomas also introduced House Bill 692, which would have allowed commercial organizations such as boards of trade or chambers of commerce to create their own grain inspection commissions and appoint grain inspectors in their municipality. Representative John Kedzie of Cook County introduced a similar bill in the House and state senator Michael Robinson, also of Cook County, introduced a similar bill in the Senate.[22] The *Tribune* had supported this type of legislation, arguing that state grain inspectors were untrustworthy patronage workers and that Chicago's grain trade had been harmed by the enactment of the creation of a State Board of Grain Inspectors. HB 692 was assigned to the warehouse committee that Thomas served on, but the committee sent it back to the House with an unfavorable recommendation, and the full House tabled the bill. Kedzie's version of the bill lost on final reading in the House and Robinson's version lost on final reading in the Senate.[23]

Thomas also sponsored House Bill 194, a compulsory education bill that required all children between the ages of seven and fifteen to attend school. This had not been an issue advocated by the Citizens' Association or the *Tribune* but was in keeping with Thomas's career as an educator. While HB 194 did not make it out of committee, another compulsory education bill, HB 247, made it to final reading where it failed to receive the required seventy-seven votes for passage on a day when approximately thirty members were absent. Republicans, including the House Speaker, supplied fifty-two of the sixty-eight votes HB 247 received. A handful of Democrats and independents also voted for the bill but a handful of Republicans, including Hopkins, the other Republican legislator from Thomas's district, joined the fifty-four who voted against it.[24]

The fact that Thomas did not pass any of his bills during the session was no shame. Few bills were introduced in the General Assembly in those days. Indeed, the 153 members of the House introduced only 735 bills during the thirtieth legislative session, an average of less than five bills per representative. Many legislators introduced only one bill during session and those legislators who introduced more than three bills generally were introducing appropriations bills at a time when the different parts of the state budget were voted on separately.[25] Of the 1,097 bills introduced in both the House and the Senate, the legislature sent only 187 to the governor.[26]

Thomas sponsored two resolutions while in the House. He offered the first on January 5, and it was perfunctory, calling for a joint session for January 8 to witness the inauguration of the state's constitutional officers. It is noteworthy only in that it may have been the first time Thomas spoke on the floor. The second resolution was equally minor. It was offered on May 2 and invited the visiting North Carolina Jubilee Singers to sing some of their plantation melodies to the House membership.[27]

Because transcripts of floor debates do not exist and newspapers often only mention that several representatives spoke on an issue, it is difficult to say how much Thomas participated in floor debate. His first time in debate, however, was recognized by the newspapers. On February 6, the House debated the revenue bill but adjourned without taking any action on it. The next day the chamber again debated the issue with no hope of resolution. In what was probably a brief speech, Thomas rose to call for the creation of a joint House-Senate subcommittee to amend the revenue law. According to the Republican *Inter-Ocean*, when Thomas was recognized, the entire House quieted down and paid attention to his remarks. Even the Democratic *Springfield Register* commented that in his maiden speech, Thomas "succeeded in enveloping the subject in a light of reasoning unprecedented." Despite this, his proposal lost.[28]

It is apparent from the bills Thomas introduced that he saw himself as a representative from Chicago and Cook County and not the representative of the state's African Americans. During his first session he did not sponsor any bills directly related to the African American community. Still, there was no forgetting that he was the first and only African American to serve in a General Assembly that consisted of many legislators born in the South and raised with the southern prejudice toward African Americans.[29]

On May 4, Speaker Shaw called on Thomas to temporarily take the chair during the session. For some of the members, having an African American in the Speaker's chair was difficult to accept. It was one thing for an African American to serve as an elected member of the House but another thing altogether for an African American to actually run the session. According to the Republican *Chicago Tribune* and *Chicago Inter-Ocean* Thomas did an admirable job in the chair. Even the Democratic *Chicago Times* wrote that "Mr. Thomas made a very good substitute for the regular presiding officer." However, the *Tribune* and *Inter-Ocean* also reported that while Thomas was in the chair, Democrats from southern Illinois began to congregate in the back of the chamber and loudly voice their indignation. The *Inter-Ocean* called these legislators "certain old negro-haters." Eventually, Shaw resumed his place in the chair, although the *Tribune* hinted that he returned early due to the anger of the Democrats. It also criticized Shaw for not rebuking the Democrats for their action.[30]

This was not the first time Thomas had seen prejudice during his first term. On February 4, the House opened its session with its customary prayer from a local minister. Two African American ministers from Springfield, Rev. George Brents and Rev. L. A. Coleman, often gave the opening prayer.[31] On February 4, shortly after Reverend Brents finished his prayer, Representative Thomas Connelly, a Democrat from downstate Hamilton County, introduced a resolution calling for the House to stop using African American ministers to say the opening prayer. Representative George Armstrong, a Democrat from LaSalle County, was presiding over the House at the time. He immediately ruled the resolution out of order. However, Thomas later said he was sorry the chair had taken that action because he would have liked to have "annihilated Connelly if an argument had been allowed." Springfield's *State Journal* also commented that had Armstrong not made his ruling, "Connelly would have received an overhauling at the hands of Mr. Thomas, the colored Representative from Cook County, that would have convinced him of his inferiority to the average 'nigger.'" While Thomas did not rebuke Connelly, the *Tribune* did. Its Springfield correspondent wrote, "Connolly [*sic*], of Hamilton, in behalf of the Democracy, which between drinks damns the nigger, this morning distinguished himself by offering a resolution that the services of colored chaplains be dispensed with in the House. Connolly represents the genuine Bourbons, who had rather be damned than prayed for by a nigger, and it was a nigger, a colored preacher, who prayed for the Solons this morning." Brents would go on to deliver the opening prayer three more times in the House that session.[32]

In Springfield, Thomas quickly acquainted himself with the city's African American community. He stayed at Reverend Coleman's house at 438 N. Fourth Street.[33] Coleman was the pastor at the Union Baptist Church and a friend of Thomas's minister, Rev. DeBaptiste. Both Rev. Coleman and Thomas attended the 1872 Wood River Baptist Association annual meeting and the two probably met there.[34] In 1883, Thomas's daughter, Justine, was born at Coleman's house.[35] On January 23, 1877, Thomas was a guest speaker at a mass meeting of the African American community that was held at Springfield's African Methodist Episcopal (A.M.E.) Church. Reverend Coleman was there as well. Although Thomas's remarks were not recorded, the meeting was held to express concerns about the situation in the South and the unresolved presidential election. The attendees passed a series of resolutions, including one declaring the loyalty of African Americans to the Republican Party. While the local Republican paper gave the meeting a favorable notice, the local Democratic newspaper the next day ran the derogatory headline "Desperate Darkies."[36]

Despite encountering some prejudice during his term, Thomas participated in many of the same social occasions as the other Illinois legislators. There were receptions at the governor's mansion, Republican meetings at the Leland Hotel and sites to see. In March, the legislature voted 68 to 27, with many representatives choosing not to vote at all, to allow a representative of the Woman's National Temperance Union of the State of Illinois to address the body. Thomas, who supported temperance but not prohibition, voted to allow the talk.[37] Other speeches given to the House during the session came from U.S. minister to France E. B. Washburne and U.S. Senators Richard Oglesby and David Davis.[38]

Near the end of the session, Thomas attended the House-Senate baseball game, an event held to raise money for Springfield's Home for the Friendless. Thomas did not participate in the game, which the House won 11 to 9.[39] The *State Register* noted that John H. Oberly, a railroad commissioner from Alexander County in deep southern Illinois, and Democrat Representative James Herrington of Kane County, gave Thomas a ride home following the game. Perhaps remembering the actions of some Democrats earlier in the session, the paper called the gesture "evidence of democratic progression." The paper also reported that Thomas was accompanied by his niece, but it is possible that it was referring to Thomas's daughter Hester, who would have been eight at the time.[40]

The *State Register* was not the only paper to look for progress on racial views among the state's southern Democratic legislators. In early May, the *Peoria Transcript* noted that Thomas Merritt, a southern Illinois Democrat, moved to suspend the rules to allow an African American singing duo, the Hyers Sisters, to enter the House chamber and sing a song. As the only African American member of the House, Thomas escorted the nationally known sisters, who were pioneers in their field, to the front of the chamber for their performance. While the Peoria paper saw the quality of the Hyers Sisters performance as proof of advances among African Americans, the *State Journal* saw Merritt's motion to suspend the rules as "strong and gratifying proof that the Democracy are advancing (or at least some of them), step by step with their sable brothers."[41]

The *St. Louis Republican*, a Democratic newspaper, used Thomas's service in the House to criticize Northern Republican policy toward the African American. Congratulating Illinois on having an elected African American in office, the paper editorialized that this was a solitary event in the North. Republicans, it said, "are very devoted to the interests of the negro in the South, but the worst Bourbon Democrat in the land is not more bitterly opposed than they to giving the negro office in any state north of Mason and Dixon's line."[42]

Many legislators utilized the railroads that serviced Springfield to return home on the weekends. The House had great difficulty achieving a quorum for its Saturday and Monday sessions. Legislators were paid $5 a day, seven days a week, from the first day of session to the last day, regardless of whether session was held on a given day or whether they attended. The newspapers began to comment on the absenteeism of the members. The *Inter-Ocean* ran a headline that read "Do Your Duty! That is What is demanded of the Lazy Legislators in Springfield." The *Illinois State Register* had a headline "A Disgraceful Performance" over an editorial criticizing a joint House-Senate committee that abandoned session to go on a junket to Chicago. The *Tribune* ran an editorial praising a bill introduced by Senator Merritt Joslyn that prohibited the acceptance of free railroad passes by members of the General Assembly during their term in office. The *Tribune* saw the bill as a way to reduce absenteeism by making legislators have to pay to leave and return to the capital.[43]

In April, Representative Moses Wentworth introduced a resolution calling for an examination of House roll calls to determine the absentee rate of the legislators. Thomas supported Wentworth on the issue but the measure failed to receive the required two-thirds vote.[44] In response, the *Tribune* conducted its own study of the roll calls of the House and listed the number of votes each House member missed. The *Tribune* examined 201 House roll calls taken since the election of a U.S. senator in January. Eighteen members missed more than 100 votes, although the *Tribune* conceded that eight of those members had legitimate excuses for missing the roll calls, such as personal illnesses, family illnesses, or work on investigative committees that took them away from the floor. Almost half the members missed almost half the votes. Only three legislators missed fewer than 10 votes of the 201 and only six missed fewer than 20.

Thomas proved to be an extremely conscientious legislator. According to the survey, he missed only eight votes, the third lowest number in the chamber behind Wentworth, who missed only one vote, and Representative Nelson Jay, who missed only five votes. Thomas remained devoted to duty through all three of his terms in the legislature. During his second term, both his wife and infant daughter died. Thomas returned to work just five days after his wife's death and just three days after his daughter's death. During Thomas's third and final term, the correspondent from the *Cleveland Gazette* would write that the "Honorable J. W. E. Thomas is accredited with being the most punctual man in the legislature."[45]

The *Tribune* story on absenteeism outraged the House. After the story appeared, the chamber argued over its facts and passed a resolution accusing the *Tribune* reporter of stealing the information. The *Tribune* took great delight in reporting on the debate, listing the number of votes missed behind the name of every speaker. The four sponsors of the resolution missed 143, 104, 93, and 68 votes. The House voted 99 to 38 to pass the resolution, which was little more than an attempt at revenge against the reporter. Thomas voted against the resolution.[46]

Thomas remained faithful to his duties in Springfield despite wanting to actively participate in the spring city and town elections. In a March letter to the *Inter-Ocean*, he stated his dilemma: "I desire to be up there to help select men to be nominated now," he wrote, "but there is such complaint about Cook County members being absent, I did not know that it would be advisable for me to leave."[47]

Most of the African American voters of the Second Ward once again strongly supported F. C. Vierling for alderman and were able to secure the Republican nomination for him at the primary election. However, several Republicans in the ward supported Addison Ballard for reelection. After losing the nomination, Ballard decided to run as an independent candidate. Thomas was able to attend a March 26 Second Ward Republican Club meeting, where he spoke on behalf of Vierling and called for harmony within the party. On April 2, Thomas was one of several hundred residents who signed a letter of endorsement of Vierling. In the April election, however, Ballard easily won reelection despite having to run as an independent. Vierling finished second and the Democratic candidate finished a distant third.[48]

Although Thomas was concerned about the split in the Second Ward aldermanic race, he was more concerned that in the city and town elections, African American voters might be lured away from the Republican Party by Democrats offering patronage jobs. Many African American Republicans in Chicago believed that they were not receiving their fair share of jobs from Republican officeholders. It was a sentiment with which Thomas agreed, although it did not diminish his loyalty to the party. In March, Thomas addressed a letter to the African American voters of Cook County in which he called for full support of the Republican Party. He wrote, "Let me again encourage you, my friends, not to turn your faces from the Republican party, but to stick close by it and help elect good men."

While Thomas addressed the letter to Cook County's African American voters, he intended that white Republicans also read it as well and so he clearly delineated the grievances of his African American constituents. "We do not feel that we ask too much when we ask for representation in the various city and county departments, for we always vote one way," he wrote, adding, "We think it is a burning shame for these men [Republicans] to treat us as they have in the past. They are very careful to select from every nationality but the black American."[49]

Thomas sent his letter to the two major Republican papers of Chicago, the *Tribune* and *Inter-Ocean*. Although the *Inter-Ocean* did not run the letter, it strongly condemned it after it appeared in the *Tribune*. In an editorial the day after the letter appeared, the *Inter-Ocean* focused not on Thomas's support of the party, but on his complaints about the lack of patronage received by African Americans. It felt that Thomas had complained too strongly on this issue. The paper noted that African Americans were a small part of the city's electorate, comprising roughly 1,200 voters. It also noted the successes of Thomas, John Jones and William Baker in securing government positions. The *Inter-Ocean* concluded that "Mr. Thomas should thank God for the Republican party, not fret and complain, in view of the fact that his 'friends' have not received all of the offices they strive for."[50]

Thomas quickly wrote back to the *Inter-Ocean* to clarify his position. He stood firm on his claims that African Americans had been slighted in their patronage requests. He also criticized the *Inter-Ocean* for not printing his original letter. In his response, Thomas again emphasized his support for the Republican Party. "I felt it my duty to at once warn my people against being led away into any independent organization, which would certainly have the tendency to defeat the Republican ticket," he wrote. But as the political leader of Chicago's African Americans, Thomas also said he wanted to apprise the party of the concerns of his community. "I felt it also a duty to report through the press the grievances of my people to the Republican party, not as a reproach to the party, but on these men who promise everything to get the votes and then, instead of giving the true and faithful and competent man of his own party something, entirely ignores him, and gives what he has to some person who voted and worked against him. This makes my people sore."[51]

The *Inter-Ocean* printed Thomas's response and backed down a bit from its criticisms. It wrote, "We never had any doubt about the purity of Mr. Thomas's motives; we doubted the wisdom and propriety of his making it appear that the question of patronage enters so largely into the calculations of the colored voter."[52]

The exchange between Thomas and the *Inter-Ocean* highlighted the problems Thomas would face throughout his career in his attempts to keep African Americans loyal to the Republican Party. Patronage was the lifeblood of political parties, and in Chicago it was distributed based in large part on ethnic considerations.[53] However, while other ethnic groups could seek patronage in exchange for their support, the *Inter-Ocean*, in criticizing patronage as entering so largely into the African American voters' calculations, implied that African Americans also owed the Republican Party their support for being the party that freed the slaves. It was an attitude that many white Republicans assumed for the duration of the century, but one that African American leaders eventually grew tired of.

While the exchange of letters showed that Thomas could be critical of the Republican Party, he would never waiver in his support of it. He believed it was the party that provided opportunity to African Americans in the North and offered the only hope for African Americans in the South. However, as the *Inter-Ocean* noted, African Americans were only a small part of

Chicago's electorate. For Thomas, this meant that politically the community needed to remain united to maximize its influence with the party. Other African Americans would argue that their vote was taken for granted by the Republican Party and the way to maximize the community's clout was to make the two parties bid for their vote.

Thomas's letters also show that he was a mainstream, nineteenth-century politician when it came to patronage. At a time when civil service reform was being discussed, Thomas knew that jobs built political parties. He also knew that many of his constituents needed jobs. In his first letter, he summed up his views: "We feel that we should, as far as we are competent, be considered as well as any other nationality. This I believe to be true 'Civil Service Reform'—give all competent men a chance, especially your friends."[54]

If in the political world Thomas was a loyal Republican and mainstream politician, so too was he in the legislative world. This did not mean he didn't have streaks of independence. As previously noted, he voted for a resolution calling for conducting a study of the House roll call votes and he voted with the minority against the resolution criticizing the *Tribune* reporter for his story on absenteeism. He also voted for a resolution to investigate the South Park commissioners, although the two other Representatives from his district, the Republican Hopkins and the Democrat Smith, voted against the resolution.[55] While he closely followed the Republican Speaker of the House on the votes for U.S. senator, Thomas and the Speaker parted ways on the revenue and warehouse bills, which were perceived as helping Cook County more than the rest of the state.

The thirtieth session of the Illinois General Assembly ended May 24, after 142 days. Most of the newspapers of the day provided harsh criticism. The *Chicago Tribune* wrote, "Taken as a whole, no General Assembly has ever been held in this State which has done more to disgrace popular government or to raise a question as to the fitness of the people to select their own lawmakers." In an editorial entitled "Another Affliction Ended," the *Chicago Times* added, "It has done more positive injury by stupid, ignorant, and malicious enactments, contrary to the public interest, than any previous legislature."[56]

In actuality, however, Thomas could take pride in the accomplishments of the session, some of which still affect the state. The legislature voted to create a State Board of Health, which was authorized to pass rules and regulations related to the health of Illinois citizens. The board of health bill mandated that physicians register their names with the county clerk of the county they resided in and that the counties register all births and deaths within their jurisdiction. The House passed the legislation, HB 485, by a 96–38 vote. In a separate bill, SB 220, the legislature created the Illinois State Historical Library and Natural Museum, charged with preserving the early history of Illinois. The House passed SB 220 by a vote of 85–32. The legislature also authorized the construction of a second state penitentiary, to be located in the southern part of the state. Thomas voted for all three bills. Both the State Board of Health and the State Natural History Museum still operate, as does the prison, which was built on 122 acres near the community of Chester, along the Mississippi River. The registration of births and deaths continues to be an important source of information for historians and genealogists.[57]

The legislature created the Illinois State Militia, which was to be known as the Illinois National Guard. While focused more on the creation of volunteer units, the legislation, HB 593, also subjected all men in Illinois between the ages of eighteen and forty-five to military duty. The House passed the bill 87 to 36, with Thomas voting yes. The National Guard received a quick baptism of fire during the great railroad strikes of July 1877, when Governor Shelby Cullom called out the guard to quell riots in Chicago and other parts of the state.[58]

In an effort to ease overcrowding on the Supreme Court docket, the legislature voted to establish the appellate court system in Illinois. The legislation, SB 279, established four Appellate Court districts. Each district consisted of three judges appointed by the Supreme Court. The House voted 103 to 35 for the bill, with Thomas again in the majority.[59] Both the Illinois National Guard and the State Appellate Courts continue to operate in Illinois.

The House voted 99 to 29 to appropriate $27,000 for the completion of Lincoln's tomb in Springfield and voted 82 to 40 to appropriate $50,000 for the completion of the Stephen Douglas monument in Chicago. It also voted 107 to 29 to appropriate $531,712 for the completion of the state capitol building. Thomas voted for all three appropriations, although under the state constitution, Illinois voters had the opportunity to vote on the statehouse appropriation, and they voted against it.[60]

By a vote of 84 to 38, the House redistricted the circuit courts outside of Cook County into thirteen districts and it voted 102 to 8 to establish a probate court in Cook County. It unanimously voted to change the way constitutional amendments could be proposed and voted to establish a Commission of Claims with the power to provide settlements for persons seeking redress against the state. By a vote of 116 to 20, it passed legislation that allowed women separated from their husbands to file suit for support if the cause of the separation was not their fault. And, by a vote of 101 to 15, it passed SB 342, legislation requiring railroads to build depots for its passengers. Thomas voted for all of these measures, all of which became law.[61]

Many of the bills supported by Thomas did not pass. As noted above, the legislature failed to pass HB 536, which would have changed the way revenue was collected in Illinois. Another controversial revenue bill, SB 114, also failed. This bill, which Thomas and most of the Cook County delegation supported, would have provided tax relief to large Illinois corporations.[62] The legislature also failed to pass a compulsory education bill. Thomas supported creating a school for deaf and mute children in Chicago, but that bill also failed. Although he was not the sponsor of the bill, he spoke on its behalf and also moved it from second reading to final reading.[63]

Most of the legislation the *Chicago Tribune* had supported before the session began failed and, coupled with the angry reaction to its reports on absenteeism, explains the severity of its postsession criticism. The *Tribune* had endorsed warehouse reform in the manner that Thomas proposed in HB 692, but that failed. It also advocated changing the way Cook County elected its board of commissioners, but that bill was defeated in the Senate. The legislature also did not pass legislation to eliminate free railroad passes for its members, something the *Tribune* had advocated.[64]

The *Inter-Ocean* had a slightly better session than the *Tribune*. It took the lead during the session in calling for a state investigation into the activities of the South Park commissioners. These were the officials who governed the parks on Chicago's South Side. Thomas spoke in favor of the issue on the floor, arguing that the commissioners themselves should want the investigation, if only to clear themselves of charges being made against them. The resolution passed 78 to 54. Of the twenty-one House members from Cook County, fourteen voted for the resolution, five voted against it and two were absent.[65] The end result of the investigation was to find only minor problems.[66]

On the last day of session, legislators exchanged gifts of canes and tobacco boxes, gave speeches of praise for their actions and sang songs, including "Auld Lang Syne," the "Star Spangled Banner" and "We Will all be Dar." The last recorded vote was on SB 184, legislation designed to prevent cruelty to animals at stockyards. The House passed the bill 87 to 21, with Thomas voting in favor of it. In the general good will of the last day, the legislature passed a resolution basically forgiving the *Tribune* reporter for his story on their absenteeism, and it ordered all references to the matter expunged from the House journal. Despite the good feelings on the last day of session, two legislators caused a storm of controversy when they announced that they had been offered bribes in exchange for their votes on the revenue bill. At a later point of the day, the members began throwing paper balls, books, and even waste paper baskets to signal their displeasure at a vote.[67]

In all, the first term was an exciting experience for Thomas. He had worked hard during the session. He had sponsored bills, served on committees, and participated in floor debate. He had proven to be a loyal Republican, a strong advocate for Chicago and Cook County and a conscientious legislator. The *State Journal* may have summed up his first term best when it wrote that he had "proven himself an able, attentive and sensible representative of the interests of his constituents."[68]

While he did not write any legislation specifically designed to benefit the African American community, he was always made aware that he was a "black" legislator. The newspapers typically referred to him as "the colored legislator." He faced prejudice in the chamber when he presided over the House. When he sought more patronage for the African Americans, he was assailed by a newspaper as being ungrateful for all the party had done for his people.

Thomas was acutely aware of his unique position as the first and only African American in the legislature, and he knew his every action would be seen in terms of representing his race. After the session, he wrote, "Deeply impressed by the duties of my new position, surrounded by friends anxious and fearful should I not well discharge those duties, and by open enemies, who would watch my course in order to criticize and find justification for the oft-repeated assertion that colored men are not qualified for official position, I conscientiously endeavored by diligent study and earnest thought to prepare myself intelligently and satisfactorily to discharge my duty as a legislator. I may have erred on some occasions; who has not? This I have, however; the proud satisfaction of knowing: No taint of personal or political dishonesty was ever or can ever truthfully be charged upon me. I was true to myself, true to my state and true to my party. And, I believe that no member of the legislature of which I was a member can be found, be he Republican or Democrat, whom will not say that I have to-day his respect as a legislator and his esteem as a man."[69]

Although both Thomas and the *State Journal* provided fair assessments of his first term in office, these assessments did not matter when it came time for reelection.

The Election of 1878

Because the Illinois legislature only met every two years, the May 24 adjournment meant that Thomas had completed his duties for his term almost a full year and a half before the next legislative election. He returned to Chicago and resumed both his teaching and his active participation in Republican politics.[70] In an effort to keep the African American community united and thus better able to compete politically with other, larger ethnic groups, he also sought to consolidate his political leadership over the community.

In the fall of 1877, Cook County elected candidates for three judicial positions, two court clerk positions, five county commissioners, and the county clerk, treasurer, and superintendent of schools.[71] Thomas and other members of the African American community participated in the election, although with limited results. W. C. Phillips continued to serve on the Central Republican Committee until that fall, when M. A. Farwell, a white business owner, replaced him as the representative from the Second Ward. The Second Ward Republican Club nominated both Thomas and Phillips to serve as delegates to the October 23 county Republican convention, but both of them lost in a hotly contested primary. The contest had nothing to do with race and, in fact, two other African American candidates were selected. In mid-October, more than 500 African Americans signed a petition in support of Louis White as the Republican nominee for probate clerk. It is not known if Thomas signed the petition. White was the only African American seriously considered for any of the nominations for office that fall but at the nominating convention he came in fifth place, receiving just 11 votes of 191 cast.[72]

Although Thomas lost his bid to serve as delegate to the county convention, he remained active. Thomas served as one of three Second Ward election judges at the primary election, held October 22. He also spoke on behalf of the Republican candidates, including S. H. McCrea, a former slave owner, for county treasurer. Thomas argued that McCrea, if elected, would appoint African Americans to positions in the treasurer's office. McCrea and the rest of the Republican ticket were successful that year.[73]

Buoyed by the success of the party at the election and seeking to become sole political leader of Chicago's African Americans, Thomas sought to make good on the promises of some Republican candidates to provide African Americans with jobs. He helped form a committee whose purpose was to recommend African Americans for jobs with the newly elected officeholders. On November 20 the committee issued a report at a meeting of African Americans at Thomas's house. The *Tribune* described it as "large and enthusiastic"; however, it also reported that the crowd repudiated the actions of the committee in making the endorsements. Thomas responded in a letter to the *Tribune* where he stated that only those who were not endorsed repudiated the committee's actions. It is not known if the newly elected officeholders hired any of the African Americans recommended by the committee or any African Americans at all.[74]

In the spring 1878 city elections, the African American community again failed to receive a nomination for an office. The Second Ward Republican

Club, with M. A. Farwell as its new president, made no endorsement for alderman and no African American sought the position. At the March Republican primary, the ward voted 436 to 407 to support Samuel Engle, a tailor, over incumbent Jacob Rosenberg. The *Times* would charge that Engle was a tool of First Ward Democratic boss Michael McDonald. Rosenberg subsequently ran as an independent candidate. The split in the party proved insurmountable, as Democrat Patrick Sanders defeated the two Republican candidates. Rosenberg, who was supported by Chicago's Democratic and Republican papers, came in a close second to Sanders. Engle, the regular nominee of the Republican Party, came in a distant third. Both the *Times* and the *Inter-Ocean* reported that the African American community supported Rosenberg.[75]

The *Inter-Ocean* also reported that spring that former Cook County Commissioner John Jones, the first African American to hold office in Cook County, was interested in running for South Town supervisor. Jones quickly denied that he was seeking an office.[76] Two African Americans, Robert M. Mitchell and A. T. Hall, were selected to serve on the nine-member Second Ward delegation to the Republican South Town convention. At that convention, which consisted of forty-four delegates from the First to the Fifth Wards, Hall was one of four candidates who sought the nomination for town clerk. He received twelve votes on the first, informal ballot, while three white candidates received eleven, ten and ten votes. On the seventh ballot, Hall only received one vote, as the convention appeared to nominate Charles L. Shorick, a German-born businessman. The *Times* reported that "the strong American wards, notably the Third and Fourth, frowned down the colored candidate."

When Hall lost, he sarcastically told the convention that the African American voters would remember the "very kind, considerate, and generous manner in which it had dealt with the colored people." Arthur Dixon, leader of the First Ward delegation, supported the African American community and said that an African American should be placed on the ticket. He also said that the First Ward's vote had been misreported, meaning that Shorick did not yet have a majority. In the balloting that followed, Hall received as many as twenty votes, just two shy of the nomination, but, as the *Times* reported, "the American wards would not swallow him." A delegate from the Third Ward, one of the "American Wards," then nominated Thomas for clerk. The nomination was declared irregular, but Thomas received ten votes anyway. Hall then withdrew his candidacy and supported Shorick, who was nominated on the 16th ballot. Shorick would go on to win the election, with Republicans electing the town supervisor, collector and clerk but losing the assessor's race.[77]

The nomination of Thomas for town clerk was the only mention of him by the daily newspapers during that election. His leadership was missed by the community, which failed to nominate a single African American as a candidate for office on the Republican ticket. The only visible honor an African American received from the party that spring and summer was the selection of Richard M. Hancock as one of four Second Ward delegates to serve at the state Republican convention in Springfield. Hancock was the only African American of the seventy-one member Chicago delegation.[78]

That fall Thomas sought renomination to the General Assembly. His candidacy was hampered early by the sudden death of his fifty-year-old wife, Maria, on August 21, 1878, less than two months before the nominating convention. According to the *Inter-Ocean*, "Mrs. Thomas, a colored woman, living on Fourth Avenue near Van Buren street, fell apparently dead outside Arcade Court about 11 o'clock last night. The woman and a number of relatives and friends had been to Farwell Hall just previous and it is thought an affection of the heart caused the fall. She was conveyed to her residence in a hack, amid the heart-rending shrieks of a young daughter." She was buried in Graceland Cemetery on Chicago's north side following funeral services at Olivet Baptist Church.[79]

With his re-election approaching, Thomas now found himself a widower and single parent. Still, he pursued renomination and could be assured of the almost unanimous support from the African American community. The African American Republicans of Chicago were scheduled to meet August 22 but they postponed their meeting due to Mrs. Thomas's death.[80] When they met five days later, on August 27, they endorsed resolutions declaring their loyalty to the Republican Party and endorsing Thomas for re-election.[81]

However, while African American voters supported Thomas, they remained a minority within the district. As in 1876, Thomas had to have the support of white Republicans to gain the nomination. And, despite his good Republican record in the House, in the world of Chicago politics incumbency offered a candidate little protection. A hint of what was to come was shown in a September 2, 1878, meeting of Thomas's own Second Ward Club, when a white candidate defeated an African American candidate for the position of secretary, a position Thomas once held. According to the *Tribune*, the white candidate won with the votes of several African American men. Thomas, attending his first meeting since the death of his wife two weeks earlier, considered the loss of the position an insult. The *Tribune* reported, "Mr. Thomas followed the announcement of the vote with a loud and violent speech, asserting that the defeat of Warren (the black candidate) was a robbery of the colored voters of the ward, and other equally plausible statements."

Thomas's speech was continually interrupted by other African Americans, who opposed him. "Between the speaking, the shouting, and the din of the Chairman's cane, the row was deafening," the *Tribune* reported. "Someone having called Mr. Thomas a scoundrel, he was about to make it a personal matter when he was pulled off and had to confine himself to talk. Just as it looked like an open row, Mr. Stapleton moved to adjourn, and the motion was unanimously carried."[82]

Clearly, while Thomas was the choice of the African American community for state representative, he was not the unchallenged leader within Second Ward politics. He blamed the activities at the Second Ward meeting on the activities of two or three African Americans and he tried to rally his community, which he saw as growing more and more apathetic. On September 4, he penned a letter entitled "An Address to Colored Citizens" that appeared in the *Chicago Evening Journal*. In the letter he encouraged more African American participation in the Second Ward Republican Club. He wrote, "It is really discouraging to go into these meetings every Monday evening and find a very large number of whites there, and only a half a dozen or so colored men. I appeal to you, if you have any interest at all in your own progress and advancement, to come out every Monday evening to these meetings, and show that you do not mean to have yourselves deprived entirely of representation by two or three unprincipled colored men who are doing all they can against your interest by assisting milk and water white Republicans to wrest from you the little you have."[83]

Although he campaigned heavily, it was apparent that things were going wrong for Thomas early in the campaign. As in 1876, the Republicans of the Third Ward gave him difficulties. At the club's regularly held weekly meeting of September 28, 1878, the *Inter-Ocean* reported that "The meeting was then addressed by Mr. J. W. E. Thomas, the colored Representative at Springfield. He felt sore, he said, because some members of the club had assailed him on account of his color and youth. He defended his character, designs and intellect in able and convincing terms. He was a candidate for re-election, not of his own accord, but in answer to the pressing invitation of his colored friends. If re-elected, he would do his best, he said."[84]

In an October 8, 1878, letter to his constituents, Thomas continued this line of reasoning for his re-election. "I am now a candidate for re-nomination and re-election at your hands. I ask an endorsement of my past conduct. If ought can be truthfully said against me, if it can be shown that I have not done my duty, as well, at least, as the average of my fellow members; if I have been unfaithful in particulars, then let me, without consideration and without pity, be disgraced and discharged from your service at the end of my first term. If such things cannot be truthfully said of me, then, as the sole representative of the colored Republicans of Illinois in its General Assembly, I confidently ask and expect at your hands a renomination and re-election. In closing, permit me to say that my own people are solidly with me. It is their battle more than mine. I am in earnest, and they are in earnest in asking that the same consideration which is shown to white Republicans, to Irish and German and Scandinavian Republicans, be shown to colored Republicans."[85]

Along with the lack of support in the Third Ward Republican organization, Thomas was hurt because there were two candidates from the Second Ward, himself and attorney Benjamin Wilson. At the Second Ward Republican primary, Wilson defeated Thomas and a near riot ensued, with the Thomas forces charging that the Wilson forces had imported Democratic voters to accomplish Wilson's victory. The police were called to the polls and it took more than three hours to count the votes.[86] At the Republican nominating convention, held the day after the primary, both Thomas and Wilson sent full delegations of eight supporters as representatives for the Second Ward. A credentials fight ensued and the matter was referred to a committee. After meeting behind closed doors for an hour the committee could not make a decision. Finally, a compromise was worked out, where each candidate seated four supporters as delegates from the ward.[87] This meant that Thomas's base was cut in half.

Also running for representative were incumbent Sol Hopkins of the town of Lake and L. D. Condee, a lawyer from Hyde Park. Because senators were elected to four year terms, there was no Senate candidate up for nomination. On an informal ballot involving all the candidates, the results were: Hopkins 18, Condee 14, Wilson 6 and Thomas 4. However, in the interests of geographical balance, Hopkins and Condee would oppose each other for the seat reserved for the candidate from the "southern" part of the district. Wilson and Thomas would vie for the seat reserved for the "northern" part of the district.

On the first ballot, Hopkins easily won re-nomination to the first legislative position, 24 votes to 17 to Condee. For the second legislative spot, Wilson defeated Thomas 28 to 13. Both nominations were then made unanimous.[88]

Thomas's defeat sparked an angry backlash against the Republican Party among African American voters in the district, who found an outlet for that anger in the independent candidacy of James Bradwell. In early October Bradwell, a judge and former Republican member of the legislature, announced that he would run as an independent for the House. Bradwell was a liberal on social issues and had many friends in the African American community. He and his wife, Myra, were leading suffragists in Illinois and were the publishers of the *Legal News* newspaper. Judge Bradwell had always been a leader on African American issues and in 1869, he used the *Legal News* to attest to the good moral character of Lloyd G. Wheeler when Wheeler became an attorney. Wheeler was John Jones's son-in-law and the first African American to pass the Illinois bar.[89]

Bradwell had made it a point to by-pass the Republican Party's nomination for the position. His supporters encouraged his candidacy in an open letter to the *Inter-Ocean, Times* and *Tribune.* The letter was signed by several voters of the Second District, including Wheeler.[90] This was done before the Republicans of the Second Senatorial District had met to nominate their legislative candidates. In other words, at least at this point, Wheeler, a prominent African American, was aiding someone who had the possibility of being an opponent of Thomas, although Thomas eventually did not receive the Republican nomination. However, the Bradwell candidacy gave African Americans a candidate they could support for state representative in retaliation for the Republicans not nominating Thomas.

Shortly after the Republican nominating convention, the Second Ward Republican Club met to ratify the ticket. Wilson attended the meeting and tried to calm down the many African American members of the club, who had been angered by Thomas's defeat. Club member E. R. Bliss said that "Republicans should never make an issue of nationality or color." Nevertheless, the meeting broke up without any ratification of the ticket.[91]

On October 21, about 200 African Americans and some whites held a large "indignation" meeting to protest the alleged slight they had received. Thomas is not listed as having attended the meeting. African American leaders who did attend the meeting included Richard M. Hancock, who presided over the meeting, A. T. Hall and Ferdinand L. Barnett, who gave speeches, and William Baker. Barnett, who was the publisher of Chicago's first African American newspaper and later married activist Ida B. Wells, also served as secretary of the meeting. According to the *Inter-Ocean*, the participants said they would put up their own candidate for the legislature, presumably African American, and would not endorse Ben Wilson. Participants at the meeting passed numerous resolutions, including one that complained about Thomas being "shamelessly deprived of the nomination." One resolution stated that by not endorsing Thomas, the Republicans had offered the "three thousand colored voters in the county an insult as unpardonable as it was unprovoked." The participants at the meeting endorsed the rest of the Republican ticket but also said they favored Judge Bradwell, as a "good, faithful and reliable man."[92]

Upon hearing that a mass meeting had been called, the regular Republicans responded with a circular addressed to the African American voters of the city. In the circular, James Root, Secretary of the Republican Cook County Executive Committee, warned African American Republicans about bolting the Republican Party, stating that it might result in a lack of white support for African American candidates in the future. Three days later the *Inter-Ocean* printed a letter to the editor, allegedly from an African American voter, which criticized Thomas for being made a fool by the organizers of the mass meeting. The letter stated, "By mixing with such parties, he clearly demonstrates his unfitness and unworthiness to be sent to Springfield again."[93]

Although the letter implied that he was working against the party, Thomas actually remained a loyal Republican. Only two days after losing the nomination, he was selected by the Republican Party's Executive Committee to serve on the Second Ward campaign committee. He spoke at several Republican meetings, including the October 21 and October 25 Second Ward meetings, sharing the dais with Wilson and Hopkins. On October 23, he told the county executive committee that he would do all he could for the entire Republican ticket and work to unite the African American people in favor of the regular legislative candidates. Thomas also said that he wanted it known that he was not sore about not getting the nomination. On October 26, he and W. C. Phillips addressed an open letter to the African American voters of the Second Ward. In the letter, which was printed in the *Inter-Ocean* and the *Tribune*, they wrote:

Fellow Citizens: You may perhaps think it strange in us to give you advice through the press, but we deem it just to ourselves and to you to appeal to you in the calm moments of reason, we having failed to achieve that representation of the Republican ticket to which we felt we were justly entitled. We felt aggrieved and we believe justly so. We have expressed our grievances and think great good has been done, as we find the great mass of the Republican party with us, and We [sic] have assurances from them that they will do all in their power to assure us representation in the various departments of the city and county offices. And we deem it best for us as a people, and for the good of the grand old party of which we form a part, to unite our forces and vote the straight Republican ticket, and thereby secure success to the party and to the election of a United States Senator. Let us trust the party once more, and then we can claim the promises which, we trust, will not be violated.

If they fail to recognize us on their tickets, or fail to give us representation in appointive positions in fair proportion as to our numbers, as they do other nationalities, then we give you our word that we will no longer ask you to give them your support. We thought today we would not write to you: but, after fully considering the matter, and advising with our friends, we conclude it best to write. Hoping you will carefully consider this matter, we remain your obedient servants.[94]

By the end of October, the revolt seems to have fizzled. On the twenty-eighth the party appointed Thomas and Phillips to serve as Republican Supervisors of Election for the Second Ward and Thomas reported to the Executive Committee that everything in the Second Ward was all right. On October 30, the *Tribune* reported that the African American voters of the Second Ward were falling in line with the Republican Party. Indeed, the African American Republicans of the Second Ward never put up a candidate.[95]

In addition, the Republican Party actively began an anti-Bradwell campaign aimed at the African American voter. Anti-Bradwell letters appeared in the October 25, 1878, and the November 3, 1878 *Tribune*. One letter, entitled, "A Word with Colored Republicans," strongly argued that Bradwell was not a proper alternative for African American voters upset about the Republicans not renominating Thomas. The letter noted that Bradwell had announced his candidacy before the nominating convention and surmised, "If Thomas, the colored candidate, had been nominated, it would have made no difference to Judge Bradwell: he would then have fought the colored voters, instead of fighting with them."[96]

The Democrats attempted to exploit the perceived split between the African American community and the Republican Party, hoping that a defection of the African American vote would affect the rest of the Republican ticket, especially in the race for sheriff. The *Times,* in reports that were probably exaggerated, wrote that there were well-attended meetings of Democratic African American voters in the Second Ward on October 30 and November 2. These meetings were led by Edward C. Dawson, an African American Democrat. The *Times* reported that at the November 2 meeting, an African American named "Mr. Remsen" said the members of his race should support the Democratic Party, rather than the Republican Party, which had "freed them and then left them to starve." Another speaker added the Republicans had treated Thomas in a "disgraceful manner."[97]

The *Times* was the only newspaper of the five major dailies in Chicago to even note that African American Democrats had held meetings. To be sure, three of the remaining four papers the *Tribune, Evening Journal,* and *Inter-Ocean*, were strong Republican papers that may not have wanted to report upon the activities of such a group. However, other than Dawson, who would campaign for the Democrats for years, the names of those African Americans who addressed the meetings are very obscure, making it likely that the *Times* exaggerated the importance, as well as the size, of the meetings.

There were other ways in which the *Times* joined with the Democrats to try to exploit a split between the Republicans and the African American community. On October 28, the *Times* in an editorial alluded to an alleged attempt by the Republican Party machine to buy off the African American community with the promise of jobs. The jobs offered, according to the editorial, were janitorial positions, plus a bailiff position at the jail. The *Times* editorialized, "It seems to be taken for granted that the colored brethren have their price, and that all that is required to induce them to abandon principle and overlook the ill-treatment they have received is to agree to appoint a few of them to wash the party pots and kettles in case of party success . . . the suggestion that the colored voters of the Second district have so little intelligence and self-respect that they will accept the offer, and sell themselves for such a handful of political pennies, shows what is the real regard of the caucus managers for the colored brother."[98]

Despite all the protests over the Republican snub of Thomas and of its failure to nominate any African American for office, on Election Day the Second Legislative District again proved to be overwhelmingly Republican. Hopkins and Wilson were easy winners, as was Democrat Patrick Barry. Wilson received 8,746 votes, Hopkins 8,246½ and Barry 6,851. Bradwell came in fourth, with 5,049½. John Gilder of the Greenback Party received 2,198 votes and Charles Burke of the Socialist Party received 1,530½ votes. J. E. Cassiday, who was a last minute entry in the 1876 election, received 230 votes.[99]

Thomas had worked hard to ensure that Chicago's African American community would stay loyal to the Republican Party and his efforts were largely successful. However, signs of future problems were appearing for him. The community had lost an important symbol with the failure of the Republicans to renominate Thomas or select any African American as a candidate. Bradwell's strong independent campaign had some African American support, demonstrating that at least some members of the community, like those of other ethnic groups in Chicago, were willing to leave the party if so provoked. While the provocation of the community in this case was the failure of the Republicans to renominate Thomas, this still did not bode well for Thomas, who saw both his and the community's best chances for advancement tied to the Republican Party. Thomas had failed in his efforts in 1877 to be the distributor of patronage in the community and now he held no elective position. In all, there could be no denying that the year 1878 represented a setback for him and the African American community.

[3]

"Justly Entitled to Representation": The Long Road Back to the Legislature

The years 1878–1880 would be a time of both political gain and loss for Chicago's African American community. While no African American would be elected to the state legislature or to a city or county office, an African American would be elected as South Town clerk. John Howard and Isaac Rivers emerged as political activists, although they were not of the caliber of John Jones or John W. E. Thomas. Jones, Chicago's first African American political leader, died in 1879.[1] More and more African Americans received government jobs, including W. C. Phillips, who began working as a clerk for the Cook County Recorder of Deeds office; Rivers, who became a Post Office carrier; and J. Q. Grant, who became a constable for the South Town.[2] Ferdinand Barnett began publishing the *Conservator*, the first African American newspaper in Chicago in 1878, and although few copies of it exist today, it once gave voice to the city's African American community. Thomas focused less on politics and more on his personal and business affairs. Despite having been a political leader of the African American community, his few efforts at politics in Chicago during this period ended in failure.

A Law Career and a Second Marriage

Following the 1878 election, Thomas began the serious study of law. He studied under the guidance of Kirk Hawes, of the law firm Hawes and Lawrence, located at the southwest corner of Dearborn and Monroe Streets in downtown Chicago. Hawes was a prominent Republican attorney in the city. In 1880, he was elected to the first of two terms as a superior court judge. Thomas received his law license on February 2, 1880, becoming only the sixth African American in Chicago to become an attorney.[3]

Lloyd G. Wheeler was the first African American attorney in Illinois when he obtained his license on April 20, 1869. By the end of the century, more than thirty African Americans from Chicago had become lawyers. As with their white counterparts, admission to the bar helped many African Americans pursue political careers. Of the first twelve African Americans in Chicago to become lawyers, three of them (Thomas, Edward H. Morris, and John G. Jones) became state representatives, and four others (Lloyd G. Wheeler, Ferdinand Barnett, S. Laing Williams, and Franklin Denison) took leading roles in community affairs. However, becoming an attorney did not mean immediate acceptance into the legal community for African Americans. The Chicago Bar Association formed in 1874, but did not admit African Americans until the 1940s. Judge Bradwell attempted to have African American attorneys admitted to the association, but he never succeeded. In 1914, fifteen years after Thomas's death, two dozen African American lawyers formed the Cook County Bar Association.[4]

Thomas worked mainly as a police court lawyer, and his practice would prove lucrative. The *Chicago Legal News* later wrote of him that, "As a lawyer, Mr. Thomas's business was principally at the Harrison Street Police Station, in defending criminals, signing their bonds and investing the proceeds in real estate." The *Legal News* seemed to apologize for the type of law Thomas practiced, stating, "Not withstanding the character of this business and the length of time Mr. Thomas was engaged in it, he was regarded by all who knew him as a man of honor and integrity." Both the *Chicago Chronicle* and the *Inter-Ocean* agreed that Thomas spent most of his time as an attorney at the Harrison Street Police Station. The *Chronicle* added, "His chief interest was in criminal work and at the Harrison Street police court, where he was almost a daily visitor for ten years, he was in demand by his clients, white and black."[5]

If the *Legal News* seemed to apologize for the type of work Thomas performed, it was because police courts were the bottom rung of the judicial ladder. Police courts were administered by police magistrates, who were also justices of the peace. Justices of the peace were elected positions everywhere else in the state, but in the City of Chicago where they were appointed by the governor by and with the consent of the state senate and following the recommendation of the judges of the superior, circuit, and county courts.[6] From the justices of the peace, the mayor of Chicago selected police magistrates, who were in charge of the courts at the police stations. The qualifications for being a justice of the peace or a police magistrate were that one had to be a male citizen of the United States, at least twenty-five years old, a state resident for at least five years, and a resident of the town, county, or city from which he would be selected. In other words, justices of the peace did not have to have a legal background, much less a law degree. The courts were often run without lawyers being present at all, as the working-class clientele often could not afford lawyers and would argue their own cases.[7] In working at a police court, Thomas would have focused his practice on minor police matters involving petty criminals, gamblers, prostitutes, and repeat offenders that were brought from the adjoining jail where they were locked up.

The appointment of the justices and magistrates was done on a partisan basis. As the *Chicago Times* editorialized in 1879, following the release of the judicial nominations for justices of the peace, "they evidently have not departed from their usual course of making nominations upon 'recommendations,' chiefly political, instead of searching inquiry into the character and qualifications of the candidates."[8] The partisan nature of the appointments created a system rife with corruption. A politician who controlled a justice of the peace or a police magistrate could use that person to further his political ends. Writing about the police courts almost one hundred years after they were abolished, historian Michael Willrich noted, "In the Levee wards, aldermen used the police courts to exact political obedience from the keepers and customers of sporting houses, cheap hotels and saloons, institutions central to the everyday life and economy of the wards."[9]

The newspapers of the day and Chicago's elite looked down on the police courts, with their corrupt police magistrates, their lack of attorneys, and their working-class clientele. The *Chicago Evening Journal* summed up this view of police courts in an 1890 editorial: "The police court system in Chicago, and other large cities, is an outrage upon law decency and humanity."[10] In the spring of 1905, under pressure from the Illinois Bar Association, newspapers, and progressive reformers, the Illinois General Assembly approved legislation abolishing Chicago's justice of the peace system and replacing it with municipal courts. Chicago's voters ratified the decision that November.

Yet, as Willrich also noted, it was before the justices of the peace and the police magistrates that the lion's share of judicial business was done. These were the courts that were the closest to ordinary people and the ones that dealt with the everyday rights of the working people. In looking at statistics for 1890, Willrich found that justices of the peace handled more than 96 percent of all criminal case in Chicago. Some justices and police magistrates were corrupt, but apparently many were not.[11]

The police stations that housed the police courts were held in a similar low esteem as the justice of the peace courts. The Harrison Street Police Station, where Thomas worked, bordered the Levee vice district and was considered the worst of the police stations. In 1894, muckraking journalist William T. Stead published a still-famous exposé on life in the city titled *If Christ Came to Chicago.* His first chapter was "In Harrison Street Police Station." He wrote,

"There is something dreary and repelling about a police station even in the least criminal districts. But Harrison Street Station stands in the midst of darkest Chicago. Behind the iron bars of its underground cages are penned up night after night scores and hundreds of the most dissolute ruffians of both sexes that can be raked up in the dives of the levee."[12] It may be assumed that those were some of the clients Thomas represented.

Thomas himself had personal experience with the dangers of the station. In 1896 Albert Abrahams, the son of former state representative Isaac Abrahams, became angry at the chief janitor of the police station. He pulled out a gun and fired two shots at the janitor. The shots missed, but one of the bullets went through the coat of George Raymond, who was working as a messenger for Thomas at the time.[13] In 1891, Thomas hired as a clerk a homeless African American youth who had been staying at the Harrison Street Police Station. One month later the clerk, named Rutherford Hayes Hicks, broke into a safe at Thomas's house, stole $300 in gold coin and $500 in cash, and fled to New York City. He was caught less than two weeks later, returned to Chicago, and in May sent to reform school.[14]

Records for the police courts do not exist, so it is difficult to discuss the types of cases Thomas worked on as an attorney. It is somewhat easier to trace his work as a bondsman. In 1887 the *Tribune* ran a story about professional bailers and mentioned Thomas. Although the article was generally negative about professional bailers, the part about Thomas was not. It discussed how Thomas made his living and operated his law practice at the police court:

> Thomas is a professional bailer, but at the same time a responsible bondsman. He schedules property worth $40,000, and no bond that he signs is ever forfeited, for the reason that he goes on none in which there is any doubt. Supposing there is a levee raid at night and a large number of people arrested. Some may be charged with selling liquor without license, others with being inmates of disreputable houses, and others for disorderly conduct. Thomas will be sent for by some of those arrested, and will give bonds for their appearance in the police court next morning. He will give bonds for anybody who has cash security sufficient to cover the fine and costs—for the fine is about the same thing in all such cases. The accused may not show up in the morning. Thomas answers for him or her, pleads guilty, and pays the fine. That is how it is worked—Thomas gets his fee as a lawyer or as a professional bailer, whichever you please.

The article maintained that several others sought to do this type of business, but "Thomas holds the best part of it."[15]

Serving as a bondsman in the levee district was not considered reputable work, yet Thomas generally kept his name clean. In 1891, Thomas signed the bonds for the owners of the House of David, a levee gambling house on Clark Street that had been raided. He also signed the bonds for the persons arrested for gambling. One newspaper complained that the gamblers did not pay their fines but that the city didn't seek to collect the bonds from the bondsman, who, in this case, was Thomas. "The whole proceeding of raiding gambling houses and putting down big fines opposite the names of the crooks and lawbreakers usually turns out to be an unmitigated farce," the paper wrote. "The law breakers do not pay their fines either in coin of the realm or by labor in prison. The professional bailer takes care of the outlaws."

While the paper's complaint may have been true in many instances, the city prosecutor denied the charges and defended Thomas, who was the professional bailer in this case. The prosecutor stated that "J. W. E. Thomas is on the bonds in the House of David Case. Within the twenty days allowed for appeal either appeals will be taken or the bonds paid, for Thomas makes his bonds good. He is one of the few in the business from whom it would be possible legally to collect anything." Thomas appears to have been the bondsman of choice for the gamblers at the House of David. A few months after the above case, police again raided the establishment and Thomas signed the bonds for sixty-five gamblers arrested in that raid.[16]

Along with associating with less-than-desirable elements of the city, being a bondsman carried with it financial risks. In 1891, Thomas and W. W. Charles signed a bond for Charles Williams, who worked as the treasurer and bookkeeper for the Windsor Theatre. The theater's proprietor, Michael Leavitt, accused Williams of doctoring the books and cheating him out of approximately $1,000. After Leavitt fired Williams, he chose not to seek the $1,000 owed him but the $6,000 bond guarantee that Thomas and Charles had signed plus damages. Thomas employed Chicago's leading African American attorney for his defense, Edward H. Morris, but lost the case.[17]

Despite the perilous nature of putting up money for persons with a less than stellar reputation, Thomas prospered in this part of his career. Thomas's sometimes nemesis, James Bradwell, would write in the *Chicago Legal News* in 1896 that Thomas had no equal as a bail bondsman. The *Tribune* in 1887 estimated that he made between $200 and $300 a week for his services as a bondsman.[18]

Thomas invested his profits in real estate, a solid investment in the rapidly growing Chicago area. As early as 1885, the *Colored Men's Professional and Business Directory of Chicago* listed him as "among the number of colored people who are in good circumstances financially, and the large owners of real estate." His law career and his subsequent work as a bondsman provided him with an income that made him the wealthiest African American in the city when he died in 1899.[19]

However, that was in the future. Along with the study of law, there were other reasons why Thomas pulled away from politics. First and foremost, he had to raise his daughter as a single parent. In this endeavor, he most certainly was helped by his parents. His mother is listed on the 1880 census as living with Thomas.[20] Also, in 1880, Thomas married for a second time. On May 4 of that year, he married seventeen-year-old Justine E. C. Latcher at St. Patrick's Catholic Church, located at the corner of Des Plaines Avenue and Adams Street. On their wedding certificate, Thomas listed his age as thirty-four. Latcher was a Canadian-born African American who lived with her mother and siblings. Her father Joseph Benjamin Latcher, a kalsominer (white washer), had passed away at the age of fifty-five just one year earlier.[21]

The marriage of Thomas to Latcher shows both the benefits and the perils of being a prominent leader. Less than two weeks before the wedding, the *Chicago Inter-Ocean* printed an accusation from an Edward Payne alleging Thomas's "intimacy with his wife." Thomas immediately protested to the *Inter-Ocean*, which printed a retraction that stated, "Mr. Thomas is too respectable a person to be mentioned in such a connection." The paper then listed the facts of the situation, stating that Payne had attempted to beat his wife outside of church on Sunday. When Thomas intervened on the woman's behalf, Payne attempted to fight Thomas and was arrested. The paper concluded by saying "Thomas was never intimate with Payne's wife and was no more to her than a distant acquaintance."[22]

More harmful to Thomas was an accusation written by George Beard, whom the *Inter-Ocean* described as an African American newspaper editor. In an article in his paper, Beard charged that Thomas was about to marry a fifteen-year-old. Thomas sued for libel but the case was discharged in a justice of the peace court. The result was to bring undue publicity to the wedding.[23]

The publicity may have led to coverage of the wedding in the daily papers, something not common for African Americans in the mainstream press. In 1878, when U.S. Senator Blanche Bruce married socialite Josephine Willson, it was the first time the *New York Times* and the *Washington Post* covered an African American wedding.[24] Similarly, the 1880 wedding between Thomas and Latcher may have been the first time the Chicago daily newspapers gave such prominence to a local African American wedding, even if the *Inter-Ocean* prefaced its article with "An event of much interest to the colored people of this city was the marriage last evening of Mr. J. W. Thomas," which was a clear reference to the scandal raised by Beard.

The Reverend Father Thomas Francis Galligan officiated at the wedding, which occurred on a clear Tuesday evening with the temperature hovering around 70 degrees. W. C. Phillips and Justine's sister, Annie, attended the couple. The newly married couple had a reception after the wedding at the Thomas home at 198 Fourth Avenue. The reception demonstrates the economic success Thomas had achieved by 1880 and the upper-middle-class Victorian lifestyle he had attained, even while living in the levee. An estimated 200 people attended the reception, including such prominent dignitaries as Judge John Jameson, Recorder James Brockway, Alderman Addison Ballard, and attorneys Edward H. Morris, J. N. Washington, and Henry Carter. The couple received many gifts, including a silver pitcher, an ink stand, a toilet box with brush and comb, a volume of Emerson's works, a dozen wine glasses, and two bottles of wine. The couple also received a set of furniture, with the *Tribune* reporting that Thomas gave the furniture to his wife and the *Inter-Ocean* reporting that Thomas's mother gave a parlor set to the couple. The following week, Justine Thomas received her friends at the home.[25]

Even with the courtship and wedding, the new career in law and the purported scandals reported by the newspapers, Thomas's mind was never too far from politics. In the spring of 1879, the Second Ward Republican Club endorsed Thomas for one of the nineteen justice of the peace positions that were open that year. Many justices received their appointments based on political considerations. A letter to the *Chicago Tribune* signed by several citizens however, noted Thomas's qualifications for the position as a former state representative and as a current student of the law. The letter concluded by stating that Thomas was the unanimous choice of Chicago's African American citizens.[26]

Despite the endorsement from the Second Ward Republican Club and the support from the African American community, the judges making the official recommendation to the governor did not recommend Thomas. The judges made their nominations based on party (eleven Republicans and eight Democrats) and area of the city (seven each for West Town and South Town and five for North Town). Ethnic considerations played a factor as well, but the African American community, comprising less than 2 percent of the city's population and located mostly in South Town, couldn't compete against the interests of the German, Irish, Scandinavian and even French communities.[27] More than 125 persons had expressed an interest in receiving an appointment, as the position paid, as the *Chicago Times* noted, "from two to seven thousand dollars a year legitimately."[28] Had Thomas, who was still a year away from passing the bar, received an appointment, it would have marked the first time an African American had served as a judge in Cook County.

While Thomas would have been qualified for the justice of the peace position, the endorsement he received from the Second Ward Republican club demonstrated that he was still a political leader. He played an active part in the spring 1879 elections. Thomas and W. C. Phillips served on the nine-member Second Ward delegation to the South Town Republican Convention. At the convention, which consisted of delegates from five of Chicago's eighteen wards, Thomas served as secretary. African American delegates attempted to have an African American, Paul Jones, selected as South Town clerk, but he lost at the convention by a vote of thirty-four to eight. Thomas also served as one of the vice presidents at a large Republican ratification meeting that was chaired by former Chicago mayor John Wentworth. He also spoke at several Second Ward Republican Club meetings and even traveled to the nearby Ninth Ward to speak to African American Republican voters there.[29]

The spring of 1879 signaled a political transition for Chicago's African American community away from the post–Civil War period of almost complete loyalty to the Republican Party. During the election, Edward Dawson established an African American Democrat Club that had a large enough following that mayoral candidate Carter Harrison spoke at one of its meetings.[30] Harrison actively sought votes from all ethnic groups, including African Americans, and his vote totals in the 1879 election and subsequent elections reflected some success within the community.[31] Even the failure of Thomas to be nominated for justice of the peace showed the perils to the community of staying within just one party. There was no incentive for the Democrats to nominate an African American and, despite its loyalty to the party, the community did not have the numbers to force the Republicans to choose Thomas.

Two other events occurred in 1879 that signaled a political transition in the African American community. The first occurred on May 21, when John Jones died. The North Carolina-born Jones had arrived in Chicago in 1845, where he established a successful tailor shop patronized by a mostly white clientele. He was friends with Frederick Douglass and John Brown, led the repeal efforts against the discriminatory Illinois Black Laws, joined Douglass as part of a five-man delegation that visited President Andrew Johnson at the White House in 1866, and became the first African American elected to office in Cook County. Jones's funeral was heavily attended, and Thomas was one of the mourners.[32] For the decade following John Jones's death, Thomas would be the most prominent African American politician in the city.

The second event of transition in 1879 was the unheralded arrival from Kentucky of Edward H. Morris, who by the 1890s would become Chicago's leading African American attorney and a man who almost all factions of Chicago's often divided African American community would see as a friend and ally. Morris arrived so poor that when he took his bar exam, he wore his overcoat to hide the shabby condition of his suit.[33]

In the fall 1879 election, African Americans played a small role. No African American was seriously mentioned as a candidate for one of five county commissioner positions that were up for election or for any of the county or judicial offices. William Landre, a janitor, served as the Second Ward representative on the Republican Central Committee and as a delegate to the county convention, and Isaac Rivers, a laborer, served on the Second Ward Campaign Committee. Thomas also served on the Second Ward Campaign Committee and spoke at a Second Ward African American Republican meeting but compared to past campaigns his involvement was small. Dawson continued his activities on behalf of the Democrats, but he was mostly ridiculed in the press.[34]

Thomas does not appear to have taken a leading role in the spring 1880 elections. Still, African Americans saw gains. A nominating committee of the Republicans of the Second Ward named W. C. Phillips as one of three suggested aldermanic candidates, but Phillips quickly stepped aside.[35] At the South Town Convention, delegates nominated African American Joseph Moore over the incumbent to serve as town clerk. Moore and the entire South Town Republican ticket won election that April, making Moore the first African American township official in Cook County. Following Moore's election, Republicans generally nominated an African American to run for the clerk position.[36]

Thomas did get caught up in the 1880 presidential campaign, where former president Ulysses S. Grant sought a third term after four years away from the White House. Grant's return to politics was met with mixed emotions from Republicans. His two terms in the White House had been marked by corruption and scandal. However, following his time in office, he had gone on a two-and-a-half-year world tour that received extensive and positive coverage in the press. In the fall of 1879, he returned to the United States, where his friends and political allies urged him to run again for the presidency. A trio of big state party bosses, Senator Roscoe Conkling of New York, Senator Don Cameron of Pennsylvania and Senator John A. Logan of Illinois, began working for Grant's nomination amid fears by others that a Grant victory would allow these "bosses" to return the federal government to the corrupt ways of the first two Grant terms.[37]

Senator James G. Blaine of Maine was Grant's primary opponent for the nomination. Blaine had attempted to win the nomination in 1876. Although he lost, he had had the support of the Illinois delegation to the Republican convention and remained strong in Illinois, Grant's home state.[38] In addition to Grant and Blaine, there were several favorite son and dark horse candidates running in 1880. In Illinois, a group of anti-third-term Republicans supported former Illinois congressman and minister to France Elihu B. Washburne as a favorite son and alternative candidate to Grant. Kirk Hawes, who Thomas studied law under, was one of the leaders of the anti-third-term movement and a strong supporter of Washburne.

Nationally African Americans, including Frederick Douglass, generally supported Grant. In Chicago, William Baker, Isaac Rivers, William Landre, R. C. Waring, and George Beard were some of the more notable supporters. But other African Americans did not support Grant. John Howard, the owner of a cigar shop, supported Blaine, as did Robert M. Mitchell. In February, Thomas attended the opening rally of the Blaine campaign in Chicago.[39]

At the May 8 Republican primary election, held to elect delegates to the county convention, the Washburne and Blaine forces combined into an anti-third-term coalition and delivered a stunning defeat to Grant in Cook County. However, the Second Ward, with its wealthy white population and large African American population, voted overwhelmingly for Grant. The ward selected a slate of eight Grant delegates to go to the county convention. The slate was led by Robert Todd Lincoln and included two African Americans, Rivers and Landre. John Howard ran and lost as a Second Ward delegate for the anti-third-term ticket.[40]

Delegates met at Farwell Hall to select ninety-two delegates to attend the state Republican convention, which was to be held the following week in Springfield. At the county convention, the Grant delegates bolted and conducted their own convention at the Palmer House. According to these delegates, Grant was due a share of the delegates to the state convention but the anti-third-term majority planned to enforce a winner-take-all rule. The bolt by the Grant forces created two delegations that would go to Springfield. With no Grant delegates at the Farwell Hall convention, delegates there selected a slate of delegates unanimously opposed to Grant. The Washburne and Blaine leaders divided the delegation to Springfield between 58 delegates pledged to Washburne and 34 pledged to Blaine. Howard was chosen as a Blaine delegate. Thomas was chosen to serve as an alternative delegate pledged to Blaine. The Grant meeting at the Palmer House selected a delegation for the state convention consisting of 92 delegates supporting Grant.[41]

Logan was in control of the state convention and was able to prevent the Cook County anti-third-term delegates from being seated until a credentials challenge could be heard. The Logan-controlled credentials committee ruled that the Grant forces should get a third of the Cook County delegation, which ensured that Grant would have a majority of the delegates at the state convention. With that majority, Logan then passed a motion requiring the state to vote as a unit for Grant at the national convention, meaning that Grant would receive all 42 votes from Illinois. The anti-third-term supporters from Cook County returned from the Springfield convention and conducted a mass indignation meeting to protest Logan's actions. Thomas served as one of the vice presidents of the mass meeting, which was so large that it was held at two separate locations.[42]

Logan did not do as well at the national convention. The anti-third-term coalition from Illinois, led by Kirk Hawes, challenged the maneuvers Logan took at the state convention and was able to defeat the unit rule. This cut the number of Grant delegates from Illinois from 42 to 24 and, combined with losses on other credential challenges, resulted in Grant's losing the Republican nomination to James A. Garfield.[43]

Following the national convention, the Republican Party united behind Garfield and his vice presidential running mate Chester Alan Arthur. In August, in a display of unity and Republican Party loyalty not seen again for a long time, African American leaders formed an African American Garfield and Arthur Club. The club appointed an executive campaign committee consisting of at least one African American representative from each city ward and from most of the county's townships. The organizational leadership read like a who's who of Chicago's African American leaders. J. Q. Grant served as chairman and Paul Jones served as secretary. W. C. Phillips served on the five member finance committee. Ward leaders included Thomas, Howard, Mitchell, Landre, Waring, Moore, S. W. Scott, John G. Jones, A. F. Bradley, George Beard, newcomer George Ecton, and dozens more.[44]

The Election of 1880

That fall, Thomas again tried for the state representative position. As in 1876, the major newspapers of the day did not mention Thomas as a prospective candidate.[45] Despite this, Thomas was out campaigning for the position. On September 6, 1880, Thomas addressed a large gathering of the Second Ward Republican Club. He spoke of the loyalty of African Americans to the Republican Party, stating that he did not think there was one African American Democrat in the city of Chicago.[46]

On September 13, thirty-three delegates met to nominate a candidate for state senator and two candidates for state representative. According to the *Inter-Ocean*, the meeting was quiet and orderly. Five ballots were held for senator, with L. D. Condee defeating incumbent D. N. Bash, S. H. Hopkins, and William S. Everett.

Nominations for the House of Representatives followed and the Republicans, as the majority party in the district, agreed to nominate two candidates. W. C. Phillips placed Thomas's name in nomination. Also nominated were R. H. White, an attorney from the Third Ward, and O. S. Cook, who was president of the Fourth Ward Republican Club. J. Q. Grant nominated Paul Jones, an African American who had been defeated two years earlier when he tried for the Republican nomination for South Town clerk. However, Jones would be a nonfactor in the nomination fight. The convention voted for one representative at a time, with seventeen votes needed to nominate. On the first ballot for the first representative position, White received 13 votes, Cook 12, Thomas 7 and Jones 1. On the second ballot, White received 13 votes, Cook 11, and Thomas 9. On the third ballot, White was nominated with 23 votes, to Thomas's 9 and Cook's 1. Ten of Cook's supporters had switched to White. Only one ballot was needed to nominate the candidate for the second representative position. Cook received 25 votes and Thomas received 8.[47]

Despite losing the nomination, Thomas remained very active in politics that fall. He addressed ward meetings and was elected vice president of the Young Men's [Republican] Central Club. He again served as a Republican supervisor of the election, representing the Second precinct of the Second Ward. Thomas even addressed a meeting of Polish citizens in the Fourteenth Ward. During a late October torchlight parade of approximately 1,000 African American Republicans, Thomas served as an aide, along with William Baker, Reverend DeBaptiste and Lloyd G. Wheeler.[48]

Some backlash did appear at the Republicans' failure to nominate an African American for a place anywhere on the Cook County Republican ticket. The Democratic *Times* attempted to exploit divisions between the African American community and the Republican Party, writing "the colored brother makes a mistake if he supposes that the party which has traded in him for 16 years has any other use for him in the North than to vote to order, or any other hope of him in the South than that some one will butcher him in order to solidify the north." The *Times* also reported, with only some probable exaggeration, that "the Negroes are in a state of insurrection because their claims to recognition [as candidates on the county ticket] were ignored." At the Republican County Convention in October, A. F. Bradley, an African American from West Town, had his name placed in nomination for county commissioner, but he came in last on the informal ballot and received no votes during the balloting. Immediately following the selection of the all-white county Republican ticket, John J. Bird, an African American leader from downstate Cairo, spoke to a meeting of Chicago African American Republicans. Bird stated that not having an African American receive a county commissioner nomination should be resented by the African American community.[49]

Coming into October, William Baker, who had helped Thomas when he ran for the legislature in 1876, announced his candidacy for the legislature from the First Senatorial District. Baker said he was running because he thought African Americans were entitled to representation on the Republican ticket. "There are twenty thousand colored voters in this state and it remains to be seen whether the Republicans will refuse to give an office to one of us," he was quoted as saying at the time. However, Baker failed in his efforts, doing so poorly in the primaries that the *Times* stated, "he was beaten shamefully."[50]

With the 1880 fall election over, African American men in Chicago had completed their first decade of having the vote. It was a decade marked with many accomplishments. There was no question that Chicago's African American community had warmly embraced participating in democracy not only as voters but as active party members. An African American had held office at the state, county, and local level during this time. African Americans had served in a variety of Republican Party posts and were being rewarded with patronage positions. Still, following 1880, there was only one African American in an elected position in Cook County and that was at the lowly town level. The losses between 1878 and 1880 seemed to outweigh the gains previously made. As political leader of the community, Thomas's losses symbolized the decline. He lost two attempts for state representative and was not nominated for justice of the peace, despite having the full backing of his community. For many of Chicago's politically oriented African Americans, it was time to reflect on their blind loyalty to the Republican Party. For Thomas, it was time to look for opportunities elsewhere.

The Election of 1882

The decade of the 1880s would mark a change in African American politics in Chicago. The coalition that Thomas had used to be elected state representative in 1876, an alliance between an African American community united behind a leader it had chosen and white Republicans sympathetic to what historian Charles Branham refers to as the "abolitionist-Republican tradition," was ending. New political activists were coming into prominence in the African American community and they were not willing to follow any one leader or, in some cases, even the Republican Party. This caused splits in the community, weakening its ability to achieve political goals. Just to succeed within their own community, African American leaders often had to make alliances with white leaders, who were less concerned about African American issues than they were about obtaining and keeping power within the party.

The practical result of this was that the white leaders were able to exploit the divisions within the community to choose who the community leaders would be, and those leaders would become dependent on their white allies. Or, as Branham notes, "Early black politicians were often willing—but sometimes petulant—captives of the power fights, patronage deals, petty squabbles, and financial machinations that characterized Chicago politics."[51] As Thomas continued his career in politics, he had to operate in this new system.

First, however, Thomas stepped away from politics. Taking advantage of what surely was a patronage appointment, Thomas moved to Washington, D.C., sometime in 1881. He accepted a position with the U.S. Treasury Department as a clerk in the Second Auditor's office, earning $1,200 a year. The salaries of the 125 clerks who worked in this office ranged from a high of $1,800 to a low of $1,000 a year.[52] In Washington, Thomas is listed in the 1882 city directory as living at 2218 I Street, NW and in the 1883 directory as living at 1922 12th St., NW. It was at the former address that his daughter, Blanche D. L. Thomas was born on September 14, 1881.[53]

It is not known how Thomas received his appointment. It is most probable that it came from Senator Logan, the federal patronage boss of Illinois. Although Thomas had been on the opposite side from Logan on the Grant fight in 1880, he had stuck with Logan in the senatorial fight of 1877. In 1879, following Logan's return to the Senate after a two-year absence, Thomas wrote him a congratulatory letter, stating that "the colored citizens generally are rejoicing in their homes because of the success of Genl. Logan." Illinoisan Green B. Raum, a Logan ally and another leader in the Grant fight, served as Commissioner of Internal Revenue and may have helped with the appointment.[54]

Thomas most likely received his appointment after the March 4, 1881, start of the Garfield administration; however, he had a difficult time leaving Chicago. On March 10, Thomas's mother, Martha, died of malarial disease at his home at 198 Fourth Avenue. One month later, on April 13, John's father, Edinboro, died of Bright's disease at the age of sixty-four. He too, passed away at the Thomas house. Both parents were buried at Oak Woods Cemetery on Chicago's south side in a plot purchased by their son. Thomas spent a good part of April in Chicago, serving as executor of Edinboro's estate. That estate was valued at a meager $41, although, as noted earlier, Edinboro owned the house at 198 Fourth Avenue until selling it to his son for $1 shortly before his death. In testimony in probate court on April 19, John testified that Martha Thomas was Edinboro's only wife and that he was their only child.[55]

African Americans continued to increase their participatory role in the Republican Party during the spring 1881 elections, although Thomas, at best, played only a limited role. At the February 7 Second Ward Club meeting,

Thomas was appointed as a member of the club's finance committee and on March 12, the *Tribune* listed him as one of the supporters of Alderman John M. Clark, a reform candidate who was seeking the Republican nomination for mayor. Clark had strong support in the African American community, including Howard, Landre, and Phillips. Joseph Moore favored Jesse Spaulding. On primary election day, Clark lost in the Second Ward, although he wound up winning the Republican nomination. Democrat Carter Harrison handily defeated Clark in the April election. In the Second Ward, Harrison received more than 60 percent of the vote and once again, Edward Dawson led a small but vocal group of African Americans in supporting him.[56]

In the Second Ward, African Americans pushed for an African American to be nominated for alderman. In all, four candidates ran for the Republican nomination for alderman, including John Howard, the lone African American. Henry F. Billings, a local merchant, won the nomination with 586 votes. While Howard came in third, receiving only 87 votes from the 1,146 cast, he did better than incumbent Addison Ballard, who only received 74 votes. Unfortunately for Howard, election judges found a batch of almost 200 ballots on the floor of the polling place and, although the ballots were marked for candidate Charles Lithgow, Howard would be the one later accused of attempting to stuff the ballot box. After losing the nomination, Howard threatened to run as an independent for alderman but Ballard actually did, resulting in a split Republican vote and the election of Democrat James Appleton, the owner of a saloon on the corner of Harrison and State Streets.[57]

After Thomas left Chicago for Washington following the spring election, no one leader united the African American community or had much stature in the political world outside of it in the way that John Jones or Thomas had. Despite an increased number of active participants in Republican politics, in many respects the community had fallen behind from the 1870s. Still, in one respect African Americans were making gains. By filling the ranks of the Republican organization in Chicago, albeit mostly on the South Side and in the Second Ward, the community had become an essential part of the Republican Party. It was with this in mind that in 1882 the community felt entitled to representation on the Republican ticket.

Thomas returned to Chicago in the spring of 1882, after just one year in Washington. Just before the April city election, he is listed as addressing an April 1 meeting of Second Ward Republicans. On June 14 his nine-month-old daughter, Blanche, died in their home at 198 Fourth Avenue. Blanche had been sickly her whole life, suffering from a heart ailment. She was buried in the Thomas plot at Oak Woods cemetery, the third burial in the Thomas plot in just over a year.[58]

That fall, Thomas again sought the Republican nomination for state representative. In the spring, the state had reapportioned the legislature, and the Thomas home was now located in the Third Legislative District. The new district had a population of 57,644 and encompassed all of the First, Second, and Third Wards, and part of the Fourth Ward.[59] For Thomas, that meant his district had lost the suburban/farm communities of Hyde Park and Lake and added, in the form of the First Ward, much of the Chicago downtown area.

By 1882, the African American voting community was no longer content to follow the Republican Party merely because it was the party of emancipation. African Americans were now demanding a piece of the political pie, in terms of patronage positions and places on the Republican slate. The patronage was coming, if slowly. Robert Waring served as a deputy in the office of county clerk, W. C. Phillips was a clerk in the county recorder's office, R. M. Mitchell was assistant clerk of the criminal court, and Isaac Rivers was a letter carrier.[60] The *Colored Man's Professional and Business Directory of Chicago and Valuable Information on the Race in General*, published in 1885, noted that there were fifty to seventy-five African Americans serving in patronage positions.[61]

The African American leadership that filled the void left by Thomas did not have the unwavering loyalty to the Republican Party as Thomas did. In July of 1880, a statewide meeting of African American activists met and voices of disapproval against the Republican Party were heard. At the end of the meeting, however, the activists passed a resolution of support for the party. Thomas did not attend the meeting, although he would play a major role at a similar meeting in 1883 and again in 1885.[62]

In 1879 and again in 1881, Democrat Carter Harrison was elected mayor of Chicago, helped by an unusually strong vote in African American areas. While the *Tribune* noted that the Third District had a solid Republican majority of 2,349, the *Chicago Times* noted that in 1881 Harrison beat his Republican challenger by 800 votes in the area encompassed by the Third District. In 1880, that same area had given Republican presidential candidate James Garfield a 1,704 vote majority over his Democratic opponent.[63]

With a newly drawn district and the fear that African American voters might not be as loyal as in the past, it was assumed that the Republicans of the Third Legislative District would nominate an African American for the legislature. As such, a number of African Americans announced their candidacies for the legislature. Just before the October nominating convention, the *Times* wrote, in its usual bigoted manner, "the number of candidates for the legislature who claim to represent the colored race are about as numerous as the nightly visitors to a plantation watermelon patch. A member of the legislature has been conceded them, and this fact has caused an unusual amount of trading." *The Tribune* wrote, "half a dozen colored brethren are in the field, and with so little prospect of an agreement by the several factions of their own race that they are not unlikely to come around and agree upon a suitable Caucasian.[64]

Thomas was to be one of the candidates but he started his campaign late. He is not mentioned in any political news stories until well into the campaign. The *Times* on September 12 reported a meeting of African American voters that featured legislative candidates William Baker, Robert M. Mitchell, and John Howard. At a First Ward meeting on September 15, white legislative candidates William Everett and Randall White spoke. At a September 18 meeting of the Second Ward Club, candidates Everett, Mitchell, and Judge Bradwell spoke. At that meeting, Isaac Rivers presented Thomas's name as a candidate for the legislature, but again, Thomas was not present at the meeting. Bradwell spoke to the First Ward Republican club on September 23, while Everett spoke at the Fourth Ward Republican Club and Everett and White both appeared before the Third Ward. On September 25, Thomas made his first appearance of the election. He gave a speech before his own Second Ward Club, where he appealed to African American voters to stand together and elect an African American representative.[65]

The Thomas campaign quickly moved forward and on September 29 a number of African Americans from the Second Ward held a meeting to promote his candidacy. At this meeting, Thomas alluded to his being gone by stating that his opponents had "circulated falsehoods about him during his absence." He also spoke out against prohibition and said he was a friend of the saloon interests and the laboring class. Among those attending the meeting were Congressman William Aldrich and Second Ward Republican boss E. R. Bliss, two white politicians from the district who supported Thomas.[66]

Jockeying for the nomination continued throughout September and into October. Both the *Chicago Herald* and *Chicago Times* reported that Bradwell would run as an independent for representative if he did not receive the Republican nomination. According to his friends, Bradwell had received a majority of the vote in the area comprising the newly drawn district when he had run as an independent in 1878. The *Herald* believed that an African American from the Second Ward would be nominated for one of the Republican slots, which, in the interest of geographic balance, would mean that the Republicans would not nominate Second Ward resident Bradwell.[67]

On October 2 Mitchell, one of the African American candidates, addressed a meeting at which Thomas was not present and criticized Thomas's record in the General Assembly. He added that he wished Thomas would meet with him to discuss the issues. On October 9, the *Tribune* reported that Walter Kercheval of the First Ward was a candidate for the state house.[68] This meant that there were at least seven candidates actively seeking the Republican nomination for state representative, four of whom were African American. Several other potential candidates watched for an opportunity from the sidelines.

The Thomas candidacy appeared to be hurt when Aldrich, who supported Thomas, lost his bid for renomination as the Republican candidate for Congress. While the *Tribune* on October 6 said this might affect the political moves in the Third District's state legislative race, in that same issue it also reported that the African Americans of the district had settled on supporting Thomas. That report was denied by Mitchell in the *Chicago Times*. That evening, both Mitchell and Baker addressed the First Ward Republicans as candidates for the legislature.[69]

The major Chicago newspapers reported that the race for the Republican nominations for the state Senate spot and the two state Representative spots would be hotly contested in the Third District. The *Tribune* and *Times* both printed articles on the nominations describing several different possibilities, which were all based on geographic considerations. Generally, it was assumed that, of the First, Second and Third Wards, whichever ward won the Senate seat, the other two wards would divide the two representative spots.[70] Because only a part of the Fourth Ward was in the legislative district, it was generally not considered a player in the proceedings.

The primary election was held October 13 and the convention for the nomination met on October 14. The delegation strengths were as follows: the First Ward, ten delegates; Second Ward, eleven; Third Ward, eleven; and the Fourth Ward, three. At the primary, the Thomas forces defeated the Bradwell forces in the Second Ward, 325 to 53, which pretty well determined that Thomas, as both the candidate from the Second Ward and the candidate of a now united African American community, would be one of the nominees. Indeed, the *Tribune* had noted before the primary that the "Second Ward primary alone can determine whether the nominee is to be white or black." Two of the eleven delegates from the Second Ward were Isaac Rivers and John Howard.[71]

At the convention, the first vote taken was that for state senate. John H. Clough of the Third Ward defeated Dan Wren of the First Ward by a vote of 25 to 10. Clough won the eleven delegates in his Third Ward, the three delegates of the Fourth Ward and the eleven delegates of the Second Ward. The vote for representative went next. The First Ward, having lost the senate race, put up Walter Kercheval for representative, while Thomas ran as the Second Ward candidate. Bradwell, also of the Second Ward, also was nominated. William Everett withdrew as a candidate because he was from the Third Ward and that ward had received the Senate spot. The other African American candidates had apparently united behind Thomas. In placing Kercheval's name in nomination, First Ward Alderman Arthur Dixon said that he had heard rumors that the First Ward might be shut out of the nomination process, and he warned the convention that this had better not be the case.

When the balloting occurred, Thomas easily won, taking one vote from the Fourth Ward, all of the eleven votes of his Second Ward and ten of the eleven votes from Clough's Third Ward. The *Times* had reported that Clough and Thomas had made a deal before the primary and this appears to be the case.[72] The final voting on the first ballot was Thomas 22, Kercheval 10 and Bradwell 3. Kercheval's votes came entirely from the First Ward, while Bradwell picked up one vote from the Third Ward and two from the Fourth.[73]

Custom and political strategy would have it that by nominating Thomas of the Second Ward for the one representative position and Clough of the Third Ward for the senate spot, the second representative position should go to Kercheval or another First Ward candidate. Indeed, Bradwell had said before the primary that he would run as an independent Republican if Thomas was nominated, under the assumption that only one Second Ward resident would receive a nomination. But Alderman Dixon had been right in fearing that the First Ward might be excluded from the proceedings. Following Thomas's nomination, the entire First Ward delegation walked over to where the Third Ward delegation was sitting to ask for its support for Kercheval. The Third Ward delegates refused. Instead, they overwhelmingly supported Bradwell for the second nomination, as did the Second Ward delegates. In all, Bradwell received ten of the eleven votes from the Third Ward, eight of the eleven votes from the Second Ward and all three of the votes from the Fourth Ward. Kercheval received the ten votes of the First Ward, three votes from the Second Ward and one vote from the Third. The final tally was Bradwell 21 to Kercheval's 14.[74]

There were several factors that played a role in how the nominations occurred. In the First Ward, Republican bosses Abner Taylor and Arthur Dixon, strong anti-Loganites, had yet to build an effective party machine. They spent the primary fending off a challenge to their authority and could not concentrate on advancing Kercheval or Wren's interests. Clough came from a fairly united Third Ward and could cut a deal with Thomas and the Second Ward. In addition, the newly elected legislature would vote for a U.S. senator to replace David Davis, and Republican powerbrokers were jockeying behind the scenes to work for legislative nominees that would be favorable to their interests. Both Thomas and Bradwell appear to have been supported by John Logan, who wanted Green B. Raum to join him in the Senate. As the *Times* reported, "After a contest fought inch by inch, the Logan men yesterday scored a victory, nominating J. H. Clough for Senator and J. W. E. Thomas and Judge Bradwell for representatives."

The actions of the delegates caused a split in the Third District Republican Party. The First Ward Republican delegates stormed out of the convention. Alderman Dixon denounced the action "as a piece of treachery which the First Ward would not stand." Failed Senate candidate Dan Wren stated that he would not support the ticket. Dixon would later calm down and at a First Ward Republican Club meeting held that evening he counseled moderation to the angry club members. Still, the *Daily News* reported just five days before the election that despite Dixon's statements that he would help the Republican ticket, he was actually working against it.[75] Kercheval, the First Ward's candidate at the convention, would run as an independent.

The *Inter-Ocean*, which was already worried about the looming U.S. Senate selection that the new General Assembly would make, stated, "the convention committed an insufferable stupid blunder, to use no harsher term, in selecting two candidates for the House from the Second Ward. There is no excuse for it and unless the mistake is rectified it is likely to work very serious mischief." The *Tribune* added, "There is no doubt that the convention made a mistake. In nominating Thomas and Bradwell and throwing the First out, the delegates have damaged the ticket." The *Tribune* also warned, correctly as it turned out, that Bradwell would have troubles with working men because he ran a nonunion shop at his newspaper, while Kercheval was a member of the printer's union."[76]

In the controversy surrounding Bradwell's nomination, very little mention was made about Thomas's nomination. It seems as if it was accepted that Thomas or another African American should be on the ticket, although the *Tribune* had endorsed Kercheval and Bradwell before the convention. Kercheval himself said he thought the African American community should have a representative. The only paper to comment on the Thomas nomination was the *Evening Journal*. It wrote that Thomas was an intelligent and wide-awake African American "who had a seat in the House in 1877 and represented his constituency with marked credit." It also said, "Mr. Thomas will be elected and will sustain the reputation he has already made as a faithful and worthy legislator." Additionally, the paper noted that the "large colored population are justly entitled to representation on the Republican ticket."[77]

For Thomas, the 1882 campaign would be just as difficult as that of 1876, only this time the issue of his race would not command center stage. Instead,

Bradwell would be the controversial Republican nominee, as all Republicans seemed to agree that the African American community deserved a state representative. Making the 1882 race even more difficult was that the Democrats nominated two candidates for representative, choosing to create a contest in the Republican-majority Third District. They would be aided by Kercheval, who ran as an independent Republican. Both the Trades and Labor Party and the Anti-Monopoly Party nominated M. L. Crawford for the state legislature. After Bradwell's nomination, Crawford dropped out of the race, in an effort to unite labor voters behind the two Democrat candidates and against Bradwell. The Prohibition Party also fielded a candidate for the legislature that year, nominating attorney George C. Christian on October 24.[78] The Prohibition Party was expected to cut into the Republican vote because most of their supporters came from the Republican Party.

A First Ward Republican meeting on October 22 highlighted the problems Bradwell faced in his own party. Thomas addressed the meeting and was well received. He encouraged the ward to vote the straight ticket and promised to serve the district to the best of his ability. Bradwell, however, was heckled from the floor. Kercheval chose that meeting to declare his candidacy as an independent candidate and he called Bradwell's nomination "an outrage to workingmen." Although the impetus for the Kercheval candidacy was the slight to the First Ward at the Republican nominating convention, the issue of his campaign became an attack on Bradwell's non-union newspaper.[79] The anti-Bradwell message would later be echoed by the Trades and Labor Assembly, where member M. L. Crawford, the former third-party candidate for legislature, passed a resolution calling on all working men to vote against Bradwell.[80]

With the field crowded with candidates, Thomas needed the support of both white Republicans and African American Republicans. At an October 24 meeting of the Second Ward Republican Club, congressional candidate R. W. Dunham mentioned a rumor that some white Republicans were in favor of scratching Thomas's name from the ticket. In other words, they would not cast their vote for him. Thomas responded, "This talk about white men scratching me, I have got to see it before I believe it. If they would scratch a man because he was black, they ought to be drummed out of the republican party."[81] Thomas had a right to be concerned. Although Bradwell was Thomas's running mate, under the cumulative voting system he was also his rival. Bradwell was extremely popular in the African American community, which could reduce the number of African Americans who might bullet vote (cast all three of their votes) for Thomas. If white Republicans scratched Thomas's name from their ticket, he would be in serious trouble.

A united African American community also was a concern during Thomas's campaign, as Democrats sought to divide the community with the promise of exchanging patronage jobs for political support. The *Times* reported the creation of an African American Democrats Club in the Second Ward, led by Dawson again and A. F. Bradley. It also reported that Democratic sheriff candidate W. G. McGarigle had offered certain positions in the sheriff's office to African Americans if they would work for the Democratic ticket. Although the *Times* probably exaggerated the importance of the African American Democrats Club, Thomas was aware of its activities. In a talk to the Second Ward Colored Republican Club on November 1, he gave several reasons why the Republican Party was the friend of African Americans. He said he "wanted the lie nailed that was being circulated that the colored people of Chicago were going to vote the Democratic county ticket because Mr. McGarigle had promised if elected to appoint five colored men to positions in the sheriff's office"[82]

That same evening, Thomas spoke before a meeting of the First Ward Republicans and gave a rousing defense of the Republican Party. He told his audience that it was the Democratic Party that had caused the Civil War and tried to keep the black man in bondage. He said that same party now sought to prevent African Americans from living in respectable neighborhoods and if the fifteen thousand African American voters in Illinois voted for Democrats, it would mean throwing 3,000 African American men out of government employment and replacing them with "rebels." He concluded by saying that the way African Americans cast their votes up North had an effect "for weal or woe" on African Americans who lived in the South and who did not enjoy any of the advantages of freedom that the African Americans in the North did.[83]

Coming into November, the *Tribune* endorsed Thomas, Bradwell, and Kercheval and predicted Thomas and Bradwell would win. The Republican-leaning *Herald* endorsed Bradwell only.[84] Election Day showed the confusion facing the voters. At a time when ballots were printed by candidates and political parties and not by the government, the *Times* reported that voters were using at least six different kinds of ballots.[85] Indeed, according to the *Times* there was a ballot being distributed in the Second Ward resembling the straight Democratic ticket, except that it included Thomas for the state legislature.[86] Early returns showed the election of Democrats Thomas McNally and Isaac Abrahams and of the Republican Bradwell.[87] In the end, however, it was McNally, Abrahams, and Thomas, with Bradwell finishing a close fourth and Kercheval finishing fifth. The official results were Abrahams 6,486, Thomas 6,373, McNally 6,115, Bradwell 6,065½, Kercheval 1,096½, and Christian of the Prohibition Party 591½.[88]

Thomas and Bradwell fared worst in the First Ward, due to the split with the First Ward Republican Club and also because the ward leaned towards the Democrats anyway. Thomas's Second Ward delivered a large vote for him and Bradwell. Thomas did well in the Third Ward and that part of the Fourth Ward that was in his district. The closeness of the election caused Bradwell to protest his defeat, taking his case all the way to the General Assembly. He did not win his appeal, however. The *Times* reported that Thomas was surprised to be elected and bitter towards Bradwell, whom he suspected of playing both sides of the fence. The *Times* quoted Thomas as saying "if Judge Bradwell had played his fiddle straight, both of them would have been elected."[89]

The path Thomas had taken to winning his second term differed from his first election. In 1876, he had been the choice of a united African American community. In this election, he had to defeat three other African American candidates for the Republican nomination. In 1876, whites from the "abolitionist-Republican" tradition helped him earn the nomination. This time, Thomas needed to forge alliances with Third Ward power broker John Clough and Illinois political boss John Logan to be selected. And, although the African American community came together after the Republican nomination to support Thomas, splits between factions in his own party jeopardized his prospects throughout the 1882 campaign. Despite this, Thomas was now headed to Springfield for a second term.

[4]

"Advising Moderation in All Things": The 1883 Legislative Session and Colored Convention

Thomas had been away from Chicago for more than a year in Washington yet came back to make a stunning return to political leadership in Chicago's African American community. The Republicans had a majority in both the House and the Senate and there was a Republican governor. As a second-term member of the House, Thomas could expect a committee chairmanship. If there was a cloud on the horizon, it was personal. His wife, Justine, was five-months pregnant when Thomas left for Springfield in January 1883. Justine had been battling tuberculosis for almost two years. She had been pregnant twice before, with one pregnancy ending before birth and the other resulting in the birth of a child who died within nine months.[1] Perhaps Justine's frail condition was why Thomas was one of the last six legislators to arrive in Springfield for the session, coming in the night before the new session began.[2]

The 1883 Legislative Session

Thomas arrived in time to participate in a House Republican caucus at the Leland Hotel. The purpose of the meeting was to select the Republican candidate for Speaker and the choices for several of the patronage jobs in the House, such as clerk, postmaster, and doorkeeper. The Republicans quickly and easily selected Lorin C. Collins Jr. of Chicago as their choice for Speaker. At least three African Americans sought House patronage positions, with the caucus selecting Archibald Ward, an African American from Peoria, as Second Assistant Doorkeeper.[3]

The Republicans had a slim 77–75 majority over the Democrats in the House. There was also one independent member of the chamber, the always unpredictable Elijah Haines of Lake County, which meant that the Republican majority was only one. The closeness of the majority meant that the often fractious party had to keep all its members in line to successfully control the House.

Early on, the Republicans were able to do this. On January 3, the first day of session, the party easily elected its choices for the temporary organization of the House. The next day, the members took the oath of office and were sworn in by State Supreme Court Justice John M. Scott. The chamber's first action was to pass a resolution of sympathy to France on the death of French statesman Leon Gambetta. After that, the House voted for Speaker and Collins won 78–75. In the tradition of the times, he voted for his Democratic opponent, who in turn voted for him. Collins carried the votes of all the other Republicans, including Thomas. The independent Haines also voted for him.[4]

As in 1877, one of the first votes Thomas cast in the new session was for U.S. senator. With Republicans having a small majority in the House but a large 31 to 20 majority in the Senate, the selection of a Republican for the spot was virtually assured. There were three main Republican candidates seeking the selection. They were Shelby Cullom, the current governor, Richard J. Oglesby, who was both a former governor and former U.S. senator, and Green B. Raum, who had led the Grant forces at the Republican state convention in 1880 and was the federal commissioner of Internal Revenue. Thomas supported Raum, who was a Logan loyalist and who may have helped Thomas get his job in Washington.[5] Cullom was the favorite, but he was hindered by a clause in the state constitution that said state constitutional officers were not eligible to serve in any other position during the term of their office.[6] While seemingly banning an incumbent officeholder from being elected to another office, it was unclear if the prohibition applied to seeking a federal office, such as U.S. senator.

The House and Senate Republicans caucused on the evening of January 11 to select their candidate. Previous to the caucus, Representative James Herrington, a Democrat, introduced a resolution in the House declaring state constitutional officers ineligible for election to the U.S. Senate. The nonbinding resolution was an obvious attempt to foster division in Republican ranks. In response, Thomas offered a substitute resolution that declared that the state constitution did not prohibit state officers from becoming U.S. senators. Thomas's resolution demonstrates that he put his loyalty to the party above his own preference. Even though he did not support Cullom for the Senate, he recognized that the Democrats were trying to split the Republican Party by wounding its strongest Senate candidate. Thomas's resolution failed however, as Herrington seemingly achieved the split in the party that he was seeking. Ten Republican representatives voted for Herrington's resolution, enabling it to pass by an 80 to 65 vote.[7]

That night, despite concerns over Cullom's eligibility, Republicans nominated him on the fifth ballot at the caucus. With 54 votes needed to receive the party's endorsement, Cullom received 44 on the first two ballots. Oglesby received 29 on the first ballot and 30 on the second, while Raum received 22 votes on the first ballot and 21 on the second. Three other candidates received a total of 12 votes on both ballots. Thomas voted for Raum on both ballots. On the third ballot, Cullom picked up 3 more votes, including 2 from Raum supporters, leaving the vote totals 47 for Cullom, 30 for Oglesby, 19 for Raum, and 11 for the rest. On the fourth ballot, Cullom moved up to 51 votes, while Raum dropped to 15. One of those switching on this vote was Thomas. On the fifth ballot, Cullom won it with 63 votes to Oglesby's 23 and Raum's 13. The vote was then declared unanimous, despite the fact that ten of the House members voting in the caucus had voted for the Herrington resolution that afternoon.[8]

On January 16, each chamber met separately to cast its vote for senator. In the Senate, Cullom won over the Democrat nominee, former governor John Palmer, 30 to 20, with Senator George Adams, Republican of Cook County, choosing not to vote rather than vote for Cullom. In the House, two Republicans did not vote due to their views on the eligibility issue and one Democrat was absent, resulting in a 75 to 75 tie between Cullom and Palmer. Since Cullom did not have a majority in both chambers, the law required the House and Senate to meet in joint session the following day. Despite all concerns, Cullom easily won election at the joint session, defeating Palmer 107 to 95, with Senator Adams again not voting.[9]

With the House organized and the vote for U.S. senator completed, the thirty-third session of the General Assembly could begin. On January 23, Speaker Collins announced the creation of forty-four House committees. Thomas was named chairman of the fifteen-member Public Buildings and Grounds Committee and as a member on the committees on Labor and Manufacturers, Warehouse, State Institutions, and Enrolled and Engrossed Bills. While none of these committees were very important, Thomas's chairmanship of Public Buildings and Grounds marked the first time an African American served as a committee chairman in the House.[10]

As the new session began, Springfield's Republican newspaper noted Thomas's presence and editorialized, "Less than a quarter of a century ago, the statute books of Illinois were marred by the existence of laws on their pages forbidding colored men from moving from other States into this under severe penalties, and the occasional appearance of a member of that then oppressed and proscribed race in our Legislature is a noteworthy token of progress in the recognition of human equality."[11]

While the "occasional" appearance of an African American in the legislature still elicited newspaper comment, it was obvious that Thomas was much more comfortable as a legislator than he had been in his first term and that he intended to play an active role in the session. He sponsored a resolution to increase the pay for two statehouse elevator operators to a dollar per day higher than *per diem* for their services during the current session. After the resolution received an unfavorable recommendation from the committee on contingent expenses, Thomas took the issue to the floor of the House and was able to have the resolution passed. In April, he successfully submitted an amendment to add $580 to an appropriations bill to pay for cleaning and restoring of five pictures in the state house and the portraits of governors in the executive mansion.[12] He also delivered reports on the floor on behalf of the committees he served on and moved bills along in the process, even if they were not his.

In March, this latter activity caused Thomas to unwittingly enter into a partisan spat when he carried HB 389 through the House, despite not being the sponsor of the bill. A mining disaster in the town of Braidwood in Will County on February 16 had killed sixty-nine miners and left behind forty-five widows and more than one hundred fatherless children. A majority of the miners and their widows were foreign born. HBl 389 appropriated $10,000 for relief for the widows and children. It also appropriated $2,000 for the relatives of the victims of an explosion at a mine disaster on January 8, 1883, in Coulterville in Randolph County. Introduced on February 19 by Representative David Littler of Sangamon County, the bill languished, a victim of the stalling tactics employed by Haines and the House Democrats on unrelated issues.

On March 6, Governor John Hamilton sent a message to the House, urging it to take action. That same day, Thomas asked the House for unanimous consent to move the bill to second reading, which was granted. An attempt to amend the bill on second reading failed and the bill moved to third reading where, on March 8, Thomas moved that the bill be passed. He spoke on its behalf, as did his fellow Third District representative, Democrat Isaac Abrahams. Despite concerns expressed by some members as to its constitutionality, the bill passed. The Senate later passed it and Governor Hamilton signed it into law.

The day after the House passed the bill, Springfield's Democratic newspaper criticized Democratic representative John O'Connell, whose district included Braidwood, for not sponsoring or moving the bill. O'Connell responded that he had attempted to bring the bill up for a vote, but that the Republican Speaker had called on Thomas instead. In defending himself, he stated that he "had always believed the Republicans were thieves, and now he was convinced of it."[13]

Overall, it was a fairly normal session. The papers complained about the legislature's ineffectiveness and about legislators leaving before the Saturday sessions and not arriving in time for the Monday sessions. The House generally met at 10 A.M. early in the session and 9:30 A.M. as the session neared its conclusion. In January, a train wreck outside of Bloomington led to members' being delayed from arriving on the 5 A.M. train from Chicago until 3:30 P.M.[14] In March, the Woman's Christian Temperance Union submitted petitions with 50,000 signatures supporting constitutional amendments to prohibit the sale of liquor and allow for woman suffrage.[15] The chamber took no action on either issue. The House was hindered by the almost even split between the parties, Republicans having only a one-seat majority, and even that margin insecure because one of the Republican legislators, James Owen of Will County, was sick for a majority of the session. Haines, an expert parliamentarian and member of the convention that drafted the 1870 state constitution, became a de facto leader of the House Democrats, leading to delaying tactics on legislation opposed by the party.[16]

Thomas sponsored three bills during session, none of which passed. HB 228, introduced on February 2, would have allowed school districts to use eminent domain to acquire land for school sites. In justifying the bill, Thomas wrote in its third article, "There is great difficulty in securing sufficient school accommodations." The bill made it through the House Committee on Education with a favorable recommendation but never moved once it went to the House floor. A similar bill was introduced in the Senate but it too failed to become law.[17]

Thomas sponsored two bills to regulate primary elections. The idea of government regulation of primary elections was new, in that political parties are not governmental entities. Still, the rising amount of corruption in primary elections led to a call for imposing the laws that governed general elections on primary elections as well. At least seven bills were introduced during session on the subject, none of which passed.[18] On February 7, Thomas introduced HB 286, which was assigned to the Committee on Elections. On April 20, following an unfavorable recommendation by the committee, the full House tabled the bill. On March 29, Thomas introduced HB 656, which had the exact same language as HB 286. HB 656 was assigned to the committee on corporations, rather than elections, and received a favorable committee report, which was delivered to the House on May 19. However, the bill did not move in the House, most likely because another primary election bill, Senate Bill 126, was sent to the House a week later. Thomas worked for that bill in the House. On June 5, he successfully added an amendment to the bill that prescribed penalties for judges who allowed unqualified electors to vote in a primary and penalties for ballot box stuffing in a primary. He took those two provisions from his bills.[19]

One issue that occupied much of Thomas's thoughts was the disputed election between McNally and Bradwell, which involved allegations of vote fraud in the Third District. Bradwell filed his intent to contest the election of McNally with the Secretary of State's office on December 7, 1882. A little more than a week later, on December 18, Bradwell also filed an intent to contest the election of Abrahams. In response, the Democrats, led by future First Ward boss Michael "Hinky Dink" Kenna, filed a notice on December 28 that they intended to contest the election of Thomas.[20] The latter two filings were designed to cover all eventualities of a recount. The real contest was between McNally and Bradwell, the third- and fourth-place finishers.

The Committee on Elections, which had a Republican majority, spent three months reviewing the case. In its majority report, given to the House on April 12, committee members found numerous cases of uncounted ballots and also precincts where there were more votes cast than eligible voters. Overall, the majority's findings increased the vote totals for all the candidates and, based on its findings, Thomas actually received the most votes in the district, receiving 6,731½ votes to Abrahams's 6,713. The report concluded that Bradwell received 6,387½ and McNally 6,335. Based on those numbers, the majority report recommended that the election of the Democrat McNally be overturned and that the Republican Bradwell be seated, having finished in the top three. The Democrats of the committee issued a minority report questioning the legality of the entire procedure and concluding that there was no evidence to overturn McNally's election.[21]

With Owen unable to attend session and Haines and the Democrats using every parliamentary means available, the Republicans did not have the votes to approve the majority report. On April 17, an ill Owen was brought to the capitol, where he actually stayed because he was too ill to make the daily trip from a downtown hotel. It was his first time attending session since the Senate election contest in January. At this point, Republicans should have had a majority, but one of their members, Jesse J. Root of Chicago, joined with the Democrats in refusing to vote for the report. He was immediately castigated in Republican newspapers as being a drunkard and a traitor. After three days of wrangling over the issue and of having an armed federal marshal on the floor of the House, the Republicans gave up. On April 20 they moved to indefinitely postpone the issue, meaning it was dead for the session and McNally kept his seat.[22]

The problems of achieving a majority on the floor kept Thomas in Springfield for extended periods, so he brought Justine to stay with him in Springfield. On April 4 Justine gave birth to a baby daughter at the Reverend Coleman's home. They were both in poor condition following the birth. When the birth certificate was filed on April 24, the baby had yet to be given a name.[23] On April 22, two days after the McNally-Bradwell contest had been settled, the *Illinois State Register* newspaper reported that Justine Thomas had gone to the Jacksonville Insane Asylum, located about thirty miles west of Springfield.[24]

According to the paper, Justine was "bereft of reason" following childbirth. What the fragile Justine suffered from was defined as puerperal mania, a catch-all phrase for exhaustion due to childbirth. Her condition was complicated because of her tuberculosis. On Sunday, May 6, at 9 P.M., just two days after their third wedding anniversary, the twenty-year-old Justine died in Jacksonville. Her body was taken to Chicago. Funeral services were held May 9 at St. Mary's Catholic Church and she was buried in the Thomas family plot in Oak Woods cemetery.[25] Two weeks later, on Monday, May 21, John and Justine's daughter, now also named Justine, died at Justine's mother's home at 88 West Van Buren Street in Chicago. Her funeral was held at the residence the next day and she too, like her mother, was buried at Oak Woods cemetery. She had lived just 47 days. Thomas included in her obituary the words, "Rest, darling rest."[26]

With the birth of his child and the illnesses of his child and wife, Thomas began missing session days. However, he attempted to work as much as possible. There were no votes taken on April 4, the day his child was born, so it is not known if he was present that day or not. He was there on April 3 and 5. He was absent on April 20, the day the House Republicans gave up on the Bradwell-McNally fight, and April 21. These were the days Justine went to Jacksonville. He returned for session days until May 4, when the House adjourned for the weekend. On May 8, the House granted Thomas a leave of absence. It also passed a resolution of condolences for Thomas and, on the motion of Abrahams, adjourned early in memory of Mrs. Thomas. Thomas returned to session on May 11, just five days after his wife's death, but then missed session days on May 21, 22 and 23, when his daughter died and was buried. He was back at work May 24 and worked through the rest of session.[27]

While Thomas was on his leave of absence, the House entered into debate on the Harper High License Bill, legislation that, in its final form, required all incorporated villages and cities and all unincorporated towns to license dram shops at no less than $500 a year for a license to sell hard liquor and no less than $150 a year to sell only beer and light wines. The goals for the High License bill were to reduce the number of saloons by regulating out of existence the unsavory ones while raising revenues for local governments. The bill split prohibitionist supporters. Some prohibition supporters saw it as a step in the right direction because it limited the availability of alcohol and removed disreputable saloons which could not afford the license fee. However, some supporters of prohibition opposed High License because it did not completely end alcohol sales and by regulating those sales the bill, in fact, assumed support for liquor.

Debate on High License would continue for more than a month, stretching the legislative session into June, well past the customary middle of May adjournment date. Haines opposed High License and worked to delay and defeat the Harper bill. Generally, the Harper High License Bill was supported by Republicans and opposed by Democrats, but a minority of each party opposed their party's position. Thomas supported the bill and on March 22 submitted a petition from his constituents in support for the enactment of the law. The bill came for a final vote in the House on June 8 and passed, 79 to 65. The bill passed with the votes of seventy Republicans, including Thomas, and nine Democrats. The Senate then quickly passed the measure and Governor Hamilton signed it into law.[28]

Passage of the Harper High License Bill was one of the two major accomplishments of the 33rd General Assembly. The other was the passage of a compulsory education bill for children. That bill required children between the ages of eight and fourteen to attend at least twelve weeks of school a year unless excused by a local board of education. Thomas had unsuccessfully sponsored a similar bill during his first term. This version of the bill passed the House 85 to 8, with Thomas voting for it.[29]

The legislature had other accomplishments as well. It adopted a joint resolution to submit for voter approval an amendment to the state constitution to allow the governor to use a line-item veto on appropriation bills. Voters approved the amendment at the November 1884 election. Legislators passed House Bill 260, which placed on the November 1884 ballot a proposal to spend $531,712 to finish construction and furnishing of the capitol. Illinois voters had twice before voted against spending more money to finish the capitol but in 1884 they would approve the referendum, allowing the building to be completed by 1888. Another bill, House Bill 261, appropriated $25,000 for building sidewalks and streets by the capitol, contingent on receiving matching funds from the City of Springfield. In light of the mining disasters at Braidwood and Coulterville, the legislature passed two mine safety bills including one creating a system of state mine inspections. Another bill passed and signed into law helped miners by providing for the weighing of coal at the mines to be done under the supervision of an agent appointed by the miners. The legislature passed into law two road bills giving voters in towns the flexibility to tax themselves to build hard roads. Finally, the legislature voted to reimburse Franklin County in downstate Illinois $1,780.56 for expenses incurred in suppressing the Ku Klux Klan. Thomas voted for all these bills except the joint resolution on the line item veto, because he was absent.[30]

On June 18, the thirty-third session of the Illinois General Assembly adjourned. House members presented Speaker Collins with a gold watch for his efforts during the year. Thomas received $835 in pay for his services, plus another $50 compensation for postage and newspapers and $37.20 for travel reimbursement for the 372 miles round trip between his house and Springfield. The $835 was based on $5 a day for the 167 days between the start of session on January 3 and adjournment on June 18, even though members were not in session for all those days and many members, such as Thomas, missed days when the legislature was in session. It had been a difficult session for all the House members but perhaps for Thomas most of all. However, the year was not to get any easier for him.[31]

The 1883 State Colored Convention

Following the 1883 session of the General Assembly, Thomas faced one of his biggest challenges as an African American leader, when he was selected to chair the 1883 Illinois Colored Convention, held October 15 to 17 at the State Capitol in Springfield. In that role, he sought to keep the state's African American community loyal to the Republican Party.

In the nineteenth century, "colored conventions" were a popular method for African American leaders to meet and discuss the needs of their race. African American leaders in the North had been conducting conventions periodically at both the state and national levels since 1830, with the movement spreading south after the Civil War. Illinois African Americans conducted three conventions before 1880, including two which were held before the Civil War. In addition, in December 1873, a statewide convention was held but its purpose appears to have been limited to appointing delegates to a national convention in Washington.[32]

In the 1880s, attorney John G. Jones of Chicago, no relation to John Jones, was the leader of the state conventions. Conventions were held in 1880, 1883, 1885 and 1889. Jones organized the state conventions of 1880, 1883 and 1889, with his friend Lloyd G. Wheeler organizing the state convention of 1885. Jones was a firm believer in community meetings. He earned the nickname "Indignation" Jones because of his organizing "indignation" meetings in Chicago, which were relatively impromptu rallies held when the community felt slighted.[33]

According to historian Lawrence Grossman, the 1880s represented the "high tide of Negro rebellion against Republican neglect."[34] The Republican Party appeared to take African American voters for granted while Northern Democrats began to seek support from African American voters. The Democratic *Chicago Times* openly predicted before the 1880 convention that the delegates would "pass a series of resolutions containing a series of complaints against the Republican Party of this state."[35]

Illinois Republicans viewed all four of the conventions of the 1880s suspiciously, feeling that the African Americans calling the conventions were intent on hurting the party. On July 20, the opening day of the 1880 convention, the Republican *State Journal* newspaper of Springfield cautioned in an editorial "we will not call in question the consistency or fidelity to Republicanism of the signers of this call in advance of their own positive action. The motives of the principal actors will be judged by the proceedings of to-day." Delegates at a meeting of African American voters in one county passed a resolution that stated, "We, the colored voters of Iroquois county, do feel we owe to the Republican party our hearty support, and that we firmly believe that the convention of colored voters called to meet in Springfield, Illinois is being used by certain colored voters to divide the colored vote and thereby aid the Democratic party in the present campaign." The resolution specifically cited Jones as a person that Republicans should not trust. Thomas, a loyal Republican, did not attend the 1880 convention, perhaps because he agreed with the sentiments expressed by the African American voters of Iroquois County. The *Chicago Inter-Ocean* opposed the 1880 convention and opined in July that "the better class of colored Republicans" did so.[36]

Nevertheless, in the spring of 1880, 287 leading African Americans in Illinois signed a circular that called for a statewide convention. Delegates were to be selected to the convention by county, with three delegates allocated per county. In addition, all persons who signed the circular had the right to serve as delegates. Not all of the signers chose to serve as delegates and not all of the state's 102 counties sent delegates. On the day of the convention, roughly 125 delegates came to Springfield, where they elected Jones as permanent chairman.[37]

The delegates at the convention passed resolutions calling for the testing of teachers who taught in African American schools, to ensure their quality. They encouraged African Americans in Illinois to join together and form local organizations dedicated to promoting their interests. And they encouraged African Americans living in the South to move to Illinois and take advantage of available land. Delegates also discussed the removal of the word "colored" following the names of African Americans in poll books and various matters of discrimination in public places.

A major issue delegates discussed was patronage in return for their loyalty to the Republican Party. While some newspapers saw the convention as a threat to the Republican Party, others saw it as an attempt to blackmail the party into granting African Americans more jobs. The *Times* noted, "The grievance of the black man and brother is that he rarely gets any of the spoils of party victory, while he is expected to cast his vote with unfailing regularity." The *Chicago Tribune* dismissed the convention as an "office-seeking convention," and noted that African Americans in Illinois had already had representation on the Cook County Board, in the state legislature and in various departments of the federal and local government. "All this is sufficient to show that there is no prejudice against them, in the Republican party at least," the *Tribune* editorialized.[38]

The most controversial issue at the convention concerned a proposal to create an African American state central committee, consisting of a representative from each of the state's nineteen congressional districts and four at-large delegates. Originally, this committee was to serve as an African American counterpart to the Republican State Central Committee, which had no African American members. However, the idea was seen by many convention delegates as potentially hostile to the regular G.O.P., and as such the proposal was modified, made less political, and given a different name.[39]

The fears of some that the 1880 convention would seek to separate African Americans from the Republican Party were not realized. Governor Shelby Cullom and Secretary of State George Harlow, both Republicans, addressed the convention and delivered fiery partisan speeches. Many of the delegates also delivered speeches expressing strong support for the Republican Party. The delegates passed a resolution that stated, in part, "As colored men who have emerged from the condition of slavery to enfranchised citizens through the agency of the Republican party, and all rights and privileges exercised and enjoyed by Republican legislation, independent of acquiescence and support from the Democratic party, we hereby affirm our devotion to said party, and pledge our hearty support in the present campaign." The resolution further stated, "We disclaim any intention or purpose to give aid or comfort to the Democracy [Democratic Party] either by thought, deed or action but on the contrary recognize in it a life-long enemy to the negro."

Halfway through the convention, the previously suspicious *State Journal* editorialized, "Those members of the Democratic party who expected to receive aid and comfort from the meeting of the Colored Convention in this city, yesterday, have found themselves grievously disappointed. The ringing speeches, and the report made by the Committee on Resolutions, leave no doubt as to the position of the colored men of Illinois with reference to the

two great political parties. The report . . . is a reiteration of a sense of obli-
gation to the Republican party for what it has done to free the slaves of the
South, of suspicion and mistrust of the Democratic party, and a declaration of
a determination to support the Republican State, national and local tickets."[40]

The convention of 1880 represented a step toward collective action by
the Illinois African American community. Delegates voiced the concerns of
the community about jobs, education, and racial discrimination. Politically,
however, the community's leaders decided it was best to conduct their actions
within the Republican Party. Although he was not present at this convention,
Thomas could have supported all of these positions.

By 1883, times had changed. Nationally, the Republican Party had aban-
doned African Americans in the South. President Chester Alan Arthur was
working with white Republican and independent organizations in the South
on patronage issues, rather than with African American Republicans. African
American leaders and newspapers in the North and Midwest began calling for
independence from the Republican Party. In Chicago, many African Americans chafed at the limited opportunities offered them by the Republican Party.
Democrat Carter Harrison was serving his third two-year term as mayor of
Chicago and had been elected and reelected with the support of many African Americans, whom he rewarded with patronage positions. The *Chicago
Tribune* estimated that he had received as many as 600 votes in the African
American community in his spring 1883 campaign. Statewide, Republican
patronage still was slow in coming and discrimination still existed.[41]

While the idea of abandoning the Republican Party for a more independent course was radical, it was in keeping with what was occurring at the
national level. In September 1883, several Illinoisans attended a national
colored convention, which was held in Louisville. The call for the national
convention gave Illinois only three delegates. The *Inter-Ocean* reported that
Thomas was one of the delegates but it is possible the paper was wrong. The
Cleveland Gazette noted that Illinois sent a few more delegates to the convention than three, so it is possible that Thomas attended the convention
but not as a delegate. At the national convention, famed African American
leader Frederick Douglass joined the growing chorus in urging the community to seek a more independent political course, stating that African
Americans should follow no party blindly. "If the Republican party cannot
stand a demand for justice and fair play, it ought to go down," Douglass said.
Following Douglass's lead, delegates shelved a resolution of support for the
Republican Party.[42]

Douglass had been a loyal Republican and his speech demonstrates
the frustrations many African Americans were having with the party. In

Illinois it came to a head with the state colored convention. Chicagoans John G. Jones, Lloyd Wheeler, Robert M. Mitchell and Ferdinand Barnett, plus Rev. Charles Spencer Smith of Bloomington and W. T. Scott of Cairo, all of whom favored pursuing an independent course from the Republican Party, were among the signers of the call for the convention. Delegates were elected by congressional districts but in a clear demonstration of the growing split in the community, as well as the political abilities of Thomas, Wheeler and Jones could not even win in their own districts at the September election, losing to Thomas and to John Howard, Charles Whiting, and R. C. Waring. As a result, Wheeler and Jones, the organizers of the convention, had to attend it using proxies of other delegates.[43]

There were two factions at the convention. Thomas, Dr. J. W. W. Washington of Chicago, and John J. Bird of Cairo led one faction, which was loyal to the Republican Party. Washington was a Chicago physician. In 1873, Bird was elected as a police magistrate and later that year became the first African American to serve on the board of trustees of the University of Illinois following his appointment by the Republican governor, John Beveridge. This faction believed that African American progress could only be found in the Republican Party and saw the Democratic Party in Illinois as the allies of the discriminatory Southern Democrats. Jones, Barnett, Wheeler, Smith, and Scott were leaders of the other faction. Jones, Barnett, and Wheeler were prominent attorneys in Chicago. Smith was a leading minister in the A.M.E. church, a gifted orator, and a former state representative from Alabama. Scott was a Democratic newspaper editor from deep southern Illinois. This faction claimed that African American loyalty was being taken for granted by the Republicans. and that if the community showed more political independence, it could reap rewards and respect from all political parties. The Springfield *State Register* newspaper correctly noted that the Thomas faction was "intent on getting possession of the convention for the purpose of preventing it from harming the 'grand old party.'" Thomas certainly had his work cut out for him.[44]

The convention began with Jones as temporary chairman. The Jones faction came in the stronger of the two factions. It possessed the temporary chairmanship and most of the committees, including the committee on credentials and permanent organization. The first battle for the Thomas faction would be over the naming of a permanent chairman and the officers of the convention.

The committee on permanent organization issued a majority report calling for Wheeler to serve as permanent chairman, Scott as first vice chairman, and Smith as second vice chairman. However, a minority report of the committee called for Bird to serve as chairman and Thomas to serve as first vice chairman. Although Cook County had sent the largest delegation to the fifty-delegate convention, obviously an appeal was being made to downstaters, with Bird as the choice of chairman for the Thomas faction and Scott and Smith on the ballot for the Jones faction.

A motion was made to adopt the majority report, which led to a lengthy and loud debate. After much shouting and disorder, Jones left the podium and handed over the temporary chairmanship to Wheeler so he could to go to the floor and participate in the debate. From the floor, he bitterly denounced Thomas, claiming that Thomas had overused his power in Chicago and had sought to prevent the convention from meeting. At this point, Wheeler cut off the debate. Frustrated with the proceedings, he withdrew as a candidate for permanent chairman. The Jones faction then named Scott as the majority report's candidate for chairman. It was now downstater versus downstater for chairman, with Chicagoans holding the strings.

Debate continued on the floor until delegates decided to adopt neither the majority or the minority report. Instead, they opted to elect the chairman and other convention officials by ballot. Thomas's, Wheeler's, and Scott's names were all placed in nomination, with Wheeler then withdrawing his name. Thomas was selected by a 32 to 17 vote over Scott, with Bird receiving one vote. Delegates then made the Thomas nomination unanimous. They also selected Bird, of the Thomas faction, as first vice chair, and Scott, of the Jones faction, as second vice chair. Delegates also selected Thomas T. Brown and Willis Wright, both of Sangamon County, as secretaries. A three-person committee escorted Thomas to the podium, where Wheeler presented him to the convention in presumably flattering, if not sincere, terms.

In his acceptance speech, Thomas thanked the convention for the honor of his appointment. He denied that he had been opposed to the convention, stating that he had advised that the best available men attend it. He then clearly laid out what he thought was the purpose of the convention. Addressing the concerns of the Republican newspapers, he said the convention had not been called for political reasons or to secure a place on the state ticket. He said it was for the purpose of securing greater freedom and better education for African Americans. He called for equality in public schools for African American children and for the opening of business opportunities to qualified African Americans.[45]

All sides praised Thomas's speech. The Republican *Inter-Ocean* said, "Mr. Thomas made a very sensible and modest address, advising moderation in all things that they might do." Even the Democratic *State Journal* wrote, "the speech was a creditable one, and if Mr. Thomas will rise above the partisan, and refuse to run the convention in the interest of any political party, it may yet be made to advance the interests of the colored people." After delivering his speech, Thomas was given a half-hour to organize the committees. He formed committees on rules, education, labor, civil rights, resolutions, and address. A few resolutions were then introduced and sent to the committee on resolutions and then the convention adjourned for the night.[46]

The efforts by some African American delegates to move the African American community away from the Republican Party had failed by the end of the first day of the two-day convention. Despite long odds, Thomas had effectively taken over the convention for Republican loyalists. Democratic newspapers conceded defeat. A headline in the *State Register* noted, "The Republican Bosses Triumphant." The *Chicago Times* wrote, "The election of Thomas as president means that the convention is composed by men who propose, at least for the present, to train with the Republican party." Jones was so upset with the result of the first day of the convention that he left Springfield and returned home.[47]

However, Thomas made one mistake on the first day of the convention. Perhaps it was in the spirit of conciliation or perhaps he did not have a choice, but he appointed several members of the Jones faction to serve as chairmen of the various committees. Wheeler was made chairman of the committee on resolutions, Barnett, the committee on Civil Rights, and Scott, the committee on state organization. The next day, these appointments would cause problems for Republican loyalist Thomas.[48]

The second day of the convention was the day that delegates were to vote on resolutions and reports and hear the convention's featured speakers. However, the day began with the news that the Republican-dominated U.S. Supreme Court had declared the federal civil rights act unconstitutional. That act, sponsored by Republican senator Charles Sumner in 1875, banned discrimination based on race in public places, such as restaurants, theaters, and hotels. Essentially the Court, in an 8 to 1 decision, ruled the law unconstitutional because it sought to regulate individuals, not states. The decision outraged the African American community, which saw the law as protection against discrimination.[49]

The outrage extended to the convention. To African Americans, the decision represented another sign that the nation, and the Republican Party, was abandoning them. Reverend Smith said the decision "sounded the death knell for the Republican party." Even Thomas is quoted as saying, "the ruling would be injurious to the Republican party."[50]

The Supreme Court's decision reenergized the Jones faction on the second day of the convention, even if Jones himself was no longer present. In firm control of the most important committees, the Jones faction issued a series of anti-Republican reports on behalf of these committees. With the Supreme Court's ruling, these reports found a much more receptive audience among the delegates.

Much of the work of the convention echoed that of the 1880 convention and of Thomas's acceptance speech. Delegates unanimously approved reports calling for nationwide compulsory education, equal funding for separate schools, and the hiring of African American teachers. The report on labor criticized unions for discriminating against African Americans, called for increased opportunities for African Americans in the industrial trades and advocated the settling of African Americans on vacant Illinois land owned by the railroads. It also recommended prohibiting the use of convict labor in Illinois.

However, following news of the Supreme Court's decision, delegates were angry at the Republican Party. As in 1880, the committee on state organization called for the creation of a state central committee, dedicated to, among other things, political organization. In 1880, this plank was watered down to be apolitical. In 1883, despite strong protests from Bird, delegates passed this report, complete with its political connotations. Along with creating the committee, the report also named its members. That membership was completely controlled by the Jones faction. Four members were to be from Cook County: Wheeler, Mitchell, Barnett, and John Howard. Only Howard was a member of the Thomas faction, and he tended to be unpredictable in his politics. The report also named Smith and Scott as members.

The Republican Party was loudly condemned on the second day. The report on state organization criticized the Republican state administration for not having hired any African Americans. Barnett's committee on civil rights introduced a majority report that questioned the Republican Party's faithfulness to the cause of civil rights. The committee's resolution stated, "We are ostracized, robbed of civil rights and denied the respect accorded to felons, and our friends tell us they can do no good." Wheeler's committee introduced a resolution that stated, "while we are proud of the noble record of the Republican party in the past in the interest in the negro, we solemnly pledge ourselves not to vote for any man for office who will not give us that recognition to which we are justly entitled."[51]

Attached to Wheeler's resolution was a document known as the Cairo Convention resolution. The document, passed September 18 at the convention held in the newly created Twentieth Congressional District in southern Illinois, offered a litany of slights faced by the African American community there. The manifesto concluded, "we denounce the bosses and managers of the republican party, in this congressional district, in the state, as well as those who manage and 'boss' the national Republican Party." All of the reports were submitted in the afternoon session. Delegates then took a break for dinner before reassembling in the evening to vote on the resolutions and to hear speeches.

Thomas and his fellow Republican loyalists certainly needed the break. The day had not gone well for Thomas, who truly believed that the best hope for African Americans lay in loyalty to the Republican Party. The tone of the resolutions had been angry and separatist. The speakers scheduled for the evening were Bird, Wheeler, and Smith, and it could be expected that the latter two would provide eloquent anti-Republican speeches. However, following dinner, Thomas was able to regain some initiative and cool some of the passions that had been released by the Supreme Court's decision.

The evening session began with a Republican loyalist delegate introducing a resolution endorsing Richard Oglesby for governor. Oglesby would indeed become the 1884 Republican nominee for governor. However, the resolution was referred to committee, never to be heard from again. Then, Republican governor John M. Hamilton was escorted to the speaker's platform, where he sat next to Thomas. Secretary of State Henry Dement and other state officials sat in the gallery. Unlike 1880, these officials were not asked to address the convention. Instead of participating in the convention, they attended as guests.

Although Wheeler was one of the evening's scheduled speakers, he chose not to address the audience. Reverend Smith spoke first. A gifted, electrifying orator, he first praised the Republican Party for its past efforts at fighting slavery. He then stated that African Americans had paid their debt to the Republican Party, if they ever owed it any, and he advised African Americans to organize and stand together. Smith said there were 25,000 African American voters in Illinois, and they gave the Republican Party its majority. African Americans, Smith said, had the right to aspire to more than spittoon cleaners and boot blacks. It was a stirring speech, although it later inspired a Springfield resident to complain in his local paper that the convention was a contest between the fellows who wanted clerkships, meaning Smith and Scott, and those African Americans who had patronage jobs as janitors, spittoon cleaners, and laborers. While Smith focused on the need for African Americans to organize, Bird, in his speech, focused on their need to be educated. In a clear demonstration of the divisions between the two factions, Bird stated that it was better for African Americans to qualify for office than to demand it.

Following the speeches, the convention voted on the various resolutions. Delegates approved all of the resolutions except for the Cairo convention, which was the most inflammatory. After lengthy and boisterous debate, the Thomas forces called for a motion to table the Cairo resolution. Thomas called for a standing vote, rather than a roll-call vote. When the vote was taken, Thomas declared the vote as 25 in favor of tabling and 22 against. Because it was a standing vote, the Thomas ruling was the official count, even though it appeared to most in the chamber, including the reporters from both the Democrat *Springfield State Register* and the Republican *Chicago Evening Journal*, that the motion to table had been defeated. Scott moved to call the roll, but Thomas refused to entertain the motion. A delegate moved to reconsider the question, but again Thomas blocked the motion. With that, the Cairo resolution was tabled. The Thomas faction had won a major victory. The Republican *Springfield State Journal* noted the success of the Thomas faction when it editorialized that "the plain truth is, a few men who desired to foist the Cairo resolutions upon this State Convention had a personal purpose to serve, and they were defeated in their object."[52]

Although the *State Journal* saw the defeat of the Cairo resolutions as a victory, other newspapers saw the convention as a whole as a defeat for the Republican Party. The Republican *Chicago Evening Journal* ran a headline stating "State Convention captured by Office-Seeking Politicians," its put-down phrase for the independents. The Democratic *Springfield State Register* took the same view as the *Evening Journal*, but from a Democratic standpoint, with a headline that read, "The Convention Captured and Run by Advanced Thinkers." The *Evening Journal* was especially harsh in its criticism of Thomas, stating that his decision to give committee chairmanships to some of the independents allowed them to carry the convention. "The 'sore-heads' as they are denominated, laughed all day at the stupidity of Mr. Thomas in giving them such an advantage. They made good use of it," the *Evening Journal* reporter wrote. In a later story, he added, "only a few of the Thomas faction were keen enough to see how successfully they had been hoodwinked and beaten by their crafty opponents.[53]

The *Evening Journal*'s comments were both unfair and untrue. The Thomas forces came into the convention in the minority yet captured the convention leadership posts and prevented the passage of the anti-Republican Cairo resolutions. They did so in an environment that at the national level was questioning blind support of the Republican Party. Indeed, that same year conventions in Rhode Island and South Carolina passed resolutions condemning the party. And, while Thomas may have erred in appointing Wheeler, Scott, and Barnett to committee chairmanships, those appointments were made prior to the Supreme Court's decision on the Civil Rights Act. Even the creation of the state central committee was softened. Although Wheeler was made chairman of the committee and Mitchell secretary, the Thomas faction made some gains here as well with the addition of Bird to the committee and Thomas as treasurer. Overall, Thomas achieved a significant victory at the convention in keeping the activities of the independents under control. However, the convention was merely a battle in a war that the factions would wage for the next two years. Relations between Reverend Smith and Thomas would become especially bitter.[54]

In January 1884, members of the state central committee met and endorsed a plan by Smith to conduct a multistate convention in Pittsburgh in April. The convention was to consist of African American delegations only from northern states, and these delegates were not to be elected but invited. The purpose of the convention was to organize African Americans in the North, where they had the power to vote, to exert pressure on northern elected officials to help African Americans who were being oppressed and denied the vote in the South. Once again, the underlying theme of the convention would be political independence from the Republican Party. The call for the convention was signed by Wheeler, Mitchell, Smith, Barnett, and Scott.[55]

The Thomas faction objected to the committee's action and in March conducted a mass meeting to protest it. Thomas chaired the meeting and among those who attended it were Phillips, Howard, Baker and Waring. Wheeler attended and spoke out in favor of the call for the convention. Despite Wheeler's presence, the meeting adopted resolutions stating that the central committee did not have the authority to call for a national convention and criticizing the call for having the delegates invited, not elected. The resolution pointedly noted that Wheeler and Jones had lost election to the 1883 state colored convention and had to attend using proxies from other delegates, despite their having issued the call to convene the convention. Finally, while "recognizing the ability of Mr. C. S. Smith as a public speaker," the resolution criticized him for being inconsistent in his actions, stating that he claimed to be a loyal Republican on some occasions and yet swore that he had no allegiance to any political party on other occasions.[56]

The protests of Thomas and the others did not prevent the Pittsburgh convention from meeting. On April 29, Smith convened the convention. Wheeler was made president and Barnett delivered a paper. Such national African American leaders as Frederick Douglass and T. Thomas Fortune were among the sixty or so delegates to attend the event. Despite meeting for two days, the convention did not achieve much. Smith was defensive at the meeting. In his opening address, in words that were perhaps aimed directly at Thomas, he stated, "A few colored office holders have been bending their energies to weaken the influence of this meeting. They have industriously circulated not only false but slanderous reports concerning the motives of those who have been its main projectors."

As a whole, the convention appears to have been a failure. Coming just eight months after the Louisville national convention, several African Americans questioned the need for the Pittsburgh convention. Douglass, while attending the convention, was mistreated at it. When a delegate introduced a resolution inviting Douglass to address the convention, a fierce debate broke out on the floor, forcing Douglass to note that as a delegate he could address the convention any time he wished. The convention's concluding statement merely called for the securing of the rights of all citizens in all parts of the country. The *Cleveland Gazette*, an African American newspaper, editorialized that "the colored people and the majority of the colored press have paid it little attention," adding, "it was not a convention but a conference, a private affair, gotten up by a few men craving notoriety and it is looked upon as such by the colored race."[57]

Thomas would also make an attempt for the national stage in 1884. That fall, he worked with five other African American leaders to bring a Colored People's World Exposition to Chicago. The purpose of the exposition was to show "the arts, mechanics and products of the colored race to the world." In December 1884 Senator Henry Blair (R-New Hampshire) introduced a bill calling for a $500,000 appropriation for such an exposition to be held in September and October 1885. According to Blair, these African American leaders came to him with the idea for the exposition and they later incorporated into an entity for the purpose of holding an exposition. Blair's bill created a board of directors that consisted of Thomas, Daniel Johnson of Mississippi, Phillip Joseph of Alabama, W. Wyatt Henderson of Illinois, Joseph W. Moore of Tennessee, and T. Thomas Fortune of New York. Presumably, these were the individuals who approached Blair. Of them, only Fortune had any notoriety. It appears as if the Senate failed to pass an appropriation and the idea for the exposition went nowhere.[58]

Although Smith at the colored conventions was trying to steer the African American community away from the Republican Party, when speaking to white Republicans he appeared a loyal supporter. In the early spring, he delivered a stirring partisan address before a Republican conference held in Chicago. In April just before he left for the Pittsburgh Colored Convention, he attended the state Republican convention as a delegate. It was here that he was able to get his revenge on Thomas.[59]

Coming in to the state Republican convention, African Americans had discussed having an African American selected to serve as a delegate-at-large to the Republican National Convention. Each congressional district in Illinois could select two delegates to attend the national convention, and the state as a whole received four additional at-large delegates. The numbers were too small in any congressional district to have an African American chosen as delegate by district, so African American leaders sought to leverage their party loyalty and use some moral persuasion to have the state convention select an African American as a statewide delegate-at-large. At the African American state executive committee meeting in Chicago, the committee endorsed Smith for one of Illinois' four delegate-at-large positions. In early April, the *Cleveland Gazette* mentioned Thomas as a possible candidate. Just before the convention, the *Chicago Evening Journal* wrote, "the colored brethren are here in force, demanding a delegate-at-large—either Bird, of Cairo, Smith, of Bloomington or Thomas, of Chicago." The *Chicago Inter-Ocean* predicted that Smith would be named as a presidential elector and Dr. James Magee of downstate Metropolis would be returned to the Republican State Central Committee to which he had been named in 1882. "This, it seems, will be sufficient recognition of the colored element," the paper wrote. Both Smith and Bird attended the state convention as delegates. Thomas served as an alternate delegate. In all, there were 792 delegates at the state convention, 11 of whom were African American.[60]

A committee issued a report recommending a delegate slate to the convention. The report named Smith as an alternate delegate-at-large to the national convention but did not name an African American as a full delegate-at-large. As the report was being debated, John Howard and some other African American delegates spearheaded a movement to have Thomas named as a delegate-at-large. In recommending Thomas to the convention, Howard stated, "I name J. W. E. Thomas, of Cook, member of the legislature, who, if he had been willing, might have sold out the Republican party in the legislature to the Democrats." The Illinois Republican Party had never nominated an African American to serve as a delegate to a national convention and, in fact, Smith was the first African American nominated by Illinois Republicans as an alternate delegate. The naming of Thomas would have been a demonstration of the gains the community was making within the party and would have served as an important symbolic victory for it.

Although the convention chairman noted that an African American, Smith, had been named as an alternate delegate-at-large, many of the participants at the convention understood the importance of having an African American serve as delegate. Following Howard's comments, a motion was made to recommit the report to committee with instructions to place an African American on it as delegate-at-large. Another delegate went further, moving to replace one of the proposed delegate-at-large candidates from Cook County with Thomas. Both proposals were met with cheers from the convention.

At the crucial moment of the debate, Smith stood and opposed the selection of Thomas, stating that the African American delegates proposed his name too late. He stated that while he wanted a African American for delegate, he wanted order, rule, and procedure. Smith added that the mistake the convention made in not naming an African American as a delegate-at-large could be fixed at another convention. The split in the small African American delegation meant the Thomas nomination was doomed. As the *Tribune* noted, "getting the colored troops to fight amongst themselves proved wise, and their dissensions were urged as the reason for not giving them all they asked."[61]

While the *Tribune* gave the convention managers the credit for the split in the African American community, the *Cleveland Gazette* squarely and correctly laid the blame on Smith. In a large headline over the story covering the convention, the paper wrote "Rev. C. S. Smith Proves Himself a Traitor to his Race."[62]

The same language could also have been applied to Smith with regards to his party loyalties. Despite serving as an alternate delegate to the Republican National Convention in the spring, Smith advocated the independent presidential candidacy of Benjamin Butler by late summer. When the Butler campaign began to fizzle, Smith supported Democrat Grover Cleveland for president. After Cleveland's election, Smith tried for a patronage position in the new administration. The Cleveland administration ignored his requests, perhaps noting that Smith had supported three different political parties during the course of one presidential campaign.

While Smith's flip flopping cost him a federal patronage appointment under the Cleveland administration, Thomas's loyalty to the Republican Party had cost him a chance to serve as a delegate to the Republican National Convention. It also had made him enemies within the now bitterly divided Chicago African American community, which threatened his hopes for a third term to the state legislature.[63]

[5]

"We Are Here as Citizens": Reelection, the Civil Rights Bill, and Another Colored Convention

The differences over strategy and the limited number of electoral opportunities available divided Chicago's African American leaders. The small African American community could not afford division if it hoped to make gains in the political world. While patronage was increasing, gains were also measured in the holding of public office. Having African Americans nominated and elected with white votes served as an important symbol to the community. Achieving this was more difficult when the community was divided and unable to unite behind one candidate. Thomas saw this firsthand in the spring of 1884 when divisions in the African American contingent at the state Republican convention cost him being selected as a national delegate.

The Election of 1884

There were other examples as well. In the spring of 1883, John Howard and an African American named Brown (probably George) ran for the Republican nomination for Second Ward Alderman but lost to the one white candidate in a low turnout primary election. Charles H. Lithgow, the white candidate, received 113 votes, while Brown received 72 and Howard 62. It is unknown if the vote was along racial lines, but combined the two African American candidates outpolled the one white candidate. Similarly that spring, two African Americans sought the Republican nomination for South Town Clerk, with the result that the one white candidate won the nomination at the town convention, although Joseph Houser, one of the losing candidates, disputed the result. The following year, one African American, H. J. Mitchell, ran for the clerk's nomination against two white candidates, incumbent D. C. McKinnon and future Speaker of the Illinois House David Shanahan. With the African American community not split, Mitchell was able to win narrowly on the fourth ballot, although William Baker, who had nominated him, promoted the light-skinned Mitchell to the convention by exclaiming, "he is almost a white man." Mitchell, however, would lose the 1884 election to Democrat Henry Malzacher.[1]

Thomas did not play a large role during the off-year elections following his 1882 victory, limited by his service in the legislature and his family problems. He did serve as a delegate to the county Republican convention in the fall of 1883, but that election only entailed nominating candidates for a superior court judge position and five county commissioner seats, none of which were located on the South Side.[2]

In the spring of 1884, despite differences over the Pittsburgh convention, Chicago's African Americans were united behind Senator John Logan's efforts to seek the Republican nomination for president. The Second Ward organized a Logan club with Thomas serving as secretary and Isaac Rivers as one of the vice presidents. On April 3, Ferdinand Barnett chaired an African American Logan Club meeting that was addressed by Thomas, Edward H. Morris, William Baker, and Robert Mitchell. Other African American Logan supporters included John Howard, W. C. Phillips, R. C. Waring, J. Q. Grant, and John G. Jones.[3]

Logan received the Republican vice presidential nomination that year, with James Blaine of Maine serving as the Republican standard-bearer. New York governor Grover Cleveland was the Democratic candidate for president, and Benjamin Butler, a former union general from Massachusetts, ran as an independent/Greenback Party candidate. With Blaine's nomination, African American unity fell apart. Lloyd G. Wheeler supported Butler for president and Democrat Carter Harrison for governor. Reverend Smith of Bloomington stated he couldn't support Blaine and by June was working for Butler. However, by the fall Smith had joined the Cleveland camp.[4]

But the real split in the community could be seen in the race for state representative in the Third Legislative District. There, Thomas ran for renomination against Robert M. Mitchell, William Baker, and John Howard, the three African Americans who had run against him in 1882. Mitchell had been a strong supporter of the Jones-Wheeler-Smith faction at the 1883 Illinois Colored Convention. While Howard had sided with Thomas in opposing the Pittsburgh Colored Convention, he had become a chronic office-seeker and had been campaigning for state representative all year. Baker was a longtime community activist who had served as a doorman for the state legislature in Springfield and run for the legislature in the old First District of Chicago in 1880 and in the Third District in 1882. H. J. Mitchell, Lloyd G. Wheeler, and Isaac Rivers were also mentioned as possible candidates.[5]

Senators were elected to four-year terms, so in 1884 John Clough of the Third Ward was not up for reelection. With Clough living in the Third Ward, that meant there would be pressure to select one House candidate from the Second Ward and one from the First Ward. The *Inter-Ocean* cautioned Third District Republican leaders not to make the mistake they made in 1882, when they nominated two House candidates from the Second Ward. It wrote, "In view of the sorry mess the district made of it in 1882 a little 'sober second thought' in advance is in order. Had the First Ward been given one of the House nominations in 1882 and the Second the other both would have been elected no doubt, but instead of that the Second Ward, in its greed, took both nominations." The result, of course, had been the election of two Democrats and one Republican in a Republican-majority district.

The *Inter-Ocean* went on to state that the logic the Second Ward Republicans used to secure both 1882 nominations was fallacious. That logic was that Bradwell had to be nominated or he would bolt the party and run as an independent (instead, First Warder Dan Wren wound up doing this), and that an African American had to be nominated so the African American community would have a representative. The *Inter-Ocean* argued that neither reason was sufficient to nominate two Second Warders. It went on to argue that nominating someone on the basis of color was especially wrong. Nevertheless, like in 1882, it was almost universally recognized that an African American would receive one of the nominations.[6]

Although the prenomination jockeying was less than it had been in 1882, there was still some. Throughout the year, Howard was mentioned favorably as a legislative candidate in the weekly column of the Illinois correspondent to the *Cleveland Gazette*, I. C. Harris. Howard, not coincidently, sold the *Gazette* out of his cigar and liquor store. On September 11, Harris chaired a small meeting of Howard supporters. The meeting adopted a resolution calling for an African American to represent the Third District and, not surprisingly, further recommended that Howard be the representative. The *Gazette* noted on September 13 that Thomas was "working earnestly and quietly for renomination to the legislature, notwithstanding there are millions in the field." On September 16, the *Tribune* reported that Republican leaders had cut a secret deal to nominate Thomas and an unnamed white candidate. Just two days later it reported that the leaders of the Third District had agreed to nominate two white candidates: George A. Gibbs and either Abner Taylor or John Lyle King.[7]

However, with the 1882 debacle fresh in their minds, the true scenario would be that the First Ward would unite behind one candidate, the Second Ward would try to unite behind an African American candidate and both candidates would probably receive a nomination. On September 18, the

First Ward let it be known that it wanted Abner Taylor nominated. While other names surfaced as possible rivals for the September 20 convention, the endorsement by the First Ward club was the equivalent to nomination for Taylor, who, with Alderman Arthur Dixon, was putting together a Republican machine in the ward. That left the second nomination up to the Second Ward, which would make its decision in a contested ward primary on September 19.[8]

All four African American candidates— Thomas, Mitchell, Howard, and Baker— fielded a slate of candidates for delegate from the Second Ward. The winner, as in 1882, would be able to claim the ward's backing and go to the district convention virtually assured of a nomination. Eleven delegates would represent the Second Ward at the district convention. Each of the four candidate's slates consisted of six African Americans and five white men. By agreement, the five white men were the same on all four slates. They had agreed to cast their votes for the African American candidate whose slate received the most votes.[9]

Although the Thomas slate apparently won the Second Ward primary, coming into the convention both the *Tribune* and the *Inter-Ocean* reported that the second spot would be a tight race between Thomas and Mitchell. No newspaper reported whom the delegates elected in the other wards favored for the second legislative nomination. Both the *Tribune* and the *Inter-Ocean* reported that there was an outside chance the split in the African American community could result in the nomination of a second white candidate.

In all, voters selected 35 delegates to attend the Third District Republican nominating convention. Both the Second and Third Wards had 11 delegates each. The First Ward added 10 delegates and the portion of the Fourth Ward in the District had 3 delegates. It would take 18 votes to win a nomination.[10]

At the Saturday, September 20, convention, Alderman Dixon nominated Abner Taylor for the first representative spot. Taylor was unanimously nominated without a formal vote. Then, all four African American candidates were placed in nomination. A. T. Hall of the Fourth Ward nominated Howard, George Gibbs of the First Ward nominated Baker, G. R. Rockfeller of the Second Ward nominated Mitchell, and E. R. Bliss of the Second Ward nominated Thomas. Of the four persons nominating candidates, only Hall was an African American. Thomas received 17¼ votes on the first ballot, just three-fourths of a vote shy of winning. Mitchell and Howard both received 6¼ votes and Baker received 5¼. The vote stayed the same on the second ballot and changed very little on ballots three through five. On the sixth ballot, Baker withdrew his candidacy. The *Evening Journal* reported that he withdrew in favor of Mitchell, while both the *Inter-Ocean* and the *Gazette* reported that he withdrew in favor of Thomas. The *Tribune* merely reported that he withdrew. In any event, Baker's delegates split their support between the remaining three candidates, but with Thomas only needing ¾ of a vote, he was able to win the nomination. The vote on the sixth ballot ended up Thomas 18¼, Howard 8½₁₂ and Mitchell 8⅚. No breakdown of delegate votes by ward exists, but it seems that Thomas's strength came from the Second and Third Wards. After Thomas won the nomination, delegates made the vote unanimous.[11]

Thomas's nomination passed with little comment. The only daily newspaper to opine on the nomination was the *Evening-Journal*, which favorably wrote, "Mr. Thomas, an intelligent colored citizen, has already represented this important district with fidelity in two terms of the Legislature." The weekly *Cleveland Gazette* added, "Let us return him for the good record that he has made in the past, with the hope that his future may be the same.[12]

The day after receiving the nomination, Thomas spoke to a meeting of the Third Ward Republican club, where he thanked club members for their support at the convention. Thomas is quoted as saying that he owed his nomination to the Republicans of the Third Ward and that he would always have their welfare in his heart. Senator Clough was from the Third Ward and he and Thomas had an alliance in 1882 that saw them both elected. Clough apparently carried that alliance into 1884, even though he himself was not up for election. In addition, former congressman William Aldrich, who had supported Thomas in 1882, headed the Third Ward delegation. The Second Ward was slightly split, even though Thomas apparently won the primary. The First Ward was probably mostly against Thomas, as he was one of the chief beneficiaries from their 1882 disaster. Also, Alderman Dixon and his candidate, Abner Taylor, were strong anti-Logan men, whereas Thomas was a Logan supporter.[13]

About the only sour note that came after Thomas's nomination came from his defeated opponents and, to some extent, his own community. At a Second Ward Republican Club meeting, Baker said that the nominating convention had been unfairly packed against him and that his delegate ticket had been tampered with. Despite this, Baker said he would still support both Thomas and the entire Republican ticket. Samuel Wright warned that there was resentment against Thomas in the African American community. On September 29, Wright spoke to the Second Ward Republican club and said, "I understand that a good many of the colored men of this ward are opposed to Mr. J. W. E. Thomas, but I tell you, brethren, I'm going to work for him tooth and nail"[14]

At the same time, in a masterful display of double-speak, Howard announced that he would run as "an independent candidate of Republican tendencies with Democratic leanings." A campaign advertisement appeared in the *Inter-Ocean* newspaper which announced a specific threat against Thomas. The advertisement read, "J. H. Howard, independent candidate for the Legislature against the Hon. J. W. E. Thomas, from the Third Senatorial District of Chicago, Republican candidate." Howard, who continually flirted with the Democratic Party, denied placing the notice when asked about it. He never did mount a third-party bid. As long as Thomas could keep the African American community united behind his candidacy, he would have no problems for reelection in the overwhelmingly Republican district.[15]

Democrats in the Second District had their own problems, which provided some help to Thomas. Although the Third District was heavily Republican, the 1882 split in the Republican Party, which resulted in three Republican candidates, had allowed Democrats to capture two of the three legislative seats. Even though the Republicans would have only two candidates in 1884, the Democrats could not just concede the second seat. It too nominated two candidates for the legislature. The first nominee was incumbent Tom McNally of the First Ward, a machine Democrat whose 1882 election had been contested by Judge Bradwell all the way to the General Assembly. The second Democratic nominee was George Cass, a lawyer from the Third Ward. Trade unions were slightly upset that the Democrats did not nominate a labor man for Cass's spot on the ticket, and Democrat antimachine "kickers" were not pleased with the growing First and Second Ward machines' involvement in crafting the ticket. That machine was led by Joseph Mackin, who would soon be sent to jail for election fraud, and Michael "Hinky Dink" Kenna, who was just starting his legendary career as a First Ward Democratic powerbroker. Added to the fall election mix would be Greenback (Butler) candidate William V. Barr and Prohibition Party candidate B. M. Davenport. Neither candidate would be much of a factor.[16]

Although the 1884 race promised to be difficult for Republicans, who had nominated scandal-plagued James G. Blaine for president, Cook County Republicans entered the campaign with confidence. At their county convention, held the same day as the Third District Republican Senatorial nominating convention, Cook County Republicans easily put together a countywide ticket. The only real dispute centered over selecting two candidates to run for the county board from the South Side. African American delegates sought to name Samuel Wright as one of the two nominees. At the convention, Republicans placed the names of four men in nomination, including Wright and African American newspaper editor George Beard. A candidate needed 108 votes to receive a nomination. On an informal ballot, F. A. McDonald of the Third Ward received 99 votes, Dan Wren of the First Ward received 75, Wright received 37, and Beard received 3. At this point, the Wright supporters made a deal with the McDonald supporters and on the first formal ballot, with 108 votes needed to nominate, McDonald received 149 votes, enough for the first nomination, Wren received 55 votes, and Beard received 4 votes. On the second ballot, McDonald reneged on the deal and supported Wren, who received 134 votes and the second nomination, while Wright received 76 votes. The African American delegates angrily refused to make the nominations unanimous.[17]

Many African Americans felt slighted that they did not have a representative on the county ticket. There were rumors that Wright and other African Americans would bolt the party. This forced Wright to send a letter to the *Chicago Inter-Ocean* stating that he would not bolt and would support the ticket from "J. G. Blaine to the last man." Still, on September 29 the Second Ward Republican Club felt the need to pass a resolution denouncing as traitors to their party and race all African American men who adopted independent or anti-Republican principles.[18]

Despite this resolution, on September 30 a group of African Americans met to form a First Ward Independent Republican Club. The only major newspaper to report the meeting was the Democratic *Chicago Times*, which had a history of exaggerating the importance of independent or Democratic African American clubs. For this meeting, it estimated the attendance to be at 500, a preposterously high number. However, a list of attendees shows that club was more legitimate than similar clubs had been in the past. Lloyd G. Wheeler chaired the meeting, John Howard served as secretary, and attorneys Edward H. Morris and J. E. Jones made addresses. The meeting was held mainly to oppose the Blaine candidacy, but Howard and Morris also expressed their disappointment over the failure of the Republicans to nominate an African American on their county ticket. There was no effort to form a third party, nor was there an effort to bolt to the Democratic Party. Attendees at the meeting merely expressed their support for Butler for president. Some would later come out for Harrison for governor. Wheeler would sign a circular of support for Harrison that brought the patronage issue to the forefront, in that it criticized Republican Richard J. Oglesby for not hiring any African Americans during his political career. After Oglesby was elected governor, Thomas would find that the circular was not far off the mark.[19]

For Thomas, the campaign proceeded like most others. He made the rounds to the various Republican clubs, giving speeches and promoting the Republican ticket. Although not a "dry," he had never been supported by the saloon interests. His support for the Harper High License Bill the previous session made him more of a target of the saloon league in 1884. That league eventually endorsed both of his Democratic opponents. The *Times* reported that he spoke for nearly an hour at an October 31 meeting of African American voters. During his talk, Thomas urged voters to vote for both himself and Abner Taylor. He also warned them not to vote for Democrat Carter Harrison for governor. In strong language, he said that African Americans who campaigned for Harrison had been bought "for a few dollars or a drink of whiskey."[20]

One of the highlights of the campaign for Thomas was when, on October 18, former Chicago mayor Long John Wentworth campaigned for the Republican ticket in front of the Third Ward Blaine and Logan Club. At that meeting, Wentworth declared that Thomas was one of the best men ever elected to the state legislature. Another highlight occurred on October 25, when Thomas served as a member of the welcoming committee for a visit to the city by presidential candidate James Blaine.[21]

Election Day was almost anticlimactic. Despite accusations on both sides that there would be major fraud at the polls, Election Day seemed to be relatively scandal free. For the second election in a row, Thomas received the most votes in the Third District. The official results were Thomas 10,691, Taylor, 10,136½, McNally, 8,344, and Cass 7,951. The official results do not break down the vote totals by ward, but the unofficial newspaper accounts do have ward breakdowns. They show that Thomas did best in the Second Ward, where he trounced the two Democratic opponents by more than 1,400 votes. In that ward, he bested fellow Republican Taylor by more than 1,100 votes, a sure sign that African American voters were plumping (casting three votes) for him. Thomas came in third in the First Ward, behind McNally and Taylor. His third-place showing reflects support among that ward's African American voters, and plumping by First Ward Democrats for First Ward resident McNally. Had that ward not plumped for McNally, Cass might have nosed him out for the third legislative position. Thomas was a distant fourth in the Fourth Ward, but that represented being behind first-place winner McNally by about 100 votes, due to the small part of the ward that was in the Third District. Thomas's votes from the Third Ward are not known, but it is reasonable to assume that he came in either first or, more probably, second to Taylor in that heavily Republican ward.[22]

The Butler rebellion against the Republican Party wound up turning in pitiful results. According to the *Inter-Ocean*, Butler received only 10 votes in the First Ward, 4 in the Second, and 5 in the Third. In all three wards, he finished behind John St. John, the Prohibition Party candidate, who also did very poorly. Butler received 21 votes in the Fourth Ward. Carter Harrison ran ahead of the Democratic ticket in the Second Ward, but still lost the ward to Republican Richard Oglesby by 600 votes. Harrison won the Democratic First Ward by 300 votes, but was crushed in both the Third and

Fourth Wards, losing the former by 800 votes and the latter by 1,900 votes. Republican Oglesby won the election for governor but for the first time since before the Civil War a Democrat, Grover Cleveland, won the presidency.[23]

For Thomas, the election of 1884 would prove to be his easiest legislative race, and the community remained solidly Republican. However, the success of his reelection only temporarily covered up the divisions among African American leaders. While Thomas had won the Republican primary in the Second Ward, he still needed alliances with white politicians from both the Second and Third Wards to win renomination. With his reelection, he had again proven to be the leading African American politician in the city, but those white politicians could have supported someone else in the nomination fight. And, if the divisions in the community appeared healed with his reelection, they would soon reopen.

The 1885 Legislative Session

The Thirty-fourth Session of the Illinois General Assembly is considered one of the most tumultuous in Illinois history. The House of Representatives took three weeks just to organize and elect a Speaker. The legislature as a whole took an unprecedented three months to elect a U.S. senator, far outdoing the eight-day senatorial standoff of 1877 in which Thomas participated. In the middle of the session, 68 legislators left for a ten-day junket to New Orleans, while a majority of the Senate passed a resolution criticizing those going on the trip.[24] At least three times fights between legislators erupted on the House floor. In June, allegations of bribery in the House led to the creation of an investigative committee, but it could not find enough evidence to pursue the issue. At the end of the session, one House member was accused of committing a sexual impropriety against a female house page.[25] And, like the Thirty-third General Assembly, the session dragged on into late June.

For Thomas too, the session would be extremely difficult. The splits in the African American community, first seen in 1883, continued to haunt him in Springfield. Thomas was unable to resolve the issue of Governor Oglesby and patronage, which had been raised by Lloyd Wheeler in the 1884 campaign. However, the community's call for a state civil rights act to replace the federal act voided in 1883 would result in Thomas's greatest legislative triumph. Yet even this triumph would be marred by the splits in the African American community.

The large Republican Senate majority of the Thirty-third General Assembly disappeared after the election of 1884. The Senate of the Thirty-fourth General Assembly stood at a very narrow 26 Republicans to 24 Democrats and 1 Greenback Democrat. In the House the margin was even closer: That chamber had 76 Republicans, 76 Democrats and 1 independent. That independent, Elijah

Haines, had generally sided with the Democrats in the Thirty-third General Assembly. Most analysts expected him to do so again for the Thirty-fourth General Assembly, meaning that the Democrats would control the House and there would be an even 102 to 102 party split when the two chambers combined to vote for the U.S. senator. None of this boded well for a productive session.[26]

Yet, there were serious issues that had to be discussed, especially in the area of election reform. At the beginning of January, a bipartisan committee of three of the leading political clubs of Chicago, the Citizens' Association, the Iroquois Club, and the Union League Club, drafted legislation to reform the state's election code. Chicago elections were notoriously corrupt. Following the 1883 mayoral election, the Union League Club hired private detectives to investigate why the reform candidate for mayor had fared so poorly. The investigation found that only 7 of the city's 171 precincts did not show signs of fraud. In 1885 Joe Mackin, secretary of the Cook County Democratic Party, was sentenced to two years in prison for vote fraud and another five years in prison for perjury related to the vote fraud charges for activities conducted in the 1884 election.[27] In general, the committee proposed registering voters, creating smaller precincts that contained no more than 300 voters, making Election Day a legal holiday, and changing the way election judges were appointed to remove partisanship.

The organizations had a joint meeting in Chicago on January 2, before the new legislative session started. The committee held the meeting at the Union League Club and invited the members of the Cook County legislative delegation. Fifteen legislators attended the meeting, including Thomas. Following a lavish dinner, the legislators heard the committee's proposals and were invited to make comments. Some legislators remained noncommittal, especially because no bill had been drafted. However, other legislators, including Thomas, spoke in favor of the proposals. Thomas said he was especially concerned about the way election judges operated, stating that he had served as an election judge and one of his fellow judges had proposed recounting the ballots to change the vote count. Remembering the two primary election reform bills he had proposed in the previous General Assembly, he encouraged the committee to consider primary election law reforms as part of the bill. To the cheers of the audience, he concluded by saying he would work to secure better election laws.[28]

In Springfield, the House convened on January 7. The night before the opening of session, the Republican members caucused at the Leland Hotel and unanimously selected Charles Fuller of Boone County as their choice for Speaker. At the Democratic caucus, conducted at the St. Nicholas Hotel, Edward Conkrite of Stephenson County defeated Haines 39 to 32 to become the Democratic choice for Speaker.[29] When the House convened for the first time the next day, the independent Haines sat on the Republican side of the chamber, sending a clear message to the Democrats that he was unhappy about their choice for Speaker. The House was unable to even effect a temporary organization on its first day.[30] On the second day of session, the Democrats, hoping to curry favor with Haines, selected him as temporary Speaker with an assist from one Republican vote. The next day, Chief Justice of the Illinois Supreme Court John Scholfield administered the oath of office to the new legislators.[31]

Despite the honor of being named temporary Speaker by the Democrats, Haines wanted to be Speaker. Because neither party supported Haines, and he held the deciding vote, this meant that the House could not permanently organize. This had several ramifications. Under the state constitution, the secretary of state was supposed to report the November election results to the Speaker of the House. Without a Speaker, the results could not be reported and the governor, secretary of state, and other constitutional officers elected in November could not be sworn into office. They were supposed to be sworn in on January 12, the second Monday of the year. Also, without a permanent organization, no bills could be introduced. Finally, the voting for a U.S. senator was scheduled to begin in February, but if the delay in organizing lasted long enough, this voting also could not occur.

Haines, the expert parliamentarian and political strategist, knew all this. For almost two weeks, from January 8 to January 21, he ruled the House as temporary Speaker, waiting for the Democrats, or even the Republicans, to come to him and make him permanent Speaker. At one point, because neither the statutes nor the state constitution mentioned the election of a "temporary" Speaker, he declared that his election as temporary Speaker was tantamount to a permanent election. This parliamentary maneuver did not work, however, and on January 21, two weeks after the start of session, he resigned his temporary Speakership. Still, he refused to support anyone else for permanent Speaker, causing a further delay in organizing the House. At one point, Haines said he could support one of four Republicans for the post, including Abner Taylor from Thomas's district. The Republicans turned down this offer, since their nominee, Fuller, was not one of his choices. Finally, on January 29, three full weeks after the start of session, the Democrats gave up and elected Haines for permanent Speaker. The following day, on January 30, the new state officers were sworn into office, fully 18 days after they were supposed to be under the Constitution. The new session had gotten off to an ominous start.[32]

Things did not get any better with the selection of a U.S. senator. The Republicans were almost unanimous in supporting John A. Logan for reelection. Logan had been elected to the Senate in 1871, but lost his reelection bid during the memorable contest of 1877. Two years later, the legislature again selected him for the Senate. Coming off of his vice presidential bid in 1884, he needed reelection to the Senate if he was to have serious consideration for the presidency in 1888.

At the Republican caucus, held February 5, the party members voted to stay with Logan for the duration of the Senate contest. The Democrats supported Congressman William Morrison for the position, although his support among the party was less than unanimous.[33] The two chambers met in joint session for the first time on February 13, but it wasn't until February 18 that the first full vote was taken. On that vote, Logan received 101 votes to Morrison's 94. Haines received 4 votes, and three other candidates each received a vote.[34] From then on brief joint sessions convened every day during the middle of session, although most of the time one or both of the parties did not vote. The Republicans remained united for Logan, although a couple of their members appeared suspect in their total support. One Republican member, Eugene Sittig of Chicago, said he opposed the idea of the party not endorsing another candidate if it appeared that Logan could not win. On the other hand, although a majority of the Democrats supported Morrison, a small minority of two or three did not, depriving him of any chance to win election. Haines also did not support Morrison. Many thought it was his goal to win election to the seat himself in the same manner that he had won the Speaker's position.

New U.S. senators were to be sworn in on March 4, but by that date the Illinois legislature still had not selected its senator. When the House had failed to organize in January, resulting in the inability to swear in the state constitutional officers, the old constitutional officers remained in office. However the Illinois Senate seat remained vacant as the Senate began its duties. As February stretched into March and March stretched into April, the deadlock continued. During the course of the voting, three members of the General Assembly died and had to be replaced by special elections. For the first two members, one Republican and one Democrat, the elections resulted in no change in the party and hence no break in the deadlock. However, on April 13 Democrat House member J. Henry Shaw died. Just under three weeks later, the Republicans in a stealth campaign were able to elect a member of their own party to replace Shaw in the heavily Democratic district. The election gave the Republicans 103 members in the two chambers, the majority needed to elect a Senator. On Tuesday, May 19, three full months after the first full vote had occurred, Logan won election with the minimum 103 votes needed.[35]

The legislators who elected Logan were later called the Logan 103. A poster with their pictures on it was commissioned and the Thomas family displayed a copy of it in their home for more than a century. In later years, there would be annual reunions of the group. In 1894 Thomas named his new born son Logan, presumably in honor of the senator.[36]

Thomas had remained a loyal Republican and supported Logan through-out the Senate contest. An African American newspaper, the *State Capital* out of Springfield, would later write of Thomas and the Senate fight that, "It is in such a crucible that the picture of pure metal proves its worth and comes out untarnished and resplendent. At that time when doubt and distrust per-vaded the very atmosphere, J. W. E. Thomas pursued the even tenor of his way, and not a whisper was heard expressive of doubt as to his loyalty. He emerged from the contest unscathed, and his course did more to command respect for the negro in this state than any event in its history."[37]

The Senate struggle occupied much of the attention of the both the House and the Senate and, coupled with the precariousness of having the unpredict-able Haines in the Speaker's chair, not much work was accomplished in the first part of the session, so Thomas had some free time to enjoy himself. He received several visitors during session, including W. C. Phillips and H. J. Mitchell.[38] In May, his seventeen-year-old daughter Hester visited Spring-field. Traveling with her was a friend identified in the papers as May Marshall. It is likely that this was Mary Marshall, whose older sister, Crittie, became Thomas's third wife in 1887.[39]

With Haines serving as Speaker, the Republicans were in the minority, meaning that Thomas had no hope of becoming a committee chair. However, since he was serving his third term, Haines assigned him to serve on more important committees than he had in the past. While Haines named him to two minor committees, Manufactures and Public Charities, he also named him to the Education committee and the Judiciary committee. The latter committee was very prestigious, especially for an attorney.[40]

Keeping to his promise of support for election reform that he made at the Union League Club in January, Thomas introduced three election reform bills in the Thirty-fourth General Assembly. The first was House Bill 46, which defined the qualifications and duties of election judges in primary elections and created penalties for stuffing a primary election ballot box. Thomas attempted to completely regulate primary elections with House Bill 85, which was an updated version of the two primary election bills he had sponsored in the Thirty-third General Assembly. The bill provided for the manner in which a political party could call a primary election, scheduled the hours that the polls needed to be open, defined the duties of election judges, and provided penalties for fraud. Both bills were assigned to the House Elections Committee. On April 17 the committee recommended that they do not pass and the full House then tabled the bills. By the time of the committee's action; however, Senate Bill 69 had been passed by the Senate and sent over to the House. Senate Bill 69 also regulated primaries and since it contained much of the same language as both of Thomas's bills, it may have been why the two

Thomas bills were not recommended. Thomas also introduced House Bill 599, which attempted to move the election of the Criminal Court Clerk of Cook County from November of odd-numbered years to the November of off-year elections. This bill was assigned to the Judiciary Committee where Thomas served as a member. The committee gave the bill a favorable recommendation and it was moved to second reading, but Thomas took no action on it after that. The legislature, however, would pass a similar bill into law.[41]

During this session Thomas also became involved in a small fight dealing with House patronage. The uncertain partisan mixture of the chamber had led to a bloated House staff of patronage workers from both sides of the aisle. Disgusted with the situation and a possible investigation, on April 1 Speaker Haines fired all of the House staff. Thomas responded the same day by introducing a resolution calling for the reinstatement of all the House pages, policemen, clerks, and janitors that had been dismissed by Speaker Haines. The resolution failed. On April 24, he again introduced a resolution to rehire these workers, and this time it failed due to lack of a quorum. It was a minor issue, but Thomas may have been motivated by the fact that one of those fired was Edward H. Wright, an African American who later became a political leader and ally of Thomas in Chicago.[42]

For the first time in his legislative career, Thomas spent most his term dealing with issues that directly affected the African American community. The split of the state African American community that emerged at the 1883 Illinois Colored Convention and in the 1884 election followed Thomas into the legislature. It played a role in his efforts to get patronage for African Americans from Governor Oglesby and affected his efforts on an issue that the entire community should have been united behind: the passage of a state civil rights law.

In the 1884 election, Illinois voters returned former governor and U.S. senator Richard J. Oglesby to the governor's mansion by only 15,000 votes. A Civil War veteran and close friend of Abraham Lincoln, Oglesby had first served as governor from 1865 to 1869. During that term, he signed legislation repealing the state's discriminatory black laws, and it was his support that made Illinois the first state to ratify the Thirteenth Amendment outlawing slavery.[43]

Any new governor in Illinois receives patronage requests upon taking office, and Oglesby was no exception. Several African American leaders applied for patronage positions. Edward H. Wright applied to be the governor's messenger. H. J. Mitchell applied to be a grain inspector. Both J. H. Magee and R. C. Waring sought a position as either a penitentiary commissioner or a canal commissioner, with Magee lobbying for a position as early as the September before the election. John J. Bird sought "any honorable position" that had a compensation that would justify his support of the Republican Party. Ferdinand Barnett sought to be a canal commissioner.[44]

It was in regard to this latter appointment that Thomas deepened the split in the community when he supported his ally Isaac Rivers over Barnett. Rivers was a loyal Republican Party worker but a street tough. In 1882, he was involved in a polling place fight that resulted in a police officer being shot and killed, and in 1884 he himself was shot and seriously wounded. In 1883 he was fined $10 for assaulting John G. Jones. In 1886, he got into an ugly saloon fight with Second Ward Alderman Jim Appleton and bit off part of the alderman's thumb and lip.[45] Barnett was the founding editor and publisher of Chicago's first African American newspaper and a leading attorney in the community. However, Rivers had worked for Thomas during the 1882 and 1884 election campaigns, while Barnett had been a member of the opposition at the 1883 convention. Thomas sent to Oglesby a petition endorsing Rivers for a canal commissionership. W. C. Phillips, Abner Taylor, Henry Hertz, and Senator William Harper of the Fifth Senate District also signed the petition, undoubtedly recognizing the first rule of patronage, which was to support loyal party workers like Rivers.[46]

Still, for Thomas to endorse Rivers over someone with the stature of Barnett was a political mistake. It alienated a potential ally in Barnett, unnecessarily antagonized those who were already predisposed to oppose him, and harmed the community as a whole, which, still in its early days of political participation, needed to demonstrate that African Americans could hold positions of responsibility. Worse, it appears that Thomas at one time supported Barnett, only to change his mind later; at least, Barnett listed Thomas as a reference for the position in a December 3, 1884, letter to Governor-elect Oglesby. Even if Thomas did not want to support Barnett, he could have supported someone other than Rivers. Phillips, a longtime ally of Thomas, had been suggested by some for a canal commissionership, and Thomas could have supported him.[47]

Instead, Thomas's action in support of Rivers strongly incited his opposition. William Baker wrote to Oglesby that Rivers was, "a drunken sot, always full of whiskey and women, of no education and one of the roughest and most abusive men he [Thomas] could have picked out of the whole city."[48] While copies of Barnett's *Chicago Conservator* newspaper no longer exist, the extent of the anger against Thomas can be seen in the articles written by the new Chicago correspondent of the *Cleveland Gazette*. That correspondent, who took over for I. C. Harris at the beginning of 1885, was strongly in the John G. Jones camp, persuaded in part, no doubt, by the fact that Jones advertised in the newspaper.[49] According to the correspondent, leading African Americans met in early February to discuss patronage. Thomas attended the meeting, which was chaired by Jones and held at John Howard's cigar shop. The correspondent wrote that Thomas defended his choice of Rivers over Barnett due to his friendship with Rivers. According to the article, the committee voted to censure Thomas for his actions. In later articles, the correspondent would criticize Thomas, writing that his "treacherous way" had led to a petition being passed around calling for his resignation and stating the Thomas's inability to get any patronage appointment for an African American had "completely disgusted" the community.[50]

The patronage issue would frustrate Thomas for the entire session. In February, the *Inter-Ocean* reported that Thomas brought a delegation of African Americans down from Chicago and took them to a Republican House caucus to press their claim for a patronage position. According to the paper, Thomas convinced the caucus to support the appointment of an African American to a patronage job. The *Tribune* reported, however, that the caucus agreed to support "the person agreed on by the colored people. Although Thomas said he could support any one of four or five people, the reality was the community was split. Thomas was on record as favoring Rivers. The committee that had met in Chicago sent a petition to the Cook County House and Senate members advocating for Barnett's appointment. The petition was signed by John G. Jones, John Howard, Robert Waring, I. C. Harris, George Beard and George Ecton. Thomas also supported Wright in his bid for the governor's messenger position and Waring's request for a position as well.[51]

By May Oglesby had not appointed an African American to any job, and Thomas was placed in an extremely awkward spot. In a letter to Oglesby, Thomas wrote of the difficult position he was in with regard to Cook County's African Americans. "I have begged and insisted that the colored people of Cook County have an appointive office from you and felt sure that we would get something," he wrote. "They have claimed that I did not do my duty toward getting a place for one from there, for the reason they say they know you would give me on their behalf the privilege of naming a man."[52]

If the issue proved frustrating to Thomas, it proved embarrassing to the proud patrician Barnett. In a letter to a supporter that was forwarded to Oglesby, Barnett outlined his position. He said he was the first African American to apply for a canal commissionership and he had the support of almost all of the African American men of political standing in Chicago. He noted that at one time Thomas had supported him. He wrote, "It is decidedly humiliating for me to contest for the place with a man who can't write the title of the place he is recommended to fill and whose record for peace and sobriety would be severely punctured by the Police Court Record."[53]

Oglesby never appointed a Chicago African American to a patronage job. He did appoint J. H. Magee of downstate Metropolis as a Third Inspector in the Sample Room for the Chief Inspector of Grain for the City of Chicago, a job that paid $110 a month.[54] In all, Oglesby proved to be a great disappointment to African American job-seekers. For Thomas, this failure severely hurt his standing within the African American community, although perhaps not so much as his unnecessary backing of Rivers over Barnett for the canal commissionership. Had Thomas supported Barnett, it is likely that Barnett would have received an appointment, as it would have avoided the type of split in the community that it could not afford.

The appointment of an African American to a responsible governmental office was an important symbol to the African American community. But while Thomas wrestled with the symbolic issue of patronage in Springfield, he also was working on a matter of much more substance for the African American community, a state civil rights bill.

The need for a state civil rights law stemmed directly from the 1883 U.S. Supreme Court decision voiding the 1875 federal Civil Rights Act. Utilizing the Fourteenth Amendment to the Constitution, the Civil Rights Act sought to ensure that no distinction be made between races in the enjoyment and use of public accommodations or amusements. The court voided the law because of its interpretation that the Fourteenth Amendment applied only to actions made by states and their political subdivisions, whereas the civil rights act was directed against individuals.[55] The implication behind the court's reasoning was that the states could individually pass their own civil rights law. The court handed down the decision during the 1883 Illinois Colored Convention that Thomas chaired. Thomas, like the other attendees at the convention, was outraged. The 1885 session represented the first chance to take legislative action on the issue at the state level.

Drafting a bill was not difficult, as it was modeled after the federal law and after a similar bill from Ohio, which that state's legislature had passed in 1884.[56] Yet, from the beginning, arguments ensued between the leaders of the two factions of the 1883 convention. Much of the discussion had to do with who wrote the bill. Less than three weeks after Thomas's reelection, the Chicago correspondent to the *Cleveland Gazette*, probably I. C. Harris, reported that Thomas was already working on writing the new law.[57] Between November and February, however, the *Gazette* changed its Chicago correspondent, replacing the neutral Harris with an unabashed ally of John G. Jones. In the February 7 issue, the new correspondent wrote that Jones had drafted a civil rights bill and given it to a committee to give to Thomas to introduce. Even earlier than that, on January 6, the *Tribune* reported that a meeting of African American masons in Chicago had passed resolutions encouraging the state legislature to approve a civil rights bill. The paper reported that the masons had been told that a committee of African Americans had drafted such legislation and given it to Thomas to introduce. John G. Jones co-chaired the meeting and probably led the discussion on the proposed legislation. In later years, B. G. Johnson of Chicago would claim he had drafted the bill, working with Jones. He said it was written after Jones had faced discrimination in securing a hotel room in downstate Illinois. Similarly, the obituary of Crittie Thomas, John Thomas's third wife, would state that she helped him draft the bill, even though it was drafted two years before they were married.[58] Considering the commotion following the Supreme Court's action during the middle of the Illinois Colored Convention, considering four states had already passed civil rights laws in 1884 and another seven would in 1885, and considering the enmity between Thomas and Jones and his allies, Jones's claim of authorship is difficult to accept.[59]

The legislation introduced by Thomas stated that all persons within Illinois were entitled to full and equal enjoyment of public accommodations or places of amusement. A person who denied another person his right to public accommodation could be fined between $25 and $500, with the money going to the aggrieved victim. In addition, the violator would be convicted of a misdemeanor and face an additional fine of up to $500 and a year in prison.[60]

Thomas introduced the legislation, House Bill 45, on February 3, the first full day for bill introductions since the House organized January 29. He worked the bill as a veteran legislator. On February 20, he introduced a petition with some 3,000 signatures in support of the bill. After Thomas introduced the petition, one Democratic legislator moved to have it referred to the Committee on Fish and Game, a motion and an insult that was ignored.[61] Instead the bill was sent to the Judiciary Committee where Thomas served and could control it. On March 3, the committee voted to favorably recommend the bill for passage. On March 12, Thomas overcame Democratic objections to move the bill to second reading.[62] On March 25, the bill moved to third and final reading "without discussion," something the *Inter-Ocean* cautioned would not happen when the final vote was taken.[63] On April 2, the House voted 83 to 19 to pass the bill to the Senate. Every Republican in the House voted for the bill. While several Democrats also voted for the bill, all nineteen "no" votes were cast by members of that party, and several Democrats did not vote rather than appear to be against it. None of the Democrats voting against the bill were from Chicago or Cook County. Most of those voting against it were from the more conservative southern half of the state. As historian Lawrence Grossman has noted about civil rights legislation being passed at the same time in other states, "urbanization and a heavy Negro population in a district would dispose a Democratic representative to favor Negro rights, and the more so the further north the district was."[64]

Thomas made a short, informative speech in calling for the bill's passage, explaining what the bill did and why it was needed. The *Inter-Ocean* wrote that his views were "temperate and well-expressed, and he was listened to with great attention." Thomas was the only Republican to speak on the bill. Democrats Frederick Baird and James Dill spoke in favor of the bill, while David Linegar, Caleb Johnson, J. Henry Shaw, and Alfred Cherry spoke against it. Linegar, Johnson, and Shaw expressed concern that the bill could be used by individuals to make up cases for prosecution in hopes of receiving financial gain. Cherry said he opposed the bill because it violated the great principle of survival of the fittest. Speaker Haines spoke in favor of it, however, saying that everyone talked about principles but no one enforced them and this bill was an attempt to enforce principles.[65]

With the bill's passage in the House, it moved over the Senate, which approved the bill on June 4 by a vote of 37 to 6. Once again, Democrats cast all of the "no" votes. Thomas's senator, John Clough, helped shepherd the bill through the Senate. There was an attempt by an opponent of the bill to send it to the Horticulture Committee, presumably where it would have been killed, but Clough easily defeated that motion. Governor Oglesby signed the bill into law on June 10.[66]

On Thursday, June 18, African Americans in Springfield held a meeting to celebrate the passage of the bill into law. Because the legislature was still in session, Thomas attended the Springfield rally, which was held in the Senate chambers. Thomas and a number of other legislators, including Speaker Haines and some of the Democratic supporters of the bill, addressed the crowd. Springfield's James Young introduced a resolution at the meeting thanking the members of the legislature who supported the bill. The level of support that Thomas had in the downstate African American community can be seen in the concluding section of the resolution, which stated that "we particularly thank our own member, the Hon. John W. E. Thomas, for his especial aid and care in introducing and fostering said bill."[67]

If Thomas was popular with Springfield African Americans, he was somewhat less so in Chicago. On the same night of the Springfield meeting, several hundred African Americans in Chicago conducted a meeting at Olivet Baptist Church. This rally reflected the divide in the community. John G. Jones chaired the meeting, while Edward H. Morris, Ferdinand Barnett, and Robert Waring served on the committee on resolutions. During the first speaker's remarks, John Howard complained from the audience about who should receive credit for the bill. He said, "I want every man, woman and child to say what he's got to say and if anybody says John G. Jones is the author of this bill, which I deny this assertion, I say it was J. B. [*sic*] Thomas, and I want his bill read." Eventually, Howard was quieted and the audience heard from several speakers. Some like Lloyd Wheeler and William Baker, seemed to belittle the bill. Wheeler cautioned that equality before the law with whites did not mean that African Americans still didn't have duties and obligations that they needed to perform to be considered respectable. Baker said his enthusiasm for the bill was tempered by the fact that it could be overturned in the courts, which is what had happened to the federal civil rights bill. Other speakers, including Thomas's friend Rev. Richard DeBaptiste, were much more enthusiastic about the bill.

In the end, the committee on resolutions came back with a diplomatically worded resolution that sought to appease all parties. The resolution stated, "We hereby extend our heartfelt thanks to the Hon. John W. E. Thomas, author of the said bill; the Hon. John H. Clough, his staunch supporter; the worthy chairman of their Citizens' committee, John G. Jones, Esq.; and all others who have in anyway contributed toward the passage of said bill."[68]

The passage of the Civil Rights bill was one of the major accomplishments of the 34th General Assembly. For all its difficulties in organizing, the legislature had several other accomplishments as well. In all 635 bills were introduced in the 153-member House, an average of four bills per member. Another 472 bills were introduced in the 51-member Senate.[69]

The legislature passed several election reform bills. Senate Bill 83 enacted many of the reforms proposed by the Union League, although it was limited to cities with a population of more than 1,000 and only after the residents of that city had voted to enact the law to govern their elections. The legislation regulated the appointment of election commissioners, election judges, and clerks, provided for voter registration, and created clear, strict provisions on how elections were to be run and how votes were to be counted. It provided restrictions on what type of facility could be used as a polling place (no saloon, dramshop, billiard hall, or bowling alley) and required election judges to meet certain qualifications, including being able to speak English. Senate Bill 139 limited the size of precincts to no more than 400 voters. The legislature also enacted Senate Bills 69 and 426, which regulated how primaries operated and provided punishments for committing election fraud during a primary election. Many of the provisions of these bills were similar to the general election reform bill. Thomas voted for the passage of all four bills. All the bills passed by overwhelming margins, with the exception of SB 83, the major election reform bill, which passed 78–56.[70]

Other bills passed by the legislature included Senate Bill 417, which created a Soldiers and Sailors Veterans' Home in Illinois. That home, eventually built in downstate Quincy, continues to operate to this day. A House Joint

Resolution set up a revenue commission to review the state's inadequate revenue laws. While the *Chicago Inter-Ocean* criticized the legislature for failing to actually reform the state's revenue codes, it wrote, "the Legislature did very well to provide for even a revenue reform commission to investigate the whole matter and report a bill to the General Assembly." The legislature also passed House Bill 426, which provided that monetary fines be set for persons convicted of cruelty to animals or children and that the money be given to support humane societies. It also passed a Senate Joint Resolution which placed on the ballot a proposed constitutional amendment to prohibit the use of state prisoners for hired labor. Illinois voters approved that amendment in the November 1886 election. The session also voted to change the name of the Illinois Industrial University in Urbana to the University of Illinois and appropriated $531,712 for the completion of the state capitol. The legislature was allowed to take the latter action only because the Thirty-third General Assembly, which Thomas had been a member of, had voted to place the issue of spending money to complete the building of the capitol on the ballot. Voters had approved it at the 1884 election. Thomas voted for all the above listed bills, with the exception of the convict labor bill, which was one of a few votes he missed. All of these bills passed by comfortable margins.[71]

Despite its accomplishments, the legislature received less than stellar reviews for its work. The Republican *Evening Journal* wrote, "the legislature deserves decisive credit for three of its acts: the re-election of Senator Logan, the passage of the elections act; the final adjournment." The Democratic *Times* said the while it wasn't the worst gathering that Illinois has ever seen, "seldom has an Illinois legislature done less legislating." The *Inter-Ocean* found more to praise than most of its contemporary papers, specifically citing the passage of the election bills and the legislation creating the Soldiers and Sailors Home.[72]

In its postsession analysis, the *Inter-Ocean* also critiqued the thirty state representatives who came from Cook County. Of Thomas it wrote, "Mr. Thomas, the only colored member . . . sustained his former reputation as a modest, honest, faithful, and intelligent lawmaker. . . . No constituent need be ashamed of such representation." The paper added, "The only bill of note which he introduced was the civil-rights bill, which, we are happily able to add, is now a law."[73]

For his efforts, Thomas received $855 in per diem, $37.20 for travel reimbursement, and $50 to pay for postage and newspapers, for a total of 942.20 in pay.[74] It was a historic, volatile, brutal session. Yet, despite Thomas's hard work, faithfulness to the Republican Party, and success in passing the Civil Rights Law, it was to be his last session in the General Assembly.

The 1885 Illinois Colored Convention

The passage of the Civil Rights bill should have made Thomas the undisputed political leader of a unified African American community in Chicago, but instead political infighting continued throughout 1885. It is worth noting that the Chicago ratification meeting was held before the end of the legislative session when Thomas could not attend. The splits in the community were evident in the resolution that gave credit to both Thomas and Jones.

Perhaps more obvious were the reports coming from the unnamed Chicago correspondent of the weekly *Cleveland Gazette*. In articles on the House passage of the bill, the signing of the bill by Governor Oglesby, and the ratification meeting, he did not even mention Thomas.[75] While fights among newspapers were common in the late nineteenth century, fights among newspaper correspondents from the same paper were less so. The *Gazette* correspondent's articles on Thomas over the patronage issue were so scathing and one-sided that the paper's Springfield correspondent, S. B. Turner, felt obliged to defend Thomas, and a fight between the two ensued in the pages of the paper.

Three weeks after the Chicago correspondent wrote that people were pressing Thomas to resign as a representative, Turner wrote that Thomas would probably be elected to the state senate. In August, the Chicago correspondent wrote that "The people demand an active and honest colored man to represent them in the legislature. Hon. J. W. E. Thomas will never again fill a position as representative of the colored people of this city." That article drew a severe rebuke from the Springfield correspondent two weeks later, who wrote, "This attack is nothing more or less than the outgrowth of prejudice and a scheme to overthrow his [Thomas's] political standing among the people of Chicago." After advising the African American citizens of Chicago to exercise a little more harmony, the Springfield correspondent concluded by writing "The citizens of Springfield desire to see Mr. Thomas returned to the legislature, where he has served his constituents so satisfactorily." Two weeks later, the Chicago correspondent roared back, charging Thomas with being a hypocrite and unfit to serve the honest and intelligent citizens of Chicago. He added, "And when we want any information concerning the people in this city, we shall solicit it from a more reliable source than Springfield."[76] With that, the fight disappeared from the pages of the newspaper, although it would reappear in a familiar form that fall, with the 1885 Illinois Colored Convention.

Despite the overwhelming support of the Republican Party in 1884 by Chicago's African American voters, in 1885 Wheeler, as chairman of the executive committee, called another state convention. He cited the election of the first Democratic president in more than a quarter of a century as the reason to meet. In many respects, this convention played out exactly like the 1883 convention. Among the issues of concern to the African American community were segregated education facilities in southern Illinois and discrimination in employment opportunities and labor unions.

Again, the state's Republican newspapers criticized the convention as either an attempt by ungrateful African American leaders to steer the African American community away from the Republican Party or an attempt to receive patronage jobs by disaffected African American office-seekers. The *Chicago Evening Journal* reported, "Certain tricky politicians of the Democratic party of Illinois have induced a few sore-headed colored men to meet in convention at Springfield to go through the motions of deserting the Republican party." In a preview of the convention, the *Chicago Times* simply titled its story "The Colored Brother Wants an Office."[77]

The times may have changed politically, but the split among Illinois African American leaders had not. Once again, two factions emerged at the convention. One faction wholeheartedly supported the Republican Party. The other faction, often referred to as the mugwumps, sought political independence. Once again, the faction favoring independence from the Republican Party came in to the convention in control. That faction featured Wheeler and Jones of Chicago, Smith of Bloomington, and Scott of Cairo. The ornery Jones would actually divide his time between the convention and a meeting of the Grand Lodge of Colored Masons, where he got into a major disagreement with members of the Grand Lodge of Iowa. Thomas once again began as a behind-the-scenes leader of the other faction and once again was called to the front as chairman of the convention. For the 1885 convention, he was able to appear less heavy-handed in his actions than in 1883. Still, he successfully wrested control away from the mugwump faction and kept the convention from turning into an anti-Republican Party event.[78]

Approximately 150 delegates from the state assembled at noon on October 16 in the Senate chambers of the state capitol in Springfield. Perhaps learning from the 1883 experience, when delegates were elected by congressional district and Wheeler and Jones both lost their elections, Wheeler's notice for the 1885 convention merely called on African Americans in the various counties to conduct mass meetings on September 28 and select as many delegates as they wished to attend the convention. Cook County selected fifty delegates.[79]

As chairman of the executive committee, Wheeler called the convention to order and gave the opening speech. He explained why he had felt the need to call a convention and discussed issues of importance to the African

American community. He decried segregated schools in southern Illinois and encouraged African American patronage of businesses that employed African Americans. He also opposed protectionism. Wheeler then complained about former Republican governor Shelby Cullom disbanding the 16th Battalion Infantry, an African American unit of the Illinois militia in which Wheeler had served. Wheeler used Cullom's action to launch a blistering partisan attack on the Republican Party and against blind loyalty by African Americans to the party. "We have tried sentiment for fifteen years," he said, referring to those who thanked the Republican Party for freeing the slaves, "and though our loyalty to party has been unquestioned we have been rewarded by being made the victims of unreasonable prejudice in the house of our supposed friends." He would add, "The negro, like a good hunting dog, is needed only when game offices are to be captured. The rest of the time he must content himself with being chained to the kennel of oblivion and fed with the scraps and waste from the master's official table."

Following Wheeler's speech, the convention chose George Hill, an attorney from Bloomington, as temporary Speaker, and South Town clerk H. J. Mitchell and Chicago attorney F. L. McGhee as temporary secretaries. Delegates formed a credentials committee, with Wheeler as the chairman, and then took a recess until 4:00 P.M. Upon the return of the delegates, the convention adopted the credentials committee report without discussion. Then came the first argument of the day. Some delegates favored creating a committee to make a recommendation on the permanent organization of the convention, while some delegates favored just having delegates nominate and elect the permanent officers from the floor. After lengthy debate, the convention decided to create a committee consisting of one representative from every county. The convention then adjourned for more than an hour to allow the committee to meet.

Upon its return, the committee on permanent organization issued a majority and minority reports. As in 1883, the majority report called for the selection of Wheeler as permanent chairman. The minority report favored Dr. James H. Magee for the post. Governor Oglesby had recently appointed Magee, of downstate Metropolis, as a grain inspector in the City of Chicago. Magee, who in 1882 had become the first African American to serve on the Republican State Central Committee, took the floor and delivered a long partisan speech defending the Republican Party. He stated, "The negro has no other father, no other home, than the Republican party. That party has given him all of the privileges he now enjoys. . . . Let me ask every black man in the house, how in the devil can you be anything else than Republican?" Magee criticized those who favored abandoning the Republican Party and took

special aim at Scott. He also withdrew his name from the chairman's nomination fight in favor of Hill. Both Scott and Smith then strongly criticized
Magee. Scott noted that Magee held a Republican patronage position and
said this meant that he had been paid to express his views. Smith was even
more direct, stating that Magee belonged to the class of African Americans
who could be kicked and cuffed and would still vote Republican.[80]

What happened next is difficult to ascertain from newspaper accounts. The
Democratic *Times* charged Hill with making parliamentary decisions and er-
rors in judgment that prevented the majority report from receiving a fair vote.
It said that, as a result, Wheeler took himself out of the race for chairman and
placed Thomas's name in nomination, which was approved by the convention.
However, the *Springfield State Journal* stated that Smith nominated Thomas
after accusing Hill of seeking his own nomination as permanent chairman.
Smith and Thomas were political enemies, so Smith's nomination of Thomas,
if it happened, had to have been a parliamentary diversion on Smith's part;
or perhaps Smith and Hill, both from Bloomington, were political rivals, and
Smith would not abide Hill being selected as chairman. According to the
State Journal, Thomas had gone to the Speaker's chair, only to be rebuffed by
Hill. However, upon Thomas's return to his seat, the *State Journal* stated, Hill
placed Thomas's name in nomination. At this point, John G. Jones nominated
Richard M. Hancock of Chicago for chairman, and Smith nominated Reverend E. C. Joiner of Springfield. In any event, after a raucous debate similar to
1883, delegates selected Thomas as their compromise choice for chairman.
The *Springfield State Journal* editorialized that the selection of Thomas, "the
author of the Illinois Civil Rights bill," was a credit to the convention. [81]

Hill introduced Thomas to the convention as "the framer of the Civil
Rights bill passed by the Illinois Legislature, one of the brightest and foremost colored lawyers of the State." As in 1883, Thomas delivered a concil-
iatory speech. After stating that he had not wanted to be a candidate and
was surprised by his selection as chairman, he pledged to run a nonpartisan
convention. "We are here not as partisans but for the purpose of advancing
our interests and promoting and securing our rights as a people. I shall know
no Democratic Party nor Republican Party, but will only recognize colored
citizens in convention assembled." He added, "We are here as citizens, not as
politicians." The convention then selected Thomas T. Brown of Springfield and
Chicagoans F. L. McGee and H. J. Mitchell as secretaries of the convention.

Wheeler and Smith could not have been pleased with the selection of
Thomas as chairman. Once again, Thomas had foiled their efforts to lead the
African American community away from the Republican Party. The *State
Journal* noted that Thomas was "a thorough and conscientious Republican."

The *Inter-Ocean* wrote, "the Republican delegates proved too numerous when the convention got down to business, and the so-called Mugwump got left. The resolutions that will be adopted hereafter in the convention will not be quite as belligerent in tone as those which have been prepared by Wheeler, Smith, and others." [82]

Still, there was a convention to be run. Thomas created committees on Education, Address, Trades and Labor, Rules, and Resolutions. Apparently learning from the 1883 convention, when he allowed the Jones-Wheeler faction to control all the important committees, this time Thomas limited their power. He gave the mugwumps a large say on the Education committee, where Smith and Scott served, and on the Trades and Labor committee, where Wheeler and Jones served. However, none of the mugwump leaders served on the rules committee or the resolutions committee, which were the two committees that controlled the convention. As a result, the committee on rules issued a report calling for all resolutions to be approved first by the committee on resolutions before going to the floor for a vote. Thomas ally I. C. Harris chaired the committee on resolutions. The convention adopted this report, essentially allowing the Thomas faction to use the resolutions committee to stifle any resolution it did not favor. [83]

Thomas could allow the mugwumps to control the committees on Education and Trades and Labor because he agreed with their positions on these issues. The Education Committee report called for the abolishment of the separate school system in southern Illinois and encouraged African Americans to send their children to school. The Trades and Labor committee's report called for the African American patronage of businesses that employed African Americans and for the creation of African American county labor committees to work with other labor organizations for the hiring of blacks. The convention adopted these reports unanimously.

True to his word, Thomas kept partisanship out of the proceedings. When delegate J. F. Dyson of Bloomington offered a resolution calling for African Americans to continue their allegiance to the Republican Party, Thomas ruled it out of order. However, he also ruled out of order a resolution offered by Brown that condemned Republican governor Oglesby and Republican secretary of state Dement for their failure to appoint African Americans to political office and called for their defeat in the next election. When Magee proposed inviting Oglesby and Dement to address the convention, Thomas took no stand and allowed Wheeler to amend Magee's proposal so that the convention merely invited Oglesby and Dement, as well as other officeholders, to attend the convention but not to speak. Neither officeholder took the convention up on its offer.

One issue that arose before the convention concerned Thomas's recently passed civil rights legislation. Just before the convention met, an African American barber in Mattoon, Austin Perry, refused to serve an African American customer because he thought it would hurt his business. Jones offered a resolution condemning Perry. Interestingly, Smith opposed the resolution, stating that a man had the right to exclude from his place of business persons of any race whose presence could hurt that business. Wheeler proposed having the executive committee, when appointed, arrange for and fund a test case of the civil rights act. Wheeler's resolution was approved, as was another resolution which called for each county to create a committee to collect money to fund such a test case. Smith suggested employing noted Illinois agnostic Robert Ingersoll to look for loopholes in the new civil rights law. According to the *Times*, Smith said the convention should ask Ingersoll "to step aside for a time from discovering the mistakes of Moses and find the mistakes in the Illinois Civil Rights law, if there are any."[84]

The convention also discussed other issues of concern to the African American community. Richard Blue from Bloomington said that the orphans of African American soldiers were not being admitted to the Soldiers' Orphan Home in Bloomington. It appears, however, that the convention did not take action on his information. Delegates passed a resolution denouncing the breakup of the 16th Battalion. They also appointed a committee to raise funds for the construction of a monument in Alton to honor Elijah Lovejoy, an early Illinois abolitionist. Scott introduced a resolution commending the North, Central, and South American Exposition for "placing exhibits by colored persons on the same footing with those of white persons." The convention passed that resolution. Finally, the convention passed a resolution introduced by S. B. Turner of Springfield commending Thomas for the passage of the civil rights bill. The resolution read, "The thanks of this convention are cordially extended to Hon. John W. E. Thomas for his manly efforts in the passage of the civil rights bill, which has secured for the colored people of Illinois equal rights before the law." The resolution also thanked those senators and representatives who helped Thomas pass the bill.

By a standing vote, the delegates approved a resolution honoring the memory of Gen. Ulysses S. Grant, who had passed away the previous July. They also unanimously approved a resolution sponsored by Smith that offered support to Ireland in its efforts to free itself from the English. Brown offered a resolution calling for a Soldiers and Sailors Home to be located in Springfield, but that resolution narrowly lost.

At the evening session of the second and last day of the convention, delegates approved a report creating a state executive committee that consisted of two delegates from each senatorial district. The report represented a complete defeat of the Wheeler, Smith, and Jones forces. Hill and Blue were named as the two committee members from the Twenty-eighth District, which was Smith's home. Thomas and his allies I. C. Harris and F. L. McGhee also were selected to serve on the committee. Other noted Chicagoans selected included William Baker, Robert M. Mitchell, H. J. Mitchell, R. C. Waring, John Howard, and J. C. Buckner. Thomas had had disagreements with many of these individuals, and some of them, notably Baker and Robert M. Mitchell, had been in the mugwump faction in 1883, but most of them were now solid Republicans. John G. Jones was not named to the committee, and he failed in his efforts to have Robert M. Mitchell removed from it. Wheeler was named but, noting the Republican tilt of the committee, gave a lengthy speech declining to be a member and proclaiming his political independence. He later stated, "The Republicans captured the organization of the convention, and after that the liberal men and measures had no show."

Wheeler was not the only one to note the victory of Thomas and the Republican supporters. The Republican *Inter-Ocean* noted, "Although a bitter fight was made by L. G. Wheeler and the Rev. Mr. Smith for the Independents, a solid Republican State Central Committee was chosen by the colored men of Illinois." The Democratic *Herald* noted that, "the independents were completely snowed under, the State Central Committee, as adopted, consisting of two from each Senatorial District, ignoring that faction completely." The Republican *Tribune* said the committee consisted entirely of Republicans, while the Democratic *Times* said it was majority Republican. The *Times* added, "Maj. Wheeler of Chicago and Smith of Bloomington were especially bitter in their denunciation of the manner in which the republican members of the convention had managed to capture it and manipulate everything in the interests of the republican party instead of honest philanthropy and an untrammeled expression of free thought."

In a closing speech, Smith said that in the future, the independents would hold their own conventions and would link their future to the younger generation. Wheeler, in his closing remarks, said that the liberal-minded and independent African American men of the state would form an organization of their own. Wheeler and Smith's attitude may explain why another state convention was not called until 1889.[85]

By 1889, and the fourth convention of the decade, relations between the Republican Party and African American leaders had been repaired. Patronage had increased during the course of the decade. Thomas's civil rights act had soothed a lot of passions. Plus, there was again a Republican in the White House. So, when in 1889 Jones called for another convention, it turned into a pro-Republican event. Delegates invited Republican governor Joseph Fifer and Republican senator Shelby Cullom to address the convention and soundly voted down a proposal to invite 1888 Democratic gubernatorial candidate John Palmer to speak. Delegates were so pro-Republican that a headline in the Democratic *Springfield State Register* read, "The State Conference Converted into a Republican Hurrah, Pure and Simple." The convention again called for more educational and occupational opportunities for African Americans. Delegates also approved a resolution condemning outrages committed against African Americans in the South and a resolution creating a Colored Men's State League. Thomas did not attend the 1889 convention and neither did Wheeler, Smith, or Scott. Among the forty-five delegates were John G. Jones, Baker, Magee, Waring, Joseph Moore, Robert M. Mitchell, J. Q. Grant, S. B. Turner, Richard Blue, John J. Bird, Edward H. Wright, and Edward H. Morris. The latter was elected chairman of the conference and would also be named president of the Colored Men's State League.[86]

Despite not attending the 1889 convention, Thomas's role at the two conventions he did attend was crucial. It was also successful. Although the 1883 convention may have been more anti-Republican than Thomas would have liked, the Supreme Court decision on the civil rights bill made that inevitable. He learned from the 1883 convention and as chair in 1885 kept a strong interest in the makeup of the committees. While the 1883 convention saw resolutions approved that were critical of the Republican Party, the 1885 convention did not. By his actions, Thomas laid the groundwork for the harmonious 1889 convention, even if he didn't attend. All four conventions highlighted the grievances felt by African Americans in Illinois and, indeed, throughout the North. All of the delegates attending these conventions, including Thomas, agreed about the many problems the community faced when it came to discrimination, unfair hiring practices, and unequal educational opportunities. The disagreements stemmed from how best to solve the problems. Politically, Thomas and his faction felt the best way to promote the welfare of his people was within the Republican Party, and at the two conventions he attended he worked hard and successfully to ensure that no rupture occurred. During the most turbulent decade of relations between African American leaders and the Republican Party, Thomas kept Illinois African Americans on record as being loyal to the party.[87] He was truly, as was written about him in the 1885 *Colored Men's Professional and Business Directory of Chicago*, "leader of the colored people in the state of Illinois."[88]

Undated photo of John W. E. Thomas.
Courtesy of the Abraham Lincoln Presidential Library and Museum (ALPLM)

The scene from one block north of the Thomas home following the Great Chicago Fire of 1871. Although the fire narrowly missed the Thomas home, three years

later another large fire in the city completely burned his house and neighborhood.
Courtesy of the Abraham Lincoln Presidential Library and Museum (ALPLM)

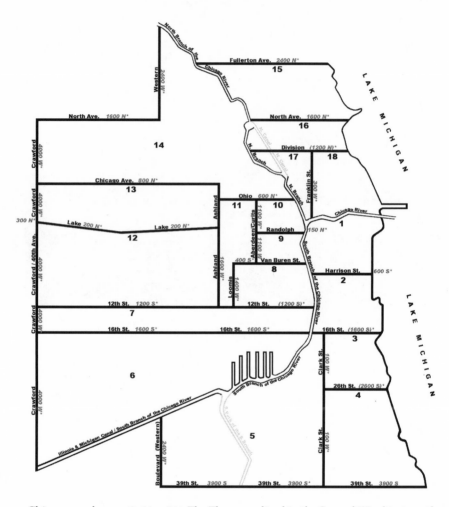

1880 CENSUS
WARD BOUNDARIES
CHICAGO, ILLINOIS

Chicago ward map, 1876 to 1887. The Thomases lived in the Second Ward just south of Harrison Street. In 1877, Thomas was elected state representative for the Second Legislative District, which included all of the Second, Third, and Fourth Wards, plus two townships (not pictured) just south of the city. Following legislative redistricting in 1882, he was elected state representative from the Third Legislative District, which included the entire First, Second, and Third Wards, plus the northern part of the Fourth Ward. Courtesy of the website alookatcook.com

4th Ward.

Hayes and Wheeler.

For Electors for President and Vice-President,

John I. Rinaker.	Peter Schuttler.
George Armour.	Bolivar G. Gill.
Louis Schaffner.	Allen C. Fuller.
Joseph M. Bailey.	John B. Hawley.
Franklin Corwin.	Jason W. Strevell.
Oscar F. Price.	Alexander McLean.
David E. Beaty.	
Michael Donahue.	Philip N. Minear.
George D. Chafee.	Hugh Crea.
Cyrus Happy.	James M. Truitt.
Joseph J. Castles.	George C. Ross.

For Governor,
SHELBY M. CULLOM.

For Lieutenant Governor,
ANDREW SHUMAN.

For Secretary of State,
GEORGE H. HARLOW.

For Auditor of Public Accounts,
THOMAS B. NEEDLES.

For State Treasurer,
EDWARD RUTZ.

For Attorney General,
JAMES K. EDSALL.

For Representative in Congress, First District,
WILLIAM ALDRICH.

For Member of the State Board of Equalization,
First District,
JAMES MORGAN.

For State Senator, Second District,
DANIEL N. BASH.

For Representatives Second Senatorial District,
SOLOMON P. HOPKINS, 1½ votes.

JOHN W. E. THOMAS, 1½ votes.

For States Attorney,
LUTHER LAFLIN MILLS.

For Clerk of the Circuit Court,
JACOB GROSS.

For Sheriff,
JOHN H. CLOUGH.

For Coroner,
EMIL DIETZSCH.

For Recorder of Deeds,
JAMES W. BROCKWAY.

For County Commissioners,
EUGENE S. PIKE.

GEORGE W. NEWCOMB.

PATRICK McGRATH.

PETER L. HAWKINSON.

An election ballot from 1876, issued by the Republican Party, showing Thomas and his Republican running mate for the state legislature, Solomon P. Hopkins. Under Illinois' unique voting system, Republican voters were encouraged to give 1½ votes to each candidate. Author's collection

HOUSE OF REPRESENTATIVES.

SPRINGFIELD, ILLINOIS.

On the _4_ day of January, A. D. 1877, before _Benj. R. Sheldon_
a Judge of the _Supreme_ Court of the State of Illinois,
appeared _J. W. E. Thomas_ Representative elect from
the _2_ District, to the _30_ General Assembly, and did
take and subscribe to the following Oath, to-wit:

I do solemnly swear that I will support the Constitution of the United States, and the Constitution of the State of Illinois, and will faithfully discharge the duties of Representative according to the best of my ability; and that I have not, knowingly or intentionally, paid or contributed anything, or made any promise in the nature of a bribe to directly or indirectly influence any vote at the election at which I was chosen to fill the said office, and have not accepted, nor will I accept or receive, directly or indirectly, any money or other valuable thing from any corporation, company or person, for any vote or influence I may give or withhold on any bill, resolution or appropriation, or for any other official act.

J. W. E. Thomas

Representative elect to the _30_ General Assembly,

from the _Second_ District.

Subscribed and sworn to before me by said _____
this _4th_ day of January, A. D. _1877_

Benj. R. Sheldon

Judge of _Supreme_ Court of the State of Illinois.

Copy of Thomas's oath of office from 1877. Thomas served three terms in the Illinois legislature. Courtesy of the Illinois State Archives

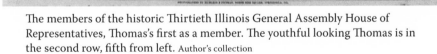

The members of the historic Thirtieth Illinois General Assembly House of Representatives, Thomas's first as a member. The youthful looking Thomas is in the second row, fifth from left. Author's collection

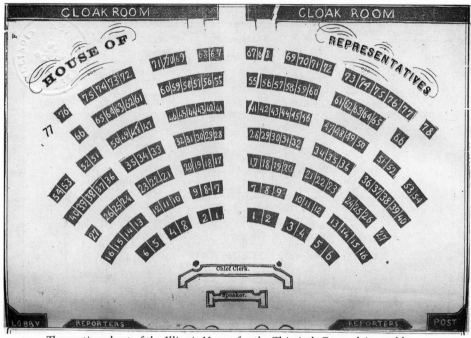

The seating chart of the Illinois House for the Thirtieth General Assembly.
Thomas sat in seat number 9 on the left side of the aisle. Courtesy of the Abraham
Lincoln Presidential Library and Museum (ALPLM)

REV. RICHARD DeBAPTISTE
A preacher of the Word in Chicago.

Reverend Richard
DeBaptiste, Thomas's
minister and friend.
Courtesy of the Abraham
Lincoln Presidential Library
and Museum (ALPLM)

Edward H. Morris, a
successful attorney,
activist, friend, and
sometimes business
partner of Thomas,
who became the third
African American
to serve in the
Illinois House of
Representatives. Courtesy
of the Abraham Lincoln
Presidential Library and
Museum (ALPLM)

George Ecton, a colleague if not a close ally of Thomas, whom he replaced in the General Assembly, where he served two terms. Courtesy of the Abraham Lincoln Presidential Library and Museum (ALPLM)

Edward H. Wright, who learned politics as an early ally of Thomas, became the leading African American politician in the city of Chicago in the 1890s, and extended his career to the 1920s. Photo from *Simms' Blue Book and National Negro Business and Professional Directory* (Chicago: J. N. Simms, 1923); ICHi-59955, courtesy of the Chicago History Museum

Lloyd G. Wheeler, the first African American attorney in Chicago in 1869 and the social leader of Chicago's African American community. A Democrat, he and Thomas opposed each other at the 1883 and 1885 Illinois Colored Conventions. Photograph by Stevens; ICHi-22386, cropped, courtesy of the Chicago History Museum

John G. "Indignation" Jones, an attorney and a leader in the movement to make the African American community more independent of the Republican Party. He and Thomas were fierce opponents in the 1880s, and there has been a dispute as to which of them actually wrote the 1885 Illinois Civil Rights Act. Photograph by Sommer; ICHi-22362, cropped, courtesy of the Chicago History Museum

Reverend Charles Spencer Smith, a gifted orator who lived in Bloomington during the 1880s. He and Thomas were strong opponents of each other at the 1883 and 1885 Illinois Colored Conventions, and Smith's efforts blocked Thomas from becoming a delegate-at-large to the 1884 Republican National Convention. Photo by C. M. Bells, Washington, D.C.; Charles S. Smith Papers, box 4, portraits folder, Bentley Historical Library, University of Michigan

Ferdinand Barnett, an aristocratic attorney and newspaper publisher who later in life married activist Ida B. Wells. Thomas did not support him for a patronage position in 1885, but the two appear to have reconciled later, as Thomas was invited to the Barnett-Wells wedding. Courtesy of Special Collections Research Center, University of Chicago Library

The Logan 103, showing the 103 state legislators who voted to reelect John A. Logan to the United State Senate in 1885. Thomas is in the fourth row from the top, the fifth person in from the right. Author's collection

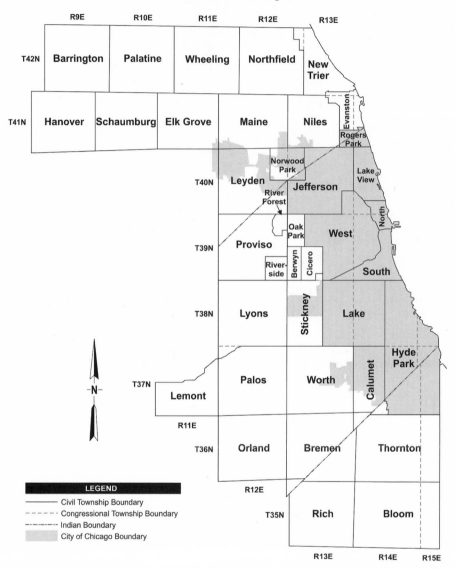

Cook County

Map of Cook County Townships, including North, West, and South Town, which were within the City of Chicago. Thomas was elected South Town Clerk in 1887. The map also shows the townships of Hyde Park and Lake, which were a part of Thomas's legislative district during his first term in the House of Representatives in 1877. Those townships have since been annexed into the City of Chicago.

Courtesy of the Illinois State Archives

Harrison Street Police station circa 1900. The majority of John W. E. Thomas's lawyer business occurred at the police court inside, with a majority of his customers coming from the petty criminals detained there. Photograph by Barnes-Crosby; ICHi-19067, courtesy of the Chicago History Museum

Election ballots from 1884, issued by the Republican Party, showing Thomas and his fellow Republican running mate for the state legislature, Abner Taylor. Under Illinois' unique voting system, Republican voters were encouraged to give 1½ votes to each candidate. ICHi-62452; courtesy of the Chicago History Museum

3d WARD

For President,
JAMES G. BLAINE,
OF MAINE.

For Vice-President,
JOHN A. LOGAN,
OF ILLINOIS.

For Electors of President and Vice-President.

ANDREW SHUMAN.	RUFUS W. MILES.
ISAAC LESEM.	JOHN A. HARVEY.
GEORGE BASS.	FRANCIS M. DAVIS.
JOHN C. TEGTMEYER.	J OTIS HUMPHREY.
JOHN M. SMYTH.	EDWARD D. BLINN.
JAMES A. SEXTON.	WILLIAM O. WILSON.
ALBERT J. HOPKINS.	RUFUS COPE.
CONRAD J. FRY.	JOHN H. DUNSCOMB.
WILLIAM H. SHEPARD.	CICERO J. LINDLY.
ROBERT A. CHILDS.	JASPER PARTRIDGE.
DAVID McWILLIAMS.	MATTHEW J. INSCORE

For Governor,
RICHARD J. OGLESBY.

For Lieutenant Governor,
JOHN C. SMITH.

For Secretary of State,
HENRY D. DEMENT.

For Auditor of Public Accounts,
CHARLES P. SWIGERT.

For State Treasurer,
JACOB GROSS.

For Attorney General,
GEORGE HUNT.

For Representative in Congress, First Congressional District,
RANSOM W. DUNHAM.

For Member of the State Board of Equalization, First Congressional District,
JAMES P. ROOT.

For Representatives, Third Senatorial District,
ABNER TAYLOR.   1½ Votes.

JOHN W. E. THOMAS.   1½ Votes.

For Clerk of the Supreme Court, Northern Grand Division,
ALFRED H. TAYLOR.

For Clerk of the Appellate Court, First District,
JOHN J. HEALY.

For State's Attorney,
LUTHER LAFLIN MILLS.

For Clerk of the Superior Court of Cook County,
PATRICK McGRATH.

For Clerk of the Circuit Court,
HENRY BEST.

For Recorder of Deeds,
WILEY S. SCRIBNER.

For Coroner,
HENRY L. HERTZ.

For County Surveyor,
JACOB T. FOSTER.

For Members of the Board of County Commissioners, First District,
FINLEY A. MacDONALD.

DANIEL J. WREN.

For the $581,712 Appropriation.

For proposed Amendment to Section Sixteen of Article Five of the Constitution.

For County Bonds.

For an appropriation by the City Council of One Hundred Thousand ($100,000) Dollars, from moneys derived from Saloon Licenses, for an

Home at 3308 S. Indiana Avenue where Thomas moved in 1893 and died in 1899.
This photo shows the house in 2001. Author's collection

[6]

"By No Means an Unimportant Position": Election to the Office of South Town Clerk in 1887

In August 1885, the correspondent for the *Cleveland Gazette* wrote that the "Honorable J. W. E. Thomas will never again fill a position as representative of the colored people of this city." The correspondent, a fierce Thomas opponent, wrote the threat on behalf of "the people," meaning the African American community. As a prediction, the statement came true. Thomas would lose the 1886 Republican nomination for state representative and he would never again serve in the Illinois General Assembly. However, the reason for his loss was due not only to opposition within the African American community but also because of old-fashioned ward politics. As historian Charles Branham wrote of this era, African American politicians often found themselves captives of the power fights and petty squabbles of white politicians. In 1886 Thomas found himself on the losing side of a power struggle between white politicians.[1]

The Election of 1886

Thomas entered the 1886 Republican renomination fight after having what was arguably his best year in public service. In the legislature, he sponsored and passed the state's civil rights bill, which was greatly lauded in the African American community. He was a member of the famous "Logan 103" that elected John A. Logan to the Senate. He had served on the Judiciary Committee. His attendance as a legislator was better than most of the other state representatives, and he did not go on a highly criticized midsession junket to New Orleans. He also chaired the 1885 Illinois State Colored Convention and managed to keep the convention a relatively peaceful one and loyal to the Republican Party.

However, intraparty loyalty, at least at the local level, was not very strong in this time period. The political system was made up less of cohesive parties and more of little fiefdoms within loosely affiliated political alliances. In Chicago, ward bosses dominated their fiefdoms and competed with other bosses within their party. However, the system was still evolving, and strong bosses or machines controlled some wards, while others were divided. Thomas, as a loyal Republican, was also a loyal member of the Republican machine. It had benefited him when he made an alliance with Third Ward leader John Clough in 1882 and 1884. In 1886, it would work against him.[2]

During this time, African Americans continued to make gains in Chicago politics, especially within the Republican Party and in the Second Ward. By 1885, Robert M. Mitchell was serving as the Second Ward representative to the city Republican central committee and often served as the committee's secretary. In April 1885, H. J. Mitchell was elected South Town Clerk and he was reelected in 1886. At party conventions, almost half of the Second Ward delegations consisted of African Americans, including John Howard, Isaac Rivers, William Baker, E. A. Payne and C. H. McCallister. Lloyd G. Wheeler became active in the Democratic Party, advocating Carter Harrison's successful reelection as mayor in 1885. In the spring of 1886 Democrats nominated an African American for South Town Clerk in an effort to defeat H. J. Mitchell. It didn't work but that they attempted such a move demonstrates the growing strength of a community active in the political world.[3]

Thomas was not as active a participant in the Second Ward organization or in the off-year elections as he had been in the past, but he was still active. In the spring of 1885 he was busy with the session in Springfield, but he gave at least one speech in Chicago endorsing the Republican ticket. The Second Ward Republicans had nominated Martin Best over John Howard for alderman, but Best went on to lose the election to Democrat James Appleton. That fall, Thomas ran for delegate to the county convention that nominated candidates for county commissioner and judge. The Second Ward split into two rival factions, with Thomas and three other African Americans running for delegate with the faction led by E. R. Bliss. Baker, Rivers, Waring, E. A. Payne, and H. J. Mitchell ran on a slate that the *Times* termed "anti-machine." After a credentials challenge, the Bliss delegation was seated at the county convention and Thomas was chosen as one of five Second Ward delegates to the county judicial convention, which nominated Benjamin Magruder for judge of the state Supreme Court.[4]

Unfortunately for Thomas, the First Ward organization, which Clough and Thomas had snubbed in 1882, was growing stronger. It was led by state representative Abner Taylor and Alderman Arthur Dixon, strong anti-Logan men. These two, having consolidated their ward, were increasing their strength in the Second Ward, where they were seen as part of the anti-machine. Former

First Ward residents George Gibbs and William Baker now lived in the Second Ward, which gave the Taylor-Dixon machine some leverage.

Thomas came into the 1886 nomination fight with the same alliance as in 1882 and 1884: one with John Clough of the Third Ward. In 1882 and 1884 Thomas was able to win his ward and combine with Clough's Third Ward to receive a nomination. In 1886, allies of the Taylor-Dixon machine defeated the Thomas forces in the Second Ward and, for reasons unrelated to race, were able to defeat Thomas in his bid for renomination.

In the Third Senatorial District, there was never any doubt Clough and Thomas would each face contests for renomination, despite the fact that they were incumbents. Also running as an incumbent was Congressman Ransom W. Dunham of the First Congressional District, which included the entire Third Senatorial District. Dunham too would face a battle for renomination.

The First Congressional District and the Third Senatorial District both held their primaries on September 17. For the Congressional race, incumbent Dunham of the Fourth Ward squared off against First Ward boss Abner Taylor, state representative William Harper of Dunham's Fourth Ward, 1885 mayoral candidate Judge Eugene Cary of the Third Ward, and Ed Maher of the town of Lake.

The congressional district primaries revealed the competitive nature of party politics of the era. Taylor and Dixon controlled the First Ward, and their slate of delegates had no trouble winning in that ward. Their machine also had a lot of strength in the Second Ward, where Taylor easily won the primary election. Among Taylor's delegates from the Second Ward were Gibbs and Baker, the former First Ward residents. The Third Ward elected a slate pledged to support Judge Cary. Clough was selected as one of the delegates attached to that slate. Harper edged out Dunham in the Fourth Ward, 582 to 534. Among the delegates on Harper's slate were Stephen A. Douglas Jr., the Republican son and namesake of the former Democratic senator from Illinois, and Thomas's old friend and ally, W. C. Phillips. Harper also won in the delegate-rich town of Hyde Park, while Dunham won the smaller townships. Lake Township went to Ed Maher.[5]

The high interest in the congressional primary greatly increased turnout in the Third Senatorial District primary. Republicans voted to select eight delegates to represent the First Ward at the Third Senatorial District convention, eleven delegates from the Second Ward, twelve delegates from the Third Ward, and four delegates from the part of the Fourth Ward in the district. The convention was held September 18, the day after the primary. Eighteen delegates were needed for nomination.[6]

In the First Ward, the ticket controlled by Taylor and Dixon won handily. Taylor was selected as a delegate to the legislative convention. Thomas and Clough did not run a slate of candidates in the First Ward. However, late in the day attorney Simeon King and Frank Warren announced they were candidates for the legislature. They were able to print ballots and get some votes for a slate of delegates pledged to them and to R. W. Dunham for Congress. Still, the Taylor ticket received 146 of the 192 votes cast in that ward. That ticket supported Gibbs for state senate. The *Times* reported the slate "claimed" to be unpledged for the two representative positions. The *Tribune* reported that First Ward party worker F. A. Brokoski was interested in the senate nomination, although he was actually a Taylor-backed candidate for the state representative. The *Evening Journal* reported that Gibbs and H. J. Mitchell had an alliance. That is possible, as Gibbs was an attorney who defended Mitchell as he tried to take office as South Town clerk in 1885. However, if they had an alliance this election, it was a much looser one than the Clough-Thomas alliance. It is also possible the *Journal* confused H. J. Mitchell with Robert M. Mitchell, whom Thomas had defeated for the state representative nomination in 1884 and who was serving in leadership roles in the Second Ward Republican organization.[7]

The Second Ward had the highest turnout in the senatorial primary, with 707 people voting. This was more than four times as many as had voted in the county Republican primaries the month before. The slates here were one for the Thomas and Clough ticket and one for Gibbs for senate. The Gibbs ticket received 425 of the 707 votes, a clear majority despite the fact that Thomas actively campaigned at the polls. The *Herald* wrote that following the election, which had required half a dozen policemen to keep order, "Lawyer Thomas and the Clough men went off in chagrin." While Thomas was unable to carry the Second Ward, the Clough-Thomas slate ran unopposed in Clough's Third Ward. Only a small part of the Fourth Ward was located in the Third Senatorial District and the Clough ticket narrowly won by a vote of 27 to 24. Included among the four delegates of the ward were Stephen A. Douglas Jr. and a relatively unknown African American named George Ecton.[8]

The Taylor-Dixon machine had conceded the Third Ward to Clough and Thomas and the latter had conceded the First Ward to Taylor and Dixon, so the race for the Third Senatorial District nomination came down to the Second Ward, which in combination with either the First or the Third Ward, was going to choose the three nominees. Knowing this, Thomas announced that he would challenge the results of the Second Ward. No doubt he was hoping that, like in 1878, he could at least be given some of the delegation.

With the Taylor-Dixon alliance having won in the First and Second Wards, they went into the convention with a 19 to 16 delegate lead over the Clough-Thomas alliance. But, as the *Evening Journal* noted in handicapping the race, nothing was set in concrete, as the legislative nominations would depend somewhat on where the congressional candidate came from. What Taylor wanted most of all was the congressional nomination, so deals could be struck. However, Taylor allies had won both the congressional and senatorial delegations from the Second Ward, leaving Thomas with very little to offer in a deal. There was also the chance that, as the *Evening Journal* surmised, Thomas would be dumped by Clough if the latter could cut a deal with Taylor.[9]

The Third Senatorial District Republican nominating convention was scheduled to be held the same day as the First Congressional District convention. Because many of the delegates to the senatorial convention were also delegates to the congressional convention, Republican leaders decided to hold the senatorial convention after the congressional convention finished its work. With a field of five candidates, however, the congressional convention was deeply divided. For four hours and fifty-seven ballots, the delegates debated, with no candidate able to achieve enough votes for nomination. Although the numbers varied throughout the balloting, the results of the first ballot and the fifty-seventh were the same, with Dunham having 29 votes to Harper's 27, Taylor's 20, Maher's 16, and Cary's 13. In the four wards that made up the city part of the district, Taylor had the entire vote from the First and Second Wards, while Cary had all of the Third Ward, and Harper all of the Fourth Ward. Thirteen south Cook County townships were also involved in the balloting, although other than Hyde Park, with nineteen delegates, and Lake, with sixteen, none of them were very large. The Lake delegation supported Maher, Hyde Park had elected a Harper slate, and all of the other townships went with Dunham.[10]

After it became apparent that the congressional convention was deadlocked, delegates or their proxies for the Third Senatorial District convention quickly met during a break. They set up a temporary organization, with Dr. Simon Quinlan of Clough's Third Ward as chairman and H. J. Mitchell of the Second Ward as secretary. It appears that some of the delegates supporting Gibbs were unable to attend the convention. Taylor made a quick attempt to adjourn the convention until after the congressional district convention was finished but failed. Thomas was allowed to file a credentials challenge to the Second Ward delegation, and delegates appointed a three-man credentials committee before adjourning. The committee consisted of a delegate from the First Ward, one from the Third, and Stephen A. Douglas Jr. from the Fourth Ward.

This was an apparent coup for Clough and Thomas. Despite being in the minority, they set up a temporary organization with a Clough delegate as chairman and they set up a credentials committee where they had a two-to-one majority. The credentials committee decided to meet on Sunday, and the convention as a whole adjourned until 4:00 P.M. Monday. The congressional convention was scheduled to reconvene at 10:00 A.M. Monday.[11]

Sunday was a day off for the delegates, but certainly not for the politicians. The *Tribune* noted that U.S. Senators John A. Logan and Shelby Cullom supported Clough (and presumably Thomas), while Gibbs was backed by Charles Farwell, Abner Taylor's law partner and Logan's chief rival in the Republican Party. Assuming that the congressional convention would remain deadlocked until after the senatorial convention, the *Tribune* surmised that if Clough lost for senate, Logan and Cullom could get their friends in the Third and Fourth Wards to retaliate by supporting Dunham for Congress. Similarly, if Clough won, the *Tribune* surmised, delegates from the Second Ward would be convinced that Abner Taylor wasn't as omnipotent as he appeared, and they might go over to Dunham. The problem with this logic, however, was that it was based on the results of the legislative race occurring before the congressional convention finished its business. With the congressional convention scheduled for 10:00 A.M., delegates there had six hours to decide a winner before the senatorial convention was slated to meet.

The *Tribune* also reported that Gibbs's supporters believed Clough had acted in bad faith at the Saturday meeting. According to a friend of Gibbs, the delegates were just supposed to meet and adjourn until after the congressional convention. Instead, Clough was able to have a challenge issued to the Second Ward delegation and take over the credentials committee. Clough's plan was to have the credentials committee recommend splitting the Second Ward delegation to 5½ delegates for each ticket. Splitting the Second Ward delegation would give Clough-Thomas 21½ votes to Gibb's 13½. Both the *Tribune* and the *Daily News* also printed a rumor that Clough men were planning to pay two delegates from the Second Ward $150 each for their support on the credentials challenge. The *Tribune* reported that the scheme was so transparent "that it is more than probable that the whole thing will fall through." It was correct. On Sunday the credentials committee, in the face of criticism, decided to let the convention as a whole handle all credentials challenges. Douglas addressed the convention on Monday and stated that there had been a misunderstanding about the role of the credentials committee. He said he would not be a part of anything underhanded.[12]

The congressional convention reconvened Monday morning and the balloting continued. For four hours, roll calls were taken, with little change in the results. On the 114th roll call, Taylor switched all of the votes of the First Ward and 8 of the 11 votes of the Second Ward to Dunham. However, Dunham still didn't have enough votes to win. On the 120th ballot, the First and Second Ward delegates went back to Taylor. Throughout the balloting, the delegates from Dunham's home ward, the Fourth, supported Harper or Maher. On the 123rd ballot, Harper released his Fourth Ward delegates and they switched to Dunham. The First and Second Wards also went with Dunham, and, combined with his strength in Hyde Park and the surrounding townships, he won the nomination. The Third Ward, where Clough was a delegate, remained with Judge Cary throughout the balloting. With the convention having finished its business before the senatorial convention, none of the *Tribune's* scenario could play out. And with Clough having backed a loser against Taylor and Dunham, things didn't look good for the Clough-Thomas alliance going into the senatorial convention. As the *Daily News* noted, "[Clough's] delegation voted for Cary regularly, and so he had a very poor chance to cultivate any friendly influences in the 1st and 2d wards."[13]

When the delegates convened for the senatorial convention, the first item of business was to hear the challenges to the delegations. Simeon King challenged the First Ward delegation, but his challenge lacked credibility. Then, John Howard spoke for the challengers of the Second Ward. Why Thomas didn't speak is a mystery. Howard was a poor choice to address the convention. During his talk, he was frequently met with shouts that he was a Democrat. He also accused H. J. Mitchell, who was serving as secretary of the convention, of corruption in the Second Ward primary. Such personal attacks were unwarranted. In the end, Taylor made a motion to seat the entire Second Ward delegation and this was done.

The convention then moved to the nominations. For senate, Gibbs and Clough were nominated. The First and the Second Wards united for Gibbs and the Third and Fourth Wards united for Clough, resulting in the selection of Gibbs by a 19 to 16 vote. The balloting for the first state representative spot then began. Brokoski, Taylor's candidate from the First Ward, won all 19 delegates from the First and Second Wards, plus the 4 votes from the Fourth Ward, to easily win the nomination. The Third Ward gave Thomas 8 votes, Robert M. Mitchell 3, and W. C. Phillips 1. Phillips's name had been put in nomination by Fourth Ward resident Douglas.

All that remained was for the convention to nominate the second representative candidate. At this point, the Republicans had a senate candidate from the Second Ward and a representative candidate from the First Ward. In the interest of geographic balance, the candidate to be nominated should have come from either the Third or Fourth Wards. Since Thomas was from the Second Ward, this was not good for him. However, the convention also needed to nominate an African American.

With the First Ward controlling the convention, Thomas was not even nominated. The nomination came down to a choice between Robert M. Mitchell, who was nominated by the Second Ward, and Phillips of the Fourth Ward. On the first ballot, the delegates nominated Phillips. He won all 8 votes from the First Ward, 10 from the Third, and 3 from the Fourth. Mitchell received all 11 of the Second Ward delegates, plus 2 from the Third Ward, while LeRoy Hayes received 1 vote from the Fourth Ward. The Fourth Ward had been unanimous for Brokoski for the first representative position, which may have been part of a brokered deal between the First and the Fourth Wards that secured the nomination for a Fourth Warder.

Phillips had the credentials of being from the right part of the district geographically, of having not alienated the Taylor-Dixon-Gibbs alliance, and of being an African American. Plus, he was a close friend of Thomas. Indeed, it is likely that Thomas stepped aside for Phillips and helped bring most of the Third Ward delegation to support Phillips over Mitchell, with whom Thomas had often clashed. The nominations were then made unanimous and the election campaign began.[14]

Far from being bitter after his defeat, Thomas worked hard for the Republican ticket. On October 4, Thomas agreed to serve on the Second Ward Campaign Committee. On October 9, he served as one of the vice presidents at a large Republican rally where John A. Logan was the featured guest. The position was an honorary one and serving with Thomas were such luminaries as Robert Todd Lincoln, *Tribune* publisher Joseph Medill, and former U.S. Secretary of State Elihu B. Washburne.[15]

The 1886 fall election quickly became a crowded campaign. By the time of the Third Senatorial District Republican convention, the Prohibition Party already had already selected senate and house candidates. One week after the Republicans met, the Democrats of the Third District convened and selected Isaac "Ike" Abrahams of the Second Ward for the senate. Abrahams had served one term in the house with Thomas in 1883, but the Republican papers dismissed him as "Three-ball Ike, the police court lawyer and professional bailer." The Democrats chose to nominate two candidates for the House. The candidates were Thomas Moran, another resident of the Second Ward and a street inspector for the city, and Dennis Kay, a saloonkeeper from the Third Ward. The socialist United Labor Party selected William A. Bruce, an African American barber, as a candidate for the state senate and Oscar Leinen, an insurance agent and former butcher at the Chicago Stock Yards, for state representative. The United Labor Party did not field a full slate of candidates and endorsed candidates from the two major parties for some offices. Another labor party, the Labor League, also put up some candidates for county office. However, it endorsed Democrats for most offices, including the entire Democratic slate in the Third Senatorial District.[16]

As the campaign progressed, the candidates for the two major parties in the Third District began having troubles. King continued his protest of the actions of the First Ward with regard to the senate nomination, but his protests merely served as an annoyance to Gibbs. Phillips was charged with owning and renting "a house used for 'disreputable purposes.'" In early October, Dennis Kay resigned from the Democratic ticket when it was discovered that he hadn't lived in the district long enough to qualify to serve. Democrats replaced Kay with Philip Koehler, who had thrice been elected South Town Constable. The *Tribune* alleged that Thomas Moran, the other Democratic legislative candidate, also hadn't lived in the district long enough to serve. While those allegations did not turn out to be true, the *Chicago Evening Journal* was moved to editorialize that "many of the chaps who are candidates for the Legislature are ignorant of the fact that they must have lived two years in the district in which they run to be eligible to the office." Kay and Moran weren't the only candidates who faced residency problems. In the second week of October, Phillips suddenly resigned his place from the Republican ticket when it was discovered that he too hadn't lived in the district for the required two years.[17]

For Thomas, Phillips's resignation meant another chance at the nomination. However, although the Republican nomination was guaranteed to an African American, Thomas still could not overcome the same drawbacks that had stopped his attempts at the convention. The Second Ward already had a legislative candidate in Gibbs, and Thomas had supported the wrong side at the convention. On October 13, Republicans chose George Ecton of the Fourth Ward to take Phillips's place. A native of Kentucky, Ecton was the headwaiter at the Woodruff House. He too would be charged with not living in the district long enough to serve, but, as was the case with Moran with the Democrats, those charges were not true.[18]

The *Times* later reported that a number of African Americans had petitioned the Republican campaign committee to have Thomas appointed in Phillips's place, but that Gibbs would not allow it. While a report like that appearing in the Democratic *Times* normally would not have much credence, the story quoted Edward H. Wright, a reputable African American leader, as bringing the charges. As such, the charges had merit.[19]

Further giving the charges merit are the actions of J. C. Buckner, who had been selected to serve with Thomas on the Second Ward Republican Campaign Committee. Buckner, a caterer, was an African American who would later serve in the legislature. On October 19, the Labor League, which had endorsed the Democrat Kay for the house before he resigned as a candidate, dropped a bombshell and named the Republican Buckner as its candidate for the house.[20]

Now, there were African American third-party candidates for both the senate and the house. A letter writer to the *Inter-Ocean* saw the nominations of Bruce and Buckner as a ploy by the Democrats to take away the African American vote from the Republican candidates. He feared that Buckner's candidacy would split the African American vote, resulting in the election of two Democrats to the House and the defeat of both Buckner and Ecton, which would leave Chicago's African American community without a state representative in Springfield. The Republican newspapers were more concerned about Bruce's senate candidacy pulling votes away from Gibbs. The *Tribune* wrote, "[The Democrats] don't care particularly about the Representatives, Brokoski or Eckston [*sic*], for they are elected for only one term, while the Senator will hold over and take part in the selection of a United States Senator in 1889." The *Journal* editorialized, "The colored voters should think twice before they throw away their votes and elect 'Ike' Abrahams to the Senate." The *Tribune*, in an appeal to the pre–Civil War era, further editorialized that "it would be a case of what might be called poetic justice if Mr. Gibbs should be defeated by a diversion of the colored votes from the Republican ticket, for in the times when Chicago had a depot on the underground railroad his father, Dr. Aaron Gibbs of the Third Ward, was one of the principal men connected with it."[21]

For Wright, however, the issue came down to the Republican Party bosses rejecting the request by the African American community that Thomas be chosen as Phillips's replacement. Wright was quoted in the *Times* as saying, "We may lose a colored representative, and we may cause the defeat of the republican candidate for state senator, George A. Gibbs, but it is the most promising move ever made by the colored citizens of this state, when we show to the world that the time has passed when the colored vote can be looked upon as so much republican merchandise to be delivered when called for."[22]

The question becomes, however, what role did Thomas play in this? In both 1878 and 1880 he worked hard for the Republican ticket after he failed to be nominated. However, after the Ecton nomination, Thomas drops from view in the mainstream press. His selection to the Second Ward Campaign Committee and as a vice president at the October 9 campaign rally occurred before he was snubbed for a second time by the Third District Senatorial Committee. While there are no newspaper articles stating that he supported Buckner, there is also no evidence that he opposed his candidacy or renounced efforts to avenge his failure to be nominated. What part, if any, he played in this revolt against the Republican Party is unknown.

Despite the machinations, on Election Day the Third District remained overwhelmingly Republican. This was best seen in the Senate race, where Gibbs handily defeated Abrahams by a total of 3,493 to 2,524. Bruce took in 814 votes, and R. A. Burrell, the Prohibition candidate, received 48 votes. Even if all of Bruce's votes had gone to Abrahams, Gibbs would have won by a comfortable 150 votes.

For the three house seats, the Republicans also had no problems. Ecton received the most votes, with 5,263½ votes. Brokoski won the second spot with 5,032 votes, and Democrat Thomas Moran won the third spot, with 4,688. Koehler, the other Democrat in the race, received 2,790 votes, and Leinen, the United Labor Party candidate, won 2,347½ votes. The Prohibition candidate, W. E. Kellett, won 143 votes. Buckner's 469½ votes do not seem to have affected Ecton's vote total, nor did they appear to do a great deal of harm to Brokoski, who came in second. In actuality, the division in the ward appears to have come more between the Democrat Koehler and the United Labor Party candidate Leinen. Even then, had Leinen not been in the race, and had his votes gone to Koehler, the two Democrats would still have only been fighting for the third representative spot.[23]

The 1886 election ended Thomas's legislative career. He had been unable to unite the African American community in the Second Ward behind his candidacy, which allowed the First Ward Taylor-Dixon machine to win the Second Ward Republican primary and dictate who the African American nominee for state representative would be. Although the community was strong enough to ensure that an African American was nominated for state representative—and it is obvious that Thomas still had several loyal supporters—the Taylor-Dixon machine was not going to allow the nomination to go to Thomas. Ironically, the following year Thomas would join the same First Ward Republican organization that had defeated him for the legislature.

1887 Election to South Town Clerk

It is difficult to say if Thomas bolted the Republican Party in 1886. All of the evidence is circumstantial. Buckner and Wright used the failure of the Republicans to nominate Thomas as their excuse for bolting the party. Both Buckner and Wright remained friends with Thomas for the rest of his life. Thomas could be critical of the Republican Party but had never bolted it. And, just five months after the 1886 election, he was nominated by the Republicans of the south side to serve as South Town clerk, with Abner Taylor, who had engineered Thomas's defeat in 1886, helping to secure his nomination.

By 1887, the labor movement was in full swing. As historians Drake and Cayton have noted, the economic upheavals that led to pitched battles between labor and capital barely touched Chicago's small African American community, most of whose members were ostracized from manufacturing jobs and employed in servant capacities.[24] However, these upheavals tore apart the Democratic Party in Chicago. The base of the Democratic Party was the large number of immigrants in the city. In the 1880s the new immigrants were moving farther and farther to the political left. The Democratic Party needed the votes of these working-class immigrants to win; yet many of the old-time leaders of the party hesitated to go as far left as many of the immigrants. It became, at best, an uneasy alliance. On May 4, 1886, a bomb exploded at a union rally at Haymarket Square on Chicago's near West Side, killing eight policemen and wounding sixty more. The mainstream media and native-born Americans, both Democrat and Republican, recoiled in horror and demanded revenge against foreign leftists and agitators. When the 1887 spring city and township elections rolled around, the Democrats faced a number of internal divisions, including a split from its large immigrant base. The only Democratic leader who could unite the party was four-term mayor Carter Harrison. However, as the election neared, Harrison played coy about whether he wanted to be renominated for another two-year term.[25]

The mayor's race would be the dominant one in the April election, but it was not the only office up for election that year. The other important city offices included the city clerk, attorney, and treasurer. Also on the ballot in the spring were the town offices.

Chicago was divided into three townships, called North Town, South Town, and West Town. The Chicago River served as the dividing line between them. It was the duty of township government to assess property in its areas and collect taxes. Thomas lived in the South Town, an area that included most of the downtown business district. The South Town collected approximately two-thirds of all the taxes of the city. More than $1.4 million had been collected in taxes in 1886 from the South Town. Of that, $971,000 went to the city, $332,000 went to the county and state, $105,000 went to the South Park Board, and $30,000 was kept by the South Town. While the town positions were not considered as important as the city positions, they still were important. Robert Todd Lincoln had served as South Town supervisor. Former Illinois governor John Hamilton was the attorney for the South Town board.[26]

Because town government in Chicago was the unit of government that both assessed property and collected taxes, it had a long history of corruption. Traditionally, Republican newspapers attempted to rally the party faithful to vote in the low-turnout elections by citing the need to prevent corruption and fraud. In 1887, the offices appeared more important, as the socialist United Labor Party threatened to win these seats and take over the reins of taxation.[27]

On February 26, the United Labor Party met to nominate its candidates. The party nominated thirty-one-year-old master iron molder Robert Nelson for mayor. Other citywide nominations went to Frank Stauber for city treasurer, John Dollard for city clerk, and Jesse Cox Jr. for city attorney. Stauber was a Swiss-born socialist who had once served on the city council. Dollard was an Irish-born member of the printer's union. Cox was a Pennsylvania-born attorney. For the South Town offices, the party nominated Frank O'Neill for town assessor, Louis Koellin for town collector, F. E. Coyle for supervisor, and James S. Nelson for town clerk. The Ohio-born O'Neill worked in the stockyards until being blacklisted for taking part in strike activities. Koellin was born in Prussia and worked as a cloth cutter. Coyle was a native Chicagoan who worked in the city railway shops. Nelson was an African American and a member of the Colored Waiters Assembly.[28]

Two days later, 175 delegates met at the Prohibitionist Party nominating convention. The party nominated a complete slate of candidates for the city offices and the South Town offices but it would not be a factor in the election.[29]

As the two third parties met in convention, Republican politicians began maneuvering for city and town nominations. Both the *Herald* and the *Times* on March 10 reported that the South Town Republican Committee had put together a slate of candidates that included B. R. DeYoung for assessor, Enoch Howard for supervisor, Frank Gilbert for collector, and Vincent Carroll for clerk. The *Times* wrote that the meeting was "secret" and that incumbents David Shannahan and R. M. Mitchell (actually H. J. Mitchell) were being dumped from the ticket. It noted that the committee representatives from four of the five wards attended the meeting. William Baker, the Second Ward representative on the committee and its only African American member, was not present.[30]

The primaries to elect delegates to the South Town Republican convention were scheduled for March 17 for the Fifth Ward and for March 18 for the First through Fourth Wards. The convention was to be held March 19, the same day as the Republican city convention, where candidates for mayor and other city offices would be selected. Polls were open from noon to 7 P.M. and each ward had one polling place. The delegate totals for each ward, which were based on the number of votes Blaine had received in the 1884 presidential election, were 8 for the First Ward, 11 for the Second, 12 for the Third, 23 for the Fourth, and 21 for Ward Five. The primary election plans drew criticism from some Republicans, who saw in them attempts to manipulate the city convention.

The *Tribune* wrote that the polling places in some wards were located in areas designed to discourage voting among the "better" elements of the party. Of the Second Ward polling place, it wrote that the machine elements of the party, which included Robert M. Mitchell, had located the polling place "at the corner of Polk street and Fourth avenue, a very tough locality." Tough or not, that was the street corner nearest to the Thomas home.[31]

African Americans were well-represented in the Republican Party in the spring 1887 election. The Third Ward Republican Club fielded a slate of delegates for the town primary that consisted of two out of twelve delegates being African American, although it also fielded a slate that had only one African American among its twelve delegates for the more important city convention. The Second Ward Republican Club endorsed Robert Waring for South Town clerk. Robert M. Mitchell was selected to serve as the Second Ward's representative on the Cook County Republican Committee. The club also debated whether or not to nominate Thomas for alderman, although when it took a vote only W. S. Babcock and J. G. Kearney, two white candidates, received votes.[32]

Despite the Second Ward Club's endorsements, the voters still had a say in who the ward supported for the different offices. And, after the voters selected a slate of delegates to the city and town conventions, those delegates were under no legal requirement to support a particular candidate. The Republican ticket selected at the town convention was a lot different than that supported by the Second Ward Republican Club.

The major races in this election were the mayor's race and the aldermanic seats. The Taylor faction had no problems in the First Ward and easily renominated Arthur Dixon for alderman. In the Second Ward, Thomas ally E. R. Bliss and incumbent Republican alderman George Mueller battled a ticket backed by Gibbs. The Bliss slate won in a contested primary election where the police had to be called out to the polling place. The slate chose a nine-person committee to select a candidate for alderman. Three African Americans, H. J. Mitchell, Robert M. Mitchell, and Dr. C. H. McCallister, served on the aldermanic committee.[33]

For the South Town convention, Alderman Dixon led the First Ward. The Second Ward delegation included three African Americans: William Baker, H. J. Mitchell, and Edward H. Wright. Each of the five wards wanted at least one of the four township positions. A total of 75 delegates attended the convention.[34]

The selection of candidates was fairly routine, with geographical balance strictly adhered to. At the city convention, Republicans nominated D. W. Nickerson of the First Ward for city clerk. This apparently satisfied Taylor, as the First Ward did not seek a nomination for one of the township offices. Instead, DeYoung of the Fourth Ward was renominated for assessor, and Frank Gilbert of the Third Ward was renominated for collector. Neither DeYoung or Gilbert had any opposition. John Dugan of the Fifth Ward, a native of Belfast, Ireland, was nominated for supervisor and also had no opposition.

The only contest for a position occurred for the clerk position. H. J. Mitchell had held the position for two terms but did not want renomination. It was assumed by some that an African American would replace him. In the interest of geographic harmony, the position needed to go to a resident of the Second Ward. Three African Americans were nominated for the post: R. C. Waring, William Baker, and Thomas. The latter's name had not even been mentioned for the position. The Second Ward delegation, under the leadership of longtime ally E. R. Bliss, nominated Thomas, the Third Ward nominated Waring, and the Fifth Ward nominated Baker. When the votes were taken, Thomas handily defeated his two rivals. Thomas received 64 votes to Waring's 9 and Baker's 2. The *Times* reported that Taylor and Dixon had put together the ticket before the convention. If so, it showed that there were no hard feelings between the First Ward and Thomas.[35]

The Thomas nomination did not receive much coverage in the press. He was the third African American to be nominated for the post by the Republicans that decade, and the nomination seemed almost guaranteed to go to an African American. The *Tribune* called him "one of the brightest and best-known colored men in the city" and stated that his record in the General Assembly had been one of "intelligence and integrity." The paper even praised his work as an attorney, which was surprising because the paper always had a low opinion of police court attorneys. The *Inter-Ocean* put things more in perspective. After noting the importance of the town supervisor, collector, and assessor positions, it wrote almost as an afterthought, "The Town Clerk is by no means an unimportant position."[36]

While the clerk's job was not as important as the supervisor or assessor positions, the *Inter-Ocean* was correct in that the clerk's job was not unimportant. A town clerk took care of all the records, books, and papers belonging to a town government and recorded all acts of town meetings and of the town board of auditors. The town clerk also annually sent to the county clerk a statement of the amount of taxes that needed to be levied in the town for that year and made sure the notice of the annual public town meeting was published in the newspapers and publicized in the town. The clerk served on the town boards of appointment, health, auditors, and equalization.[37]

Following the nominations, the convention selected a town campaign committee, consisting of a representative from each of the wards. The Second

Ward chose Baker as its representative on the committee. The committee also consisted of one representative from each candidate. Later Edward H. Wright would be added to the committee, most likely as Thomas's choice.[38]

Four days after the nominating convention, the Republicans held a large ratification meeting in support of the ticket. As always, the speakers waved the bloody shirt. Stephen Douglas Jr., in reference to the United Labor Party, managed to combine the 1860s Civil War and the labor issues of the 1880s when he stated, "The Republican party was the original and only labor party in this country. The first great strike was originated by it, and conducted by Lincoln and Grant—the strike to raise the wages of the negro in the south." While Douglas reminded the crowd of the party's role in freeing African Americans, no African Americans were listed in any of the papers as appearing on the stage during the campaign rally or as one of the 136 vice presidents of the affair.[39]

On the same day the Republicans were holding their ratification meeting, Democrats were meeting in convention to select their city ticket. The party nominated Carter Harrison to a fifth term as mayor and also nominated candidates for treasurer, clerk, and city attorney. The day after the convention, Harrison turned down the nomination. John McAvoy, whom the Democrats had nominated for city treasurer, also declined his nomination. With that, the Democrats ceased to exist for the 1887 citywide elections. The mayor's race was left between the Republican John A. Roche and the Socialist Robert Nelson.[40]

While Democrats would run for and win other offices, including aldermanic seats, the breakup of the party echoed on the lower end of the ticket. In the South Town, Democrats met four times in convention and could not nominate a ticket. As such, the situation for the South Town elections was the same as for the city elections. The campaign was between the Republicans and the socialist United Labor Party.[41]

With only a week to go between Harrison's withdrawal and the election, Democrats flocked to the Republican ticket. The newspapers sounded the alarm on what the election of the socialists would mean. The *Times* editorialized, "Only eleven months since that awful event [Haymarket], the public safety is again menaced by the same lawless class, the same socialist propaganda against property." Its front-page story on Election Day was entitled "Crush the Reptile." The *Tribune* editorialized, "On the one hand the issue is law, order, peace, and property; on the other, industrial disintegration and the chaos which must sooner or later result from the revolutionary and destructive methods of Socialism as carried out by Anarchism."[42]

The results on Election Day were a foregone conclusion. The entire Republican ticket easily won the citywide offices. Roche received slightly more than 51,000 votes to Nelson's slightly more than 23,000 votes. In office, Roche appointed Robert M. Mitchell to be chief clerk at the Harrison Street Police Station and James Porter to be the night clerk force of the Chicago Water Works Department. In all, Republicans won 13 of the 18 aldermanic seats. The Democrats won 4 seats. Socialists won the aldermanic position in the Fifth Ward. James Appleton, the incumbent Democrat, retained the aldermanic seat in the Second Ward. The *Tribune* alleged this was done with the collusion of African American voters.[43]

In both South and West Towns, where there were no Democrats running, the Republicans swept all the offices. All of the Republican candidates for South Town office received more than 12,000 votes and won by pluralities of at least 6,500 votes. However, all of them lost in the Fifth Ward to their socialist counterparts.[44]

While the victory restored Thomas to public office, much of 1887 was occupied by personal matters. On Monday, April 4, the day before the South Town and city elections, Thomas's 18-year-old daughter Hester married 22-year-old Edward R. Morrison, who was originally from Colorado. Rev. T. W. Henderson of the Quinn Chapel A.M.E. Church officiated at the wedding. At the same time, Thomas was preparing for his own wedding. On Tuesday, July 12, 1887, the forty-year-old Thomas married twenty-three-year-old Virginia native Crittie E. O. Marshall. Richard DeBaptiste, Thomas's long-time friend, officiated. The marriage took place at the home at 198 Fourth Avenue. Unlike Thomas's 1880 marriage to Justine Latcher, this wedding received little media attention. However, the couple did host a series of receptions in the days following the wedding, the first of which the *Western Appeal* noted "was largely attended by the elite of the city."[45]

Although Thomas married his third wife at the 198 Fourth Avenue home, Thomas had not lived there much since the 1883 death of his second wife, Justine. By the mid 1880s, successful African Americans such as John G. Jones, Ferdinand Barnett, Edward H. Morris, S. Laing Williams, George Ecton, and W. C. Phillips were living well south of the levee and downtown areas, in the Third and Fourth wards and even the suburb of Hyde Park. Thomas, who in 1885 the *Cleveland Gazette* estimated to be worth $100,000, could easily have afforded to live outside the levee.[46] For either political or professional reasons, Thomas stubbornly chose to stay in the Second Ward, despite the worsening conditions of the levee and the area's industrialization. However, since the death of Justine, he had moved around in the ward. The 1885 and 1886 city directories list Thomas as boarding at 181 Third Avenue, now Plymouth Court. The 1887 directory has him boarding at 197 Third Avenue.[47]

In early 1884, Thomas allowed his home to be used as the meeting place for a literary society composed of young boys and girls from the area. The club called itself "the Young Philosophers."[48] But in December of 1884, Thomas sold the house to Elizabeth Marshall, the widowed mother of two daughters: Crittie and Mary. The purchase price was $15,000 and the record of the sale was notarized by attorney Edward H. Morris. In February of 1886, Thomas bought the house back for the same $15,000. By 1888, Thomas and Crittie had moved into a three-story brick home located at 444 S. Clark Street. Despite the street number, the home was located on the block just behind the house at 198 Fourth Avenue, still in the levee. The first floor contained a store, which served as Thomas's law office.[49]

The newlyweds quickly settled in to a domestic life befitting a well-to-do couple. Shortly after their own marriage, they attended a marriage reception for African American attorney James E. Jones, where they gave a china tea set as a wedding present. The following April, they attended a wedding of Lucy Meade and Adolphus Harris, where they gave a chenille table cloth as a present. One year after their marriage, in July 1888, Crittie gave birth to their first child, a daughter named Ethel. In short succession, she gave birth to Martha in January 1890, John W. E. in 1891, Joseph in July 1892, and Logan in January 1894. Daughter Grace would follow in 1898. Martha would live only six months and John W. E. only five months. Both children were buried in the Thomas family plot in Oak Woods Cemetery.[50]

Although the Thomas family was doing well financially, Thomas and his wife did not participate in many of the events conducted by the elites of the African American community. In January 1888, the Prudence Crandall Study Club, a literary club organized by S. Laing Williams, Barnett's law partner, held a reception at the home of John Jones's widow. Among the prominent members who attended the reception with their wives were Williams, Barnett, Wheeler, Ecton, and Dr. C. E. Bentley. Thomas does not appear to have been a member of this exclusive group. He also was not a Mason, so when in February Williams, Edward H. Morris, John G. Jones, J. H. Magee, and others formed a joint stock company to build a Masonic Hall, he did not participate. In 1891 he did attend a meeting of the National Grand Lodge of the United Brothers of Friendship, a secret order of African American men, and gave the closing address on its first night before approximately 1,000 delegates. John G. Jones was a leader in that organization, although generally most social events that featured Jones, Wheeler, or Barnett did not have Thomas in attendance. Historian Christopher Robert Reed notes that about this time Lloyd Wheeler, John Jones's son-in-law, had become the social leader of black Chicago. If so, the longtime political rivalry between Thomas and Wheeler may have been what prevented Thomas from entering the most elite social circles of Chicago's African American community.[51]

If Thomas was not a social leader in Chicago's African American community, he was still the political leader. When President Grover Cleveland made a visit to Chicago in October 1887, Thomas served as one of three African Americans on the reception committee, along with George Ecton and Dr. Daniel Hale Williams. In the spring of 1888, he went to Springfield to attend a gathering of leading Republican politicians of the state. When the Porters and Janitors Union Number 1, an African American union, held its inaugural reception in 1889, Thomas gave one of the addresses. In May 1889, Thomas joined Edward H. Morris, W. C. Phillips, and several others at a reception and banquet honoring George Ecton.[52]

One of the events Thomas attended around this time demonstrates how a typical social event was structured among African American elites. In early May 1889, local African Americans held a grand banquet for nationally known African American civil rights leader John M. Langston. The evening began with Langston giving an address at the Colored Men's Library Association meeting at Quinn Chapel. Following the meeting, at 11:00 P.M., the all-male assembly moved to the prestigious Palmer House for a banquet. The banquet was illuminated by electric lights, which were still a new enough invention to deserve a mention by the reporter covering the event. The menu featured little neck clams, consommé, broiled shad, spring lamb, cakes, ice cream, fruit, cheese, coffee, and cigars. Ferdinand L. Barnett presided, and at 1:30 A.M. he gave the first toast of the evening, entitled "Our Guest." Several others gave toasts as well, including Thomas, whose toast was entitled "Our Girls and Boys," Among those attending the banquet were Ecton, Morris, Wright, Howard, Robert M. Mitchell, H. J. Mitchell, and doctors Daniel Hale Williams, Charles E. Bentley, and C. H. McAllister.[53]

In the fall of 1887, African American leaders selected Thomas as one of their two choices for a county commissioner position. The election marked a change in the way county commissioners were elected. Rather than one-third of the board being elected every year to a three-year term, the new election law had the entire fifteen-member board elected annually to one-year terms. As in the past, the city was allotted ten members of the board and the county five members. In October, South Side African American voters met and settled on supporting either Thomas or Samuel Wright for county board.[54]

However, support within the community did not translate into support within the Republican Party. At the Republican convention, the only African American whose name was placed in nomination for commissioner was William Baker of the Second Ward, who was nominated by Robert M. Mitchell. Republicans at the convention determined that 3 of the 10 city commissioners should come from the South Side. They voted against a proposal that would have allowed only the delegates from a section of the city to select their own candidates. This meant that the entire city delegation to the convention voted on the all nominees for the 10 city spots, even though 3 of the nominees had to come from the South Side, 5 from the West Side, and 2 from the North Side. The West and North Town delegates to the convention did not have the African American population that the South Side did and, as such, had less reason to vote for an African American candidate. The 259 city delegates took three separate votes to select the three candidates from the South Side. Baker received a maximum of six votes on one ballot, all from the Second Ward.[55]

The exclusion from the ticket provoked mild protest from the community. After the convention, Baker conducted a poorly attended protest meeting at Bethel Church. It was aimed as much at the eleven-member Second Ward delegation, which had said it would stand united for an African American commissioner candidate and then gave Baker only six of its eleven votes, as it was at the county party as a whole.[56]

Things became worse when one of the candidates nominated by the Republicans turned down the nomination. Rather than select a Republican to replace the nominee, the party's executive committee decided to endorse one of the Democrat candidates, incumbent Thomas Brenan. The committee did not seriously consider an African American for the spot. Both Thomas and Baker later addressed the First Ward Republican Club and protested the actions of the party. However, both also pledged the full support to the Republican ticket. On Election Day, the Republican candidates, including the Democrat Brenan, swept into office.[57]

As the fall campaign was winding down, the Chicago City Council redistricted the city's wards. The redistricting plan did not go into effect until after the fall 1887 election. The plan increased the number of wards from 18 to 24 and increased the size of the city council from 36 to 48, with 2 aldermen elected from each ward.[58]

For Thomas, redistricting had a number of implications. Whether by intention or not, the makers of the plan split Chicago's South Side African American community. Under the 1880 census, the Second Ward had a population of 20,127, of which 2,309, or roughly 11 percent, were African American. Those numbers increased through the decade. By concentrating its vote in the Republican Party, the community for almost two full decades had influence in Second Ward Republican politics greater than its numbers would indicate. This translated into strength on the South Side, as seen by the nominations of African Americans to state legislator and South Town clerk.

However, the redistricting plan extended the First Ward's boundary south to Twelfth Street, deep in the Second Ward's territory. Under the previous plan, the old First Ward had an African American population of 761, the second largest amount in the city after the Second Ward but only 5 percent of the ward's population. Statistics from 1890 show that following redistricting the new First Ward had an African American population of 3,381, the largest in the city. The new Second Ward had an African American population of 2,744, the third largest in the city behind the First Ward and the Third Ward's 2,997. This meant that African Americans made up approximately 11 percent of the population of the First Ward, 12 percent of the Third Ward, and 10 percent of the Second Ward. In the Second Ward, then, the strength of the African American bloc hadn't grown but several of its leaders were now located in another ward. For the First and the Third Wards, although the African American community now represented a fairly large percentage of the overall population, its leaders had to start anew within established ward organizations.[59]

This is what happened with Thomas, whose home was now located in the First Ward, where the Republican Ward organization of Abner Taylor and Arthur Dixon was firmly entrenched. Thomas had not always gotten along with that organization. He had been a strong Logan man at a time when the First Ward was opposed to the Logan machine. The nomination of Thomas and Bradwell for state representative in 1882 had angered the First Ward and it had exacted its revenge on Thomas in 1886 when Taylor and Dixon controlled the Third District Senatorial Convention and denied Thomas renomination to the house and Clough renomination to the senate.

The first test of this new relationship occurred in the 1888 city and town elections. It proved awkward. Taylor controlled the South Town Republican convention in March. The clerk's position was conceded to go to an African American. Rather than wade in to the unfamiliar territory of African American politics, at the convention Taylor nominated four African Americans for the position. They were Thomas, Robert Waring, Dr. Charles McCallister, and J. T. Taylor. All four candidates lived in the newly drawn First Ward. The township of Hyde Park, which was soon to be annexed by the city, had voting delegates at the convention, swelling its size to more than 100 delegates. On the first ballot, McCallister received 42 votes to 37 for Thomas, 22 for Taylor, and 10 for Waring. McCallister won the nomination on the second ballot with 62 votes to 19 for Thomas, 10 for Taylor, and 1 for Waring. The Republican Party would continue its dominance in local elections, with the entire South Town Republican slate easily defeating their Democratic opponents. With the Democratic Party back in the field, the candidates for the fading labor party finished a distant third in the elections.[60]

It is difficult to gauge how much Thomas wanted the position of South Town clerk. The *Times* reported before the convention that the spot had been promised to an African American and that there were several candidates for the spot. It noted that while Thomas was the most likely choice, the community was divided, and he would have his hands full retaining the position. None of the newspapers reported that Thomas worked particularly hard to get the nomination. In commenting on the nomination fight, none of the papers note how Thomas did as clerk, leading one to assume the duties were noncontroversial and rather mundane.[61]

If Thomas was angry at losing the nomination or at Taylor for not supporting him, his actions following the convention do not demonstrate this. A week after the convention, Thomas was appointed to a committee designed to broker an agreement on the aldermanic race in the First Ward. Thomas would not have been appointed to the committee without the First Ward machine's support. In addition, he gave a strong partisan speech at a First Ward meeting right before the election. Thomas, whose legislative career ended in 1886 at the hands of the Taylor-Dixon machine, now found himself a part of it.[62]

[7]

"You Ought Not to Insult the Colored People!":
Final Bids for Office

Politically, the year 1888 would be difficult for Chicago's small African American community. The ward redistricting had split it politically and temporarily diluted its strength in Republican councils. Electorally, it would make no gains. A strong effort to have Thomas named as a Republican county commissioner candidate was rebuffed in an embarrassing manner. Worse, a murder case involving a young African American named Zephyr Davis demonstrated that even a united African American community had limited political power. For Thomas, much of the year would be spent solidifying his new position within the First Ward Republican organization. That organization had remained independent of John A. Logan and his Republican machine. Logan had died in December 1886 but the ward continued its independence from the city and state's new Republican boss, Congressman George R. Davis. The split in the community, the Zephyr Davis case, and the fact that the First Ward Republican machine was independent of the county machine all cost Thomas a Republican nomination for county board in 1888.

The Election of 1888

In early March, Thomas was one of several African Americans, including Edward H. Morris, Hannibal Carter, and James Porter, who attended a meeting of representatives of Republican clubs in Illinois that was held in Springfield. Morris was named to one of two assistant secretary positions at the meeting and then named to be a vice president representing the First Congressional District.[1] Although in late March Thomas lost the South Town clerk nomination to C. H. McCallister, in late April he was elected to serve as a delegate to the state Republican convention. It was the first presidential election year state convention Thomas had attended as a full delegate. In 1880, he had been selected as an alternate delegate by the anti-Grant forces but was not allowed to serve by the pro-Grant party leaders. In 1884, he served as an alternate delegate.

Thomas served as one of six African American delegates from the old Second Ward to attend the county Republican convention. Although the new ward boundaries had been put into effect, Republicans decided in 1888 to select delegates to the county convention based on the old ward boundaries. The Republicans of the old Second Ward showed surprising unity. Only one slate of candidates ran for delegate to the county convention. The Second Ward had 11 delegates to the county convention, and these included Thomas, Robert M. Mitchell, and Hannibal Carter. Six of the 11 delegates would go on to serve as delegates at the May 2 state Republican convention in Springfield. Thomas, Mitchell, and Carter were included among the six. This representation demonstrates the political influence that African Americans had developed in the ward before it was split. Both the old First and the old Third Wards sent all-white delegations, while the old Fourth Ward's delegation included Morris.[2]

Before the county convention met, Chicago's African American leaders called a mass meeting to request the Republican State Convention select an African American to serve as a delegate-at-large to the national convention. Thomas was one of the signers of the call. Lloyd G. Wheeler, John G. Jones, and Ferdinand Barnett did not sign it. Almost every other African American political leader in Chicago signed the call, including Edward H. Morris, Edward H. Wright, George Ecton, C. H. McCallister, Samuel Wright, James E. Jones, John Howard, James Bish, Robert Waring, James Porter, W. C. Phillips, and William Baker. McCallister served as chairman of the meeting, and Edward H. Wright served as secretary. Thomas served on a five-member committee to draft a resolution.

The absence of Wheeler and John G. Jones can be seen in the nonconfrontational nature of the resolution, which was written by Thomas and the committee. The resolution stated, in part, "We, the colored voters of the State of Illinois, in mass meeting assembled, most respectfully petition you to grant to us a delegate-at-large to the national convention." After noting that the African American voter had remained faithful to the Republican Party, the resolution further discussed the difficulties within the community of providing such loyalty without reward. The resolution stated, "[We] have been told by those who, like prodigals, have wandered from us, that we will never receive any representation in this regard from Republicans in this state."[3]

The 1888 state convention was a harmonious affair for the Illinois Republican Party. Morris and J. H. Magee served as assistant secretaries at the convention. The delegates endorsed Judge Walter Q. Gresham for president and a platform that stated that his service as a soldier in the Civil War had won him a warm place in the hearts of the emancipated race. With strong support from Cook County, the convention nominated another Civil War veteran, Joseph "Fighting Joe" Fifer of McLean County, for governor. The convention did not select an African American as a delegate-at-large but J. H. Lott, an African American attorney from rural Paxton, in Ford County, was named as an alternate delegate-at-large. This, apparently, was enough for the African American delegates, as they cancelled a planned convention of their own that was to be held during the regular Republican state convention to press the claims for a delegate-at-large.[4]

Thomas had a quiet convention but continued to cement his alliance with the Taylor-Dixon organization. Membership to most committees at the convention was by congressional district. Delegates from each district selected who they wanted to be represented by on the committees. When the delegates from the First Congressional District met to select its members to the various convention committees, two factions appeared. Thomas sided with the Taylor-Dixon organization and was named as its choice as the district's representative on the committee on credentials. However, the supporters of the Taylor-Dixon organization were in the minority in the First Congressional District and Thomas lost out to Robert M. Mitchell.[5]

Thomas continued his alliance with the Taylor-Dixon organization that summer, when in June he served as a First Ward Delegate to the First Congressional District nominating convention. The First Congressional District consisted of most of Chicago's South Side, plus the south suburban Cook County townships. There were 106 delegates at the convention. The First Ward had 16 delegates, all pledged to Abner Taylor for Congress. Thomas, Edward H. Wright, and Hannibal Carter were three of the delegates from the First Ward. The Second Ward supported Judge Eugene Cary for the position. Also in the race were State Senator William Harper and incumbent Congressman Ransom Dunham. Taylor won the nomination on the second ballot, with Cary coming in second.

The congressional convention also was charged with choosing the district's two delegates and alternate delegates to the Republican National Convention. The First District was about evenly split between city wards and county towns, so it was decided to elect one delegate from the city and one from the county. The convention easily chose former state senator William J. Campbell as a delegate from the county towns. For the city delegate, Thomas nominated his old ally E. R. Bliss, former boss of the Second Ward. The convention, however, in the spirit of party harmony, chose Cary, the runner-up for the congressional nomination.

The African American community, largely based in the city, realized that an African American wouldn't get the coveted delegate position from the city but decided to try to have an African American selected as an alternate delegate. Divisions within the community, however, caused this plan to fail. Three African Americans were nominated. Edward H. Morris nominated James E. Jones, John G. Jones nominated William Baker, and Edward H. Wright nominated Hannibal Carter. On the first ballot, H. H. Kohlsaat of the Third Ward received 42 votes, to Carter's 30, Jones's 27, and Baker's 6. On the second ballot, Kohlsaat received 59 votes and the nomination. Jones received 34 votes on the second ballot, Carter received 9 and Baker received 4. Thomas moved to make the nomination unanimous. Although the second alternate position should have gone to a county resident, the race became one between H. V. Freeman, of Hyde Park Township, and city residents Carter, Jones, and Baker. On the first ballot, Freeman received 54, the minimum needed to win the nomination, while Carter, Baker, and Jones split the remaining vote. In discussing both alternate positions, the *Inter-Ocean* later editorialized, "If only one colored candidate had been named, he probably would have been nominated." Although fairly well represented at the convention, the community still did not have the numbers to succeed if it was not unified. The *Times*, seeking to promote a rift between African Americans and the Republican Party, sniffed that the alternate delegate position was an empty honor anyway.[6]

A week after the First District Congressional Convention, the Republicans held their national convention in Chicago. The Chicago African American community hosted a reception for the African American delegates. Thomas presided over the reception, which was attended by such nationally known African American leaders as Frederick Douglass, John M. Langston, and John R. Lynch. Although Illinois, including its African Americans, was united for Gresham for the presidential nomination, nationally African American leaders supported a number of different candidates. In the end, the convention chose Benjamin Harrison of Indiana to carry the party's standard in the fall campaign.[7]

Thomas entered the fall 1888 campaign as a new member of the First Ward Republican organization but with limited options. The First Ward Republican organization already controlled one of the two legislative seats with George Brokoski, a man termed by the Chicago *Times* as "one of Arthur Dixon's First-ward heelers."[8] George Ecton was the other incumbent legislator and he both remained popular in the African American community and provided geographic balance to the ticket. So, Thomas had no chance to run again for his old seat. The senate seat held by George Gibbs was not up until 1890.

With nowhere to turn, Thomas decided to run for county commissioner. Under the 1887 reorganization of the county commissioner form of government, all fifteen of the county commissioners were elected annually. Ten commissioners came from the city and five from the county. The Republicans reserved three of the city's ten commissioner spots for the South Side where Thomas lived, although once again at the convention all of the city delegates, and not just the South Side delegates, voted on who those three would be. To win the nomination, Thomas needed to unite the African American community behind him, receive the support of the First Ward organization, and win support in the wards that were controlled by the Davis faction of the party. In many respects, he was able to accomplish all three tasks. However, he still did not receive the nomination.

Like the General Assembly, the Cook County Board was held in low esteem by the press. In the mid-1880s, its reputation was at an all-time low. In 1883, a small group of commissioners and other county officials formed a ring to bilk the county. The ring expanded in 1886 after other county commissioners claimed that the ring was hogging all the boodle. However, that year the ring was exposed and seven incumbent commissioners, twelve former commissioners, and several other county officials were indicted. In August 1887, all of the defendants were found guilty in what became known as the Great Boodlers Trial. The result of the Great Boodlers Trial had been to change the way the board was elected.[9]

The board that served immediately after the Great Boodlers trial had acquitted itself well. The *Tribune* editorialized, "There never has been a better municipal board in this city and county." Of the ten city members on the board, nine were Republican and one Democrat. The Democrat, Tom Brenan, had been elected with Republican support in 1887.[10]

Following the socialist defeat in the spring 1887 city elections, the local Democratic Party had rebounded. The socialists would not be a factor in the 1888 fall election. The Union Labor Party nominated an African American, R. S. Bryan, to run for state representative in the Third Legislative District but, unlike the party's nominations of African Americans as candidates in 1886, this did not cause a stir in the mainstream papers.[11]

In 1888, Congressman George Davis led the countywide Republican machine. Davis was angling to solidify his base in Cook County in hopes of receiving the 1891 legislative election to the U.S. Senate. Incumbent coroner Henry Hertz was a member of this machine. One Republican organization that was independent of Davis was the First Ward Taylor-Dixon organization. Although the two First Ward leaders did not necessarily oppose Davis's plan for a county slate, Davis did not trust their independence. He sought to oust

Dixon as First Ward committeeman by running his ally, former alderman George Mueller.[12]

Republican primaries were held for the county convention on September 7, with the convention held the next day. A total of 349 delegates were to be selected for the convention. The *Tribune* predicted a harmonious convention. With all of the countywide offices up for election and most of the county board seats held by Republicans, Davis wanted to put together a ticket that consisted only of the incumbents.[13]

On primary election day, the Davis slate of delegates won most of the city but lost in the First Ward, where the Taylor-Dixon organization elected a slate of sixteen delegates. The election was boisterous, with fifteen policemen needed to control the single polling place. As noted above, the Taylor-Dixon machine was fighting to keep Dixon as ward committeeman. It claimed to be undecided for other county offices. Among those elected as delegates from the First Ward were Taylor, Dixon, and Brokoski. African Americans on the First Ward slate included Thomas, Carter, McCallister, and John Howard.

Several other African Americans were selected as delegates from the other wards, including J. E. Bish and Isaac Rivers from the Second Ward and Morris and Phillips from the Third Ward. Edward H. Wright is not listed in any of the papers and yet he apparently attended the convention as a delegate. John G. Jones was a delegate from the Fourth Ward. The *Times* would report that there was a total of thirteen African American delegates at the convention.[14]

The convention was called to order at 10:30 A.M., September 8, at the Madison Street Theater. Gen. H. H. Thomas served as chairman of the convention, and Edward H. Morris served as one of the secretaries. As the *Tribune* predicted, the convention was mostly harmonious. There were no credentials battles and all incumbent countywide officers were renominated, including Hertz, who won renomination as coroner. However, it was on the Hertz nomination, and in its spillover effects on the commissionership nominations, that the major fight of the convention occurred.[15]

The forty-one-year-old Hertz was a native of Copenhagen, Denmark. A member of the Davis faction, he had served as West Town clerk and had held patronage positions in the county recorder's office before being elected coroner in 1884. In that election, he led the Republican ticket by 2,000 votes. Although the *Tribune* insinuated he had personally profited from the position of coroner, for the most part it appears he had done a good job in that office. For the African American community, however, Hertz was the enemy. The reason was a seventeen-year-old African American named Zephyr Davis.[16]

On February 28, 1888, Davis was arrested and accused of hacking to death co-worker Maggie Gaughan the previous day. Gaughan was a fourteen-year-old Irish American girl, and Davis was her supervisor at Greene's Boot Heel Factory at 1319 South State Street, on the edge of the levee district. Within three months of his capture, Davis was hanged for the murder. Davis pleaded guilty to the murder and no one doubted that guilt. For the most part, Chicago's African American community did not come to his defense.

However, the African American community was outraged following the actions of the coroner's jury, which met shortly after Davis's capture. The duty of the jury was to determine the cause of death and whether or not a crime had been committed. During questioning of John Greene, owner of the factory where both Davis and Gaughan worked, Deputy Coroner W. E. Kent, a Fifth Ward Republican politician, criticized the idea of having African American supervisors in places where white girls work. The jury determined that Gaughan had been murdered and that Davis should be held for the crime. But, influenced by Kent, the jury added to its official decision a criticism of Greene for employing African American and white labor, both male and female, side by side. The African American community could not abide by such an overtly racist decision or its implications. When Hertz refused to fire or punish Kent, it vented its frustrations on him.[17]

Immediately following the coroner jury's verdict, a delegation of leading African Americans visited Hertz to complain about the decision and Kent's role in it. It is not known if Thomas attended this meeting, but it is probable that John G. Jones was one of the leaders. Hertz brought Kent to the meeting. Kent stated that he did not think the jury intended to insult the African American community. Hertz chose to support Kent, and the African American leaders left the meeting dissatisfied. On March 6, Jones conducted an indignation rally. Again, it is not certain if Thomas attended the meeting. Newspaper accounts do place Lloyd G. Wheeler, Hannibal Carter, and Edward H. Morris there. At the rally, participants passed a resolution calling for Hertz to fire Kent and then resign himself. The resolution also condemned the coroner jury's verdict as a "vicious, slanderous and wholly unwarranted attack on a law abiding class of citizens."[18]

Davis was hanged on May 12, 1888, inside the Cook County jail in front of a fairly large crowd that included a sheriff's jury, which was a specially selected panel who had the duty to attest that Davis had been executed.[19] The four months in between the execution and the Republican County convention had not cooled the resentment of African American leaders toward Hertz. It was a blinding anger they held toward him, and one that would cost Thomas.

When Hertz's name was placed in nomination, the African American delegates immediately protested. Morris, Wright, and Carter led the charge, with Carter stating that if Hertz was nominated "the colored voters would cut him from soda to hock." Chairman H. H. Thomas was able to quiet the protests for a moment, until John W. E. Thomas mounted a chair and announced, "You ought not to insult the colored people by nominating Hertz." Protests continued. A delegate from suburban Evanston nominated E. L. Lewis of that city for coroner. Carter seconded the motion and other African American delegates spoke on his behalf. Lewis received 9 of the 16 votes of the First Ward and 4 of the 16 votes of the Second Ward. Overall, however, Hertz easily defeated him, 305 to 46. When a delegate moved to make the vote unanimous, the African American delegates protested. Wright stated, "As long as I have one vote this nomination will not be made unanimous." With that, the motion was withdrawn.[20]

The African American delegates were still in an angry mood when it came time for the nominations for county commissioner. As noted above, party leader George Davis wanted to select a ticket that included all incumbents. Of the ten incumbent county commissioners from the city that were up for office, nine were Republican. The lone Democrat was Tom Brenan. With the boodle scandal in the very recent past and with the way the board had conducted itself, Davis wanted to nominate the entire slate of incumbents, including Brenan. Delegate W. S. Elliot made a motion to nominate all ten incumbents. Speaking on the motion, delegate Pliny Smith noted that the current board had resolved the financial problems caused by the boodlers. Because of this, he argued that the entire board should be renominated and reelected, even though one of the members was a Democrat. The resolution was immediately opposed by several delegates.

Charles Andrews, an African American from the Twenty-first Ward, moved to amend the resolution to insert Thomas's name in place of Brenan's. At least two other names were also proposed to be exchanged for Brenan's. Then Fred Wilke, a white ally of Hertz, seconded the nomination of Thomas. Philip Knopf, a white committeeman from the Sixteenth Ward and another Hertz ally, also strongly supported Thomas. Wright took the floor on behalf of Thomas and asked, "Isn't a colored man as good as a Democrat?" Despite this, two other names were proposed by delegates as well. Abner Taylor then took the floor on behalf of Thomas, declaring, "The Constitution gave the colored man the same right as the white man, and I believe a colored man has more rights than a Democrat in a Republican convention. Therefore, I hope the motion to substitute the name of Mr. Thomas, whom I know to be an honest man, will prevail."

With so many motions and proposed amendments, the chairman lost control of the convention. After a half an hour delay, the chair called for a vote on a motion to substitute Henry Peterson to replace Tom Brenan. That motion failed 89 to 222. He then called an amendment motion to substitute John W. E. Thomas to replace Brenan. That motion also failed, by a close vote of 123 to 139. After another lengthy delay, the original motion to endorse all of the commissioners, including Brenan, was put to a vote. That motion passed 171 to 91. The entire First Ward Delegation voted against it. For the second time at the convention, the African American delegates had lost a crucial battle.[21]

The *Tribune* would later state that African Americans could have received a nomination if someone other than Thomas had been their candidate, stating that Thomas's connections with the police court "had given him an unenviable notoriety." While this is a telling comment on the low regard with which police court lawyers were held, it is not a true statement on why an African American did not receive a place on the ticket. In hindsight, it appears that they could have won the fight to nominate Thomas as a commissioner. Thomas had a strong base in the First Ward, and the African American leaders had a strong case to make both in nominating an African American and in not nominating a Democrat. More importantly, it seems that Hertz, a member of the George Davis alliance, was seeking to patch the rift with the African American community by having his allies, Wilke and Knopf, work for the Thomas nomination. As the *Inter-Ocean* noted in an editorial, "Many delegates who voted for Hertz were glad to placate this animosity by voting for the Honorable J. W. E. Thomas for county commissioner in place of Brenan, a Democrat who had been elected with Republican votes a year ago." Contrary to the *Tribune*'s denigrating Thomas as a disreputable police court lawyer, it was probably principle that cost Thomas the nomination. Thomas and his supporters did not appear to be interested in working out a deal with Hertz, even though such a deal was apparently offered. Instead, they would oppose Hertz all the way through the general election. Thomas and the other African American delegates could not be bought for a commissionership nomination.[22]

The African American community, at least those of a political bent, did not forget the efforts of the African American delegates at the convention. The Eighteenth Ward Colored Harrison and Morton Republican Club passed a resolution of support for the actions of the African American delegates at the Republican convention, citing the insult the community had received by Hertz and Kent as ample justification for opposing Hertz's renomination. The John A. Logan Second Ward Colored Republican Club met two days after the convention, and members expressed their dissatisfaction over the both the renomination of Hertz and the nomination of Brenan over Thomas. In the First Ward, African American voters formed two new campaign clubs.

The first was the Arthur Dixon Club, named after the ward's committeeman. The second club, probably containing many of the same members as the first club, was named the John W. E. Thomas First Ward Republican Club. This was high praise indeed for Thomas. He did not hold an office and had just lost a nomination fight for commissioner. However, his community recognized his leadership. Hannibal Carter served as president and Edward H. Wright served as treasurer.[23]

Shortly after the convention, the newspapers reported that Brenan had turned down the nomination. This seemingly opened up the door for Thomas. The *Times* reported that at least three ethnic groups had candidates they wished to have replace Brenan. It said that Thomas was the choice of the African American community. However, within a day or two of the convention, all of the newspapers reported that while the Republican Central Committee would select an African American to replace Brenan if he stepped down, that person would be Ferdinand Barnett. Barnett's strength over Thomas was that he did not belong to any faction or organization within the Republican Party. As such, he had not alienated the Davis-controlled central committee, which would make the choice on who would replace Brenan on the ticket. Thomas, of course, belonged to the First Ward Republican organization, which was independent of Davis. In the end, however, Brenan accepted the Republican nomination, although his acceptance did not come until after he had been renominated by the Democrats.[24]

With Brenan's acceptance of the nomination, the only African American to appear on the ballot for the two major parties was George Ecton, who ran for reelection to the Third Legislative District house seat. Although Morris was mentioned as a possible candidate and the John A. Logan Second Ward Colored Republican Club actually endorsed J. E. Bish for the legislature, Ecton had no difficulty being renominated. There was a split in the district between the pro-Davis faction and the anti-Davis faction, but Ecton and the African American community were not drawn into the conflict. The result of the split was that each faction conducted a separate primary legislative election and a separate legislative convention. Stephen A. Douglas Jr. led the pro-Davis faction, and Marcus Farwell led the anti-Davis faction. The Dixon-Taylor organization in the First Ward was part of the anti-Davis faction. That faction conducted its primary first, and Ecton and Brokoski were easily reelected and then nominated at the convention. The pro-Davis faction nominated Ecton and Douglas. The county Republican campaign committee had to resolve the dispute. It asked Douglas to withdraw his candidacy, which he did. Although the Democrats would nominate two candidates to make a contest of the district, the resolution of the dispute in the Republican ranks guaranteed Brokoski's and Ecton's reelection.[25]

Thomas spent the campaign working for the entire Republican ticket, with the exception of Hertz for coroner. His opposition to Hertz marked the only time he was ever officially recorded as bolting from the Republican Party, and it had nothing to do with his own personal gain or loss, but came about because of the insult to the African American community of having Hertz on the ticket. In going against Hertz, Thomas was in accord with most of the African American community. In early October, the Third Ward Independent Colored Republican Club met and endorsed the entire Republican ticket, except for Hertz and Brenan. On October 15, African American Republicans met to denounce Hertz. Morris presided over the meeting and Wright served as secretary. An estimated two thousand African Americans attended it. Even Thomas remained outraged against Hertz. In addressing the meeting, he stated that in the past African Americans had tamely submitted to any and all wrongs or given the impression that they could be bought off. He said that day was past and it was time to discipline the Republican Party a little. The meeting endorsed the Republican ticket, except for Hertz. Other speakers included Morris, Carter, Isaac Rivers, E. R. Bliss, and Rev. J. M. Henderson. On Election Day, Hertz's vote totals would be much lower than the rest of the Republican county ticket in the First and Second Wards.[26]

Still, although not supporting Hertz, the African American community was not going to leave the Republican Party. In August, the *Western Appeal* noted that the Cook County Colored Democrat Club had only nine members, all of them officers. Of the club, it wrote, "There are no privates. Only nine Colored Democratic votes will be cast in November." Bryan, the African American United Labor candidate for state representative, said he entered the race because of the insults the community had received at the Republican county convention. He lost the race, although he received a respectable 1,527 votes, with most of his votes coming from the First Ward. Perennial candidate John Howard ran as an independent for county board from the city district but received only 913 votes out of the more than 170,000 votes cast in the city district.[27]

Perhaps the highlight of the fall campaign for Thomas came on November 3, when he shared the stage with Joe Fifer, the Republican candidate for governor. Fifer chose to give his final speech of the campaign in front of the African American Republicans of the First Ward, meaning it was probably the John W. E. Thomas First Ward Republican Club. Thomas and Carter both gave partisan Republican speeches before Fifer spoke. Fifer then spoke about Lincoln and the Republican Party freeing the slaves, the voting problems African Americans faced in the South and the need for protectionism.

At one point during his talk, Fifer received an invitation asking him to go to a Republican rally in nearby Hyde Park after he was finished speaking. Instead, Fifer stated that was going to "wind up my campaign right here with my colored fellow-citizens. And I am not going to make another speech until I am elected governor of Illinois."[28]

With that, all that remained was for the voters to go to the polls. For African Americans and Republicans the results were mixed. Ecton, the only African American on the Republican ticket, easily won reelection and received the most votes in the Third District. Brokoski and Democrat William Buckley also were elected. At the national level, Benjamin Harrison won election as president, winning Illinois in the process, and Fifer won election as governor. In Cook County, the entire Republican countywide ticket won, including Hertz, who led the ticket. Despite the success of the countywide ticket, eight of the ten Democratic candidates won the county board seats from the city. Brenan, endorsed by both parties, received the highest number of votes. Had Thomas been nominated by the Republicans, he most likely would have lost in the fall election.[29]

The Election of 1890

Following the 1888 election, Thomas and other leaders of the African American community realized that if they were to win nomination for office, they had to be a part of the inner workings of the party. In the 1870s, this is how the community had gotten started in electoral politics, when Thomas, Phillips, and others had participated in Second Ward Republican politics. In the 1880s, Robert M. Mitchell took this even further, serving as the Second Ward's representative on the city central committee and becoming president of the Second Ward Republican Club. At the state level, James Magee of Metropolis served on the state central committee from 1882 to 1884.

Redistricting, however, split the community's base. The Second Ward lost many of its African American leaders and saw its percentage of the population in the ward decrease. After spring 1889, Mitchell no longer served as Second Ward representative to the city central committee, as he no longer lived in the Second Ward. Mitchell, Thomas, and other leaders of the community, such as C. H. McCallister and John Howard, found themselves in the First Ward, which had an entrenched political machine. A similar situation existed in the Third Ward, where Edward H. Morris resided. New Republican power brokers of the county, such as George Davis, William Lorimer, and Henry Hertz, did not come from Chicago's South Side, meaning they did not have a large African American constituency that they had to answer to. They also did not try to appeal to the African American community like John A. Logan had before his death in December 1886. So, by 1889, African Americans were scarce as Republican decision makers in Cook County and the state.

Thomas had pulled back from Second Ward club politics in the mid-1880s. By 1889, not holding an elective office and finding himself a part of a new party organization, Thomas returned to active participation at the ward level. When the First Ward organization opposed the location of its precinct polling place for the spring 1889 Republican primary, Thomas served as one of twelve club members named to a committee to protest to the decision. He presided over at least one ward meeting and spoke at several others. He served on a five-man committee to select the ward's delegates to attend the county convention, on the seven-member First Ward campaign committee, and as a First Ward delegate to both the South Town Republican convention and the city Republican convention. As a delegate to the city convention, he also was a delegate to the judicial convention, charged with selecting candidates for the bench. The South Town delegation included former United Labor Party house candidate R. S. Bryan, while the First Ward delegation to the city convention included Robert M. Mitchell, Hannibal Carter, and John Howard. Mitchell actually almost lost the race for delegate when a number of African Americans, upset by remarks he purportedly made to the *Chicago Times*, scratched his name off the ballot in favor of Edward H. Wright.[30]

At the Republican city convention, delegates nominated Mayor John Roche for a second term. The convention also nominated Samuel Raymond for city treasurer. Raymond defeated Hertz ally Fred Wilke for the nomination. Every African American delegate voted against Wilke. African Americans were still letting their anger over the Zephyr Davis case be known and taking it out on anyone associated with Hertz.[31]

At the South Town Republican convention, three of the four incumbent officers were renominated, including C. H. McCallister for town clerk. Delegates replaced incumbent collector George Bass with Frank P. Barnard. Thomas placed McCallister's name in nomination, and he was chosen without opposition.[32]

On March 10, 1888, Thomas, along with H. J. Mitchell, Hannibal Carter, John T. Thomas, and George Shaw formed the Logan Hall Association, an African American political club whose mission was to "advance the interest, success, and perpetuate the Republican Party in its great American idea of human liberty." By spring of 1889 the club had enough influence that the Democratic *Chicago Times* felt the need to poke fun at it and its support of First Ward alderman Arthur Dixon for reelection.[33]

At the city level, 1889 proved to be a mixed year for the Republicans. They lost all the city offices, including mayor, by wide margins. They fared better on the lower part of the ticket. Arthur Dixon won reelection to a two-year term as alderman, defeating Democrat Jim Appleton in a race where two incumbents were pitted against each other because of redistricting. The entire South Town Republican ticket also won. The *Inter-Ocean* noted that the Republicans had had a lock on the South Town offices for a while and editorialized, "Whether the Assessor was Drake or De Young, the Supervisor Oldenburg or Dugan, the Clerk McAllister or Thomas, it was all the same, and general satisfaction has been given."[34]

The fall 1889 elections would continue to show the balance between the two parties in Cook County. There were only four countywide offices up for election: two judgeships, the presidency of the county board, and Cook County recorder of deeds. The judicial candidates, one Democrat and one Republican, ran unopposed. Democrats captured the most important office, the county board presidency, while Republicans won the recorder's office. Democrats again captured eight of the ten city county board seats from the city district, while Republicans won two seats from the city and all five from the county district.[35]

African Americans were again unable to make gains in running for elective office. African Americans had touted W. C. Phillips, who had worked in the Cook County Recorder of Deeds office for several years, for the recorder's job, but his name was not placed in nomination at the Republican county convention. Instead, Phillips became a contender for county board. However, the outcome for Phillips was the same as it had been for Thomas in 1888. Again, the South Side was allotted three of the ten city nominations, but unlike previous years the convention let the South Side delegates caucus to choose their own candidates, rather than have all the city delegates vote on the South Side representatives. This change would have helped Thomas in 1888 because of the stronger African American influence on the South Side than in the city as a whole. Approximately 11,300 of the city's 15,000 African Americans lived in the wards of the South Side at a time when the city's population had topped the one million mark.[36] The effect of the change on Phillips's chances in 1889 was diluted, however, because during the previous year the city had annexed several outlying townships, including Hyde Park and Lake on the South Side. The annexation increased the population and geographic size of the South Side area and made the relative strength of the South Side African American community that much smaller. It also affected geographic balance for the ticket. George Spencer, one of the three South Side nominees, for example, was an incumbent county board member from Hyde Park. He had been elected from the county district in 1888 but was nominated in 1889 from the city district, due to the annexation of Hyde Park.

Thomas attended the county convention, but it was John Howard who repeated the complaint of unrewarded loyalty. "You want our votes on election day and you have got to listen to us now. We have 1,200 votes in the First, 800 in the Second and 600 in the Third Ward, and you want all of those on election day. Now you had better look out," Howard told the convention. Despite the protests, African American voters again fell in line on Election Day.[37]

Thomas continued to be a loyal First Ward Republican in the spring of 1890, serving on a First Ward committee to find a candidate for alderman. Dixon had few troubles winning election as alderman as a Republican but the other aldermanic seat in the ward had traditionally gone Democrat and few Republicans were willing to run for it. For example, Thomas's name was mentioned for the Republican nomination but he turned down the chance at the ward convention. The delegates eventually selected businessman J. Frank Lawrence who, after giving the matter some thought, turned down the nomination. Several other Republicans were approached, but they too turned down the nomination. The party finally settled on hotelier John T. Major, who was badly beaten by his Democratic opponent.[38]

Thomas again served as a First Ward delegate to the city and town conventions. At the town convention, Republicans split over the renomination of four-term assessor B. R. De Young. Arthur Dixon of the First Ward Taylor-Dixon machine allied with Senator George Gibbs of the Second Ward to oppose De Young, as the First Ward machine sought to gain more influence over the South Side and to reduce possible opposition to Congressman Taylor. After a hotly divided convention, South Town Republicans replaced three of the four incumbents on the ticket, including De Young. Clerk C. H. McCallister was the only Republican renominated. His nomination was opposed by four African Americans, including J. E. Bish, now the leader of the African Americans of the Second Ward. With the support of the entire First Ward and its allies, however, McCallister's was the one nomination that was assured. Thomas served on the South Town campaign committee, serving as one of three First Ward representatives. However, that spring proved to be a Democratic year and the splits in the party resulted in the complete defeat of the Republican South Town ticket. The defeat of McCallister meant that for the first time in six years, an African American was not elected as South Town clerk.[39]

In June, Thomas again attended the Republican state convention but it was Morris and Wright who made the biggest splash there, when they were able to have Morris placed on the state central committee. The state central committee ran the party. Its members were elected by congressional district every two years at the state convention. However, as Morris noted, "There were not enough colored people in any one Congressional district to entitle the colored people of Illinois to a representation on the state central committee."

Morris had articulated the problem faced by the African American community in Chicago and the state since given the right to vote. In an era of ethnic politics, a balanced ticket often meant a ticket balanced ethnically, and African Americans often did not have the numbers to muscle their way to political positions. It took political skill and work to achieve political success. Thomas and others had laid the groundwork following the passage of the Fifteenth Amendment by becoming involved in ward organizations and getting out the vote. In the 1880s, Thomas worked to maximize the strength of the community by keeping it loyal to the Republican Party. However, smart politics was needed as well. Here, Morris and Wright demonstrated that skill.

At the convention, Morris moved that in addition to having one committeeman per congressional district, the party should create two committeemen-at-large positions. His resolution passed. Immediately after passage of the resolution, Wright nominated Morris for one of the two positions. The *Times* reported "There was loud laughter at Messrs. Morris' and Wright's little scheme, but the convention had gone too far to recede." A. M. "Long" Jones, a very popular and powerful white politician in the state who had lost favor within his own congressional district, was nominated for the other position. Morris and Wright knew this would occur, making the idea of two committeemen-at-large positions more acceptable to the convention. Both Morris and Jones were then elected by the delegates to the two positions. With his nomination, Morris, who was a friend and ally of Thomas, eclipsed Thomas as the most prominent African American politician in the city and the state and certainly as the best political strategist.[40]

Thomas remained a force to be reckoned with, however. He was a member of the Cook County Republican League Campaign Committee and still active in both ward politics and the Logan Hall Association. Tragedy again struck Thomas that summer when on July 19 his six-month old daughter Martha died at his home at 444 S. Clark Street after a short illness. Despite this tragedy, that fall Thomas continued his political efforts, making one final bid for the legislature. This time, he ran for a state senate seat.[41]

The Third Legislative District had three Republican incumbents coming into the 1890 election. George Gibbs of the Second Ward, the senator elected in 1886, would seek renomination. He had been nominated in 1886 with the support of the Taylor-Dixon First Ward machine but entered the renomination fight unsure of continued support. He also could not rely on the support of his own ward, where he had made enemies of E. G. Keith, the new Second Ward Republican boss. F. A. Brokoski, although still a valued member of the First Ward machine, decided not to seek renomination to the house. George Ecton also did not seek renomination in 1890, having moved out of the district in the summer of 1889.[42]

Thomas, on the other hand, made it known early that he wanted to be nominated for the senate, which meant challenging Gibbs. To win, he would need the strong backing of the First Ward organization that he now belonged to and of the African American community. While most of the papers thought he would not have much of a chance for the position, the *Times* thought he would, calling him the "well-known colored disciple of Republicanism."[43]

The legislative elections in the Third District began on a mixed note. The rift in the party in 1888, which had led to rival senatorial committees for the Third District, had not completely healed. On September 3, the faction opposed to the regular organization issued a call for the Third District Senatorial Committee to conduct a primary election on September 12. However, under the election law, the call was issued too late to conduct a primary on that day, so the call had to be retracted. Still, the *Inter-Ocean* noted the potential for catastrophe for the party if the split were to reoccur.[44]

Thomas was now an essential member of the Taylor-Dixon First Ward organization. At a First Ward Republican meeting in September, Dixon, D. W. Nickerson, and Brokoski sought to appoint a committee to select a slate of delegates for the county convention. The five-person committee was to include Thomas. In this endeavor, Dixon and his allies were unsuccessful, with the majority of club favoring a different way to select delegates. Thomas wound up not being selected as a delegate to the county convention. Despite this, the convention selected Thomas as the First Ward member of the Republican Party County Central Committee, a selection that could not have occurred without Dixon's support. With the Thomas selection, the African American community was represented by Morris on the state central committee and Thomas on the county central committee.[45]

Among the delegates to the county Republican convention were Wright for the First Ward, H. J. Mitchell from the Second Ward, and Morris and Robert Waring from the Third Ward. At the convention William Lorimer, the "Blond Boss" from the West Side, sought the party's nomination for county clerk. One of Lorimer's allies was Hertz, who had higher aspirations than coroner. In a few short years, Lorimer would become the Republican boss of Chicago, but he lost the clerk nomination to Henry Wulff. He was selected as the county committeeman from the Seventh Ward, meaning both Lorimer and Thomas served on the same central committee.[46]

The delegates also selected county commissioner candidates. As in 1889, the city delegates divided up the candidates for county commissioner from the city by town, with North Town allotted two candidates, South Town three, and West Town five. Each section of the city was allowed to vote for its own candidates and then those candidates were to be ratified by the convention as a whole. Franklin Denison, an African American attorney from the Second Ward, tried for one of the nominations, but came in fourth out of eight candidates. He received 65 votes, while the three winning candidates received 99, 88 and 83 votes.[47]

With the county convention over, Thomas turned his attention to the Third District legislative nominations. In early September, the Democrats nominated Lawrence Boyle for the senate, and Sol Van Praag and S. D. May for the house. Boyle and May were attorneys and Van Praag a saloon keeper and First Ward politician who was virulently opposed by both the Republican and the Democratic newspapers. During the course of the campaign, there was a shooting due to a confrontation that started in front of Van Praag's saloon and Van Praag was charged with perjury for allegedly inducing men to swear to bogus papers of citizenship. Republican papers had a field day with his candidacy and with the nominations of several other Democrats who were also saloon keepers.[48]

The Third District Republican Convention was scheduled for October 21, the day after the primaries. Both factions issued the call for the convention. By issuing a joint call, it meant that the two factions had agreed on a time for the election, polling places, and judges and clerks for each polling place. Among the potential candidates for the senate spot were Gibbs, Douglas, Alderman Dixon, Second Ward resident and attorney George Bass, attorney Pliny Smith, D. V. Parrington, and Thomas.[49]

Then, as in 1888, dissension struck within the party. The *Times* reported that Douglas thought he had the support of Abner Taylor for the state senate. According to the *Times*, Douglas had been considering a run for Congress against Taylor, but withdrew when Taylor promised him support for the senate nomination. When it appeared that Taylor would not deliver his support, an angry Douglas threatened to run as an independent against Taylor for Congress. The *Times* further stated that when the Third District committee met to discuss the primary and convention, it locked out Douglas's sole representative on the committee because he was intoxicated. The *Times* later said that representative was Hannibal Carter, who would play a major role in the Third District election.[50]

By primary election day, the only candidates who appeared still interested in the senate nomination were Gibbs, Bass, and Thomas. The *Tribune* predicted before the primary that Bass would probably be the nominee and that Thomas would probably have to settle for a nomination to the house. In one of the few times the *Tribune* complimented Thomas late in his career, the paper wrote, "Mr. Thomas will probably be satisfied with the House nomination as a representative of the colored people. He certainly ought to be. He served acceptably before in the House."[51]

Dixon ran a slate of delegate candidates in the First Ward, and E. G. Keith did the same in the Second Ward, where he was boss. Both slates won. The *Times* reported that the two power brokers had cut a deal and would select the legislative ticket. The paper stated that this meant that either Bass or Dixon would succeed Gibbs in the senate and the race for the first house nomination would be between J. C. Wallace and W. H. King, both of the First Ward. For the second nomination, which by now was supposed to go to an African American, it mentioned Hannibal Carter or a William Goggins, both of the Third Ward. The *Tribune* predicted that Bass would receive the senate nomination and that Morris and Thomas would be the two leading candidates for the second house nomination. Reverting to style, the *Tribune* wrote that both were objectionable and suggested Robert M. Mitchell as a better candidate than either Thomas or Morris. The *Inter-Ocean* also saw Bass as the probable senate nominee. However, it mentioned that Thomas had done well at the polls, implying that either Thomas ran a slate of candidates for delegate on Election Day or he ran with the support of the First Ward slate. In any event, the *Inter-Ocean*, like the *Tribune* earlier, said Thomas was likely to be the house nominee. Nothing indicates, however, that Thomas ever sought anything but the senate nomination, and he and Morris were probably allies and not competitors.[52]

At the convention, Thomas lost the nomination to Bass on the second ballot. On the first ballot, Thomas received votes from the First Ward, but Bass was stronger in the Second, which was never the same after the redistricting. Dixon flipped the First Ward to Bass on the second ballot, and Bass won nomination, receiving 22 votes to 9 for Thomas and 7 for Addison Ballard, the former Second Ward alderman. For the house, Wallace received the first nomination, defeating King 22 to 15. Although vote totals by ward were not printed in the papers, more than likely Wallace was Dixon's choice. Morris, who lived in the Third Ward, received the second nomination. His nomination came after Keith delivered a speech complaining about how African Americans were being treated and stating that they should have a spot on the ticket. As an African American was going to receive a place on the ticket anyway, it appears that Keith, who had torpedoed Thomas's bid for the Senate nomination, was doing a bit of grandstanding for his Second Ward African American constituents.[53]

Thomas had the support of a united African American community but fell victim to ward politics. Ward bosses Taylor and Dixon placed Taylor's needs for renomination to Congress ahead of Thomas's efforts for the state senate. Thomas also was probably hurt in his efforts to seek a senate nomination by geography, in that for the First Ward to have had the two top positions, that of U.S. congressman and state senator, would have been difficult to accept by the other wards. The legislative ticket consisted of a senate candidate from the Second Ward and house candidates from the First and Third Wards, so it was geographically balanced. Finally, a race for state senate was a large step up for an African American candidate. Unlike a state representative race, where three candidates were elected, or a county commissioner race, where ten candidates ran as part of a citywide slate, a state senate race represented a one-on-one campaign. Republican delegates may not have been willing to risk losing a state senate race by nominating an African American. Not until 1924 would an African American be elected state senator in Illinois.

Thomas did not seem upset at the party by his failure to be nominated for the state senate. One week after the convention, both Thomas and Morris were featured speakers at a meeting of the Young Men's Logan Club that was held to ratify the Republican ticket. On October 31 Thomas joined Bass, Morris, and other Republican candidates in giving campaign speeches to the Anchor Line "longshoremen."[54] In addition, when the *Daily News* printed an article that questioned African American support for the Republican ticket, Thomas ally J. E. Bish responded with a letter to the *Tribune* that, while referencing the disappointment in the community at Thomas's not being nominated, declared the community's support for the Republican Party. "While it is a fact that we were not overly enthusiastic for some of the Republican nominees, while we feel we have not been fairly treated by the party, we are going to (so far as lies in our power) elect the ticket . . . The party has selected Mr. George Bass of our ward as state senator and we will elect him," Bish wrote.[55]

By not being nominated, at least Thomas avoided what would have been the most vicious campaign of his career. The partisan press of the time had a field day attacking the legislative candidates. The Republican press specifically lambasted Van Praag, who eventually was indicted for perjury related to voter fraud. The *Evening Journal* wrote, "The Democratic candidates for the Legislature are generally as bad men as could be picked out for any office of place." The Democratic press returned the favor against the Republican nominees; however, they reserved their most venomous attacks for Morris. The *Times* wrote, "The notorious negro Edward H. Morris was yesterday nominated by the Republicans in the Third District. Nearly everybody in Chicago knows Morris well enough to be quite sure that he will not have the support of decent people." Both the *Times* and the *Herald* accused Morris's mother of running houses of "an unsavory character." The *Evening Post* called him "a middle-colored levee tough."[56]

The Republican papers, of course, supported Morris, especially the *Evening Journal*. It called his nomination "a good piece of work" and predicted that he would be an "efficient, influential and honest member of the Legislature." Right before the election, it wrote that his style "reminds elderly men of Fred Douglass's forty years ago." While the *Tribune* appeared a little cooler toward the Morris candidacy, it did write an article refuting the charges made by the Democrats against Morris's mother. The *Inter-Ocean* initially wrote that the nominations of Morris and Wallace would not produce a great deal of enthusiasm or materially strengthen the ticket, but it too increased its support later in the campaign.[57]

Race played a role in the 1890 election, in large measure because the Democratic Party was attempting to pry the African American vote away from the Republicans. In September, six African Americans were charged with illegally registering to vote. They were initially defended by Ferdinand Barnett and E. R. Bliss. Later, according to the *Inter-Ocean*, H. J. Mitchell and former Illinois governor John Hamilton determined that the charges of voter registration fraud were part of a Democratic Party plan to discredit the Republican Party. The Democrat press made a similar claim of a Republican conspiracy against Sol Van Praag. In October, the *Conservator* wrote an editorial against Republican country treasurer candidate Louis Hutt, accusing him of having a bad attitude toward African Americans. Thomas defended Hutt, stating that "a better friend to the Colored people never ran for office." On November 2, the *Times* printed an appeal from LeRoy Hayes that urged the African American community to vote for Democrat Roger Sullivan over Republican Tom Sennott for probate court clerk, calling Sennott an "enemy of the colored race." Finally, late in the campaign, Hannibal Carter ran as an independent Republican candidate for one of the Third District state representative seats.[58]

The Carter candidacy split the African American vote and helped the Democrats. Although Bass easily won election to the senate, Carter's independent house campaign drew a surprisingly strong 1,344½ votes. Van Praag received the highest number of votes, with 6,941½, followed by Morris with 6,336½ and May with 5,706½. Wallace came in fourth with 5,430½, meaning May beat him out for the third legislative seat by 276 votes.[59] It is safe to assume that a good number of Carter's 1,344½ votes would have gone to the

Republican Wallace if Carter had not been in the race, so Carter probably cost the Republicans a second seat in the district.

Worse for the Republicans, Wallace's defeat may have cost them a U.S. Senate seat. The 1890 election resulted in an evenly divided legislature that elected Democrat John M. Palmer to the Senate after 154 ballots. Had Wallace been elected, it might have been possible for the Republicans to win that Senate seat.[60]

The 1890 election was split in Cook County, with Democrats winning three of the contested countywide offices and Republicans winning three. The Republican candidates that the *Times* had said had problems with the African American community both lost. Louis Hutt lost the county treasurer position to Charles Kern and Thomas Sennott lost the probate court clerk's position to Roger Sullivan. Although the papers of the day supported their party's candidates, that support was tepid. The *Inter-Ocean* described the Republican county candidates as a disappointment and described the county ticket as "made up almost wholly of what is known as practical politicians." Public opinion reflected this dissatisfaction with the two parties as well. In September, a group of wealthy activists who supported "traditional American values," known as the Committee of One Hundred, ran candidates for some county offices. The slate represented a coalition of interests, including the British American Council, the Prohibition Party and the Patriotic Order Sons of America. One of their nominees was Lloyd G. Wheeler who ran for probate court clerk. Wheeler received 12,039 votes in a race where Sullivan defeated Sennott 72,471 to 66,434.[61]

Where Thomas stood on the Wheeler and Carter candidacies is not certain. Thomas and Carter had worked together in the past but Carter was a member of the Douglas wing of the party and Thomas belonged to the First Ward organization, so it is doubtful Thomas would have supported Carter. It is also unlikely that Thomas would have supported Wheeler, as the two do not appear to have ever been friendly toward each other and Wheeler's third-party candidacy seemed to be based more on wealth than on race.

In any event, these independent candidacies do not appear to have been part of a larger strategy to seek independence from the Republican Party. Indeed, 1890 had seen the emergence of new African American leaders whose loyalty to the Republican Party was deep. These new leaders included Morris, Wright, and Bish. Thomas would continue to play an active role in politics, but the torch was being passed to a new generation of leadership.

[8]

"Forget Personal Grievances": Uniting the Community as Elder Statesman

Throughout his career, Thomas supported the Republican Party in the belief that it offered the best opportunity for African Americans to achieve political equality. Given the small numbers of African Americans in Chicago and Illinois, he saw efforts to divide the African American vote as injurious to the cause of African American equality. Although in the 1880s the Democratic Party in the North made appeals for the African American vote, Thomas never lost sight that the party's southern wing was increasingly enacting discriminatory Jim Crow measures in the South. He recognized that the Republican Party was far from perfect. In the 1880s and 1890s the party appeared to be abandoning the cause of the African American, as seen in the 1883 Supreme Court ruling on the civil rights bill, Republican president Chester Alan Arthur's dealing with white Southerners on patronage questions, and the failure of the Republicans to enact voting right protections and school funding measures for the South.[1] Thomas had often noted the party's failings in its dealings with African Americans at Republican conventions and party caucuses. Despite being a loyal Republican, he himself had suffered defeats at the party's hands, both electorally and in his efforts on behalf of others. In letters to the editor and in public comments, he had proven that he could be highly critical of his party when he thought it was betraying his community or the cause of civil rights.

The Creation of the Afro-American League

With that in mind, it was not surprising that when in 1889, T. Thomas Fortune, an African American journalist from New York, called for a national convention of African Americans to discuss the problems facing the African American community, Thomas supported the idea, even though Fortune was known as an independent in politics and had supported Democratic candidate

Grover Cleveland in the 1888 presidential election. Unlike the 1883 and 1885 state "colored conventions," where it was obvious the convention organizers were seeking to attack the Republican Party, Fortune, despite his political record, appeared to be focused on issues of community self-help, something Thomas could support. In an editorial in his newspaper, the *New York Age*, Fortune described those supporting him as "Afro-American Agitators" who expected their rights and, like their abolitionist predecessors, would not stop until they achieved success. In describing these "agitators," Fortune wrote, "the 'Afro-American Agitator' expects that his rights under the Constitution as amended shall be conceded to him, not grudgingly and in part, but freely and in whole." Thomas qualified as an agitator by this definition.[2]

Fortune was one of three African Americans who called for a national convention to discuss race concerns in 1890. John G. Jones had also called for a convention, as had Washington, D.C., hotelier Perry Carson. All three individuals worked separately on their proposed conventions instead of working together to hold one convention. Ironically, Jones opposed Fortune's convention because he felt "it would divide the colored vote." Despite his stated reason for opposing the Fortune convention, Jones appears to have opposed it because it rivaled his proposed convention and because he felt Fortune had stolen his idea.[3]

Fortune wished to use his convention to create an Afro-American League, which was to be a national umbrella organization composed of state branches. The focus of the league was on the deteriorating conditions in the South, where Jim Crow laws, segregation, and disenfranchisement were occurring. Fortune proposed five measures the league could take to help African Americans. These measures included creating an Afro-American emigration bureau to "scatter the race through the different parts of the country," creating an Afro-American bank, and creating committees to promote legislation favorable to African Americans. He also proposed forming committees to promote technical education and industry in the African American community. Fortune wanted the league to be nonpartisan. These were ideas that Thomas could support.[4]

Although Jones opposed Fortune's convention, most of Chicago's African American political activists, such as Ecton, Bish, Morris, Howard, Baker, Robert M. Mitchell, and H. J. Mitchell supported it. Several of Chicago's African American social leaders did as well, including Dr. Daniel Hale Williams, Dr. C. E. Bentley, and attorney S. Laing Williams. Even Lloyd G. Wheeler, Jones's ally at the Illinois conventions, supported the Fortune convention, and Ferdinand Barnett signed the initial call. Fortune would later write that Jones appeared to be the only African American in the city who opposed the League convention.[5]

Fortune was extremely critical of Jones. He arrived in Chicago the week before the convention and, after surveying the situation, he wrote, "The citizens of Chicago refuse to take Mr. Jones seriously. They regard him as a huge standing joke, and that fact breaks Mr. Jones all to smash." He added, "He must call conventions, whether he has any object in view or not." When Jones held his convention in June, only seven delegates appeared.[6]

Fortune originally called for the Afro-American League convention to be held in Nashville, Tennessee, but concern over hotel accommodations in that southern city had him move the convention to Chicago. Chicago's African American community was excited about hosting the event and it sent the largest delegation to the convention. Fortune would write that there were nine local branches of the Afro-American League in Cook County and that their members all wanted to be delegates. He later added, "The citizens of Chicago took the liveliest interest in all sessions and attended them in large numbers."[7]

Although the community strongly supported the Fortune convention, the Illinois delegation was divided and in turmoil. On one occasion, a delegate from Ohio made a motion instructing the Illinois delegation to make less noise. The motion passed. Another motion approved by the convention required the sergeant at arms seat the Illinois delegation. Illinois delegate A. Boyd noted that there was dissatisfaction in the Illinois delegation and he successfully passed a motion so that for each vote taken the Illinois delegates would be polled separately, rather than allow its chairman, whom he apparently mistrusted, to announce the vote totals. Another Illinois delegate felt compelled to ask the convention chairman who the Illinois chairman was. Perhaps summing up the view of the other delegates at the convention, H. J. Mitchell said, "It has been said the Illinois delegation was almost a mob."[8]

While several Chicagoans played prominent roles at the convention, including H. J. Mitchell, Robert M. Mitchell, Morris, Barnett, and James Porter, the largest honor was given to Thomas. Three large portraits adorned the stage at the convention, which was held in the Madison Street Theater. In the center of the stage was a portrait of Frederick Douglass, who since before the Civil War had been the leading African American activist in the nation. To the right of the Douglass portrait was a portrait of Fortune, the person who called the convention. To the left of the Douglass portrait was one of Thomas, which was appropriate in that he was the leading African American activist in the host city.[9]

Thomas served as chairman of a citizens committee created to make arrangements for the convention and to host a reception for the delegates. H. J. Mitchell and George Ecton served as officers on the committee. The reception for the approximately 140 delegates was held on the first night of the convention at the First Regiment Armory. The reception, which consisted of a banquet where speeches were given in the lower room of the armory and dancing and socializing in the upper room, began at 9:00 P.M. and lasted until after midnight. Thomas's sister-in-law, Mary "Mollie" Marshall, sang a song as part of the entertainment. Thomas gave the address of welcome to the delegates and congratulated them on their mission. On behalf of the delegates, Fortune gave the response to Thomas's words of welcome and outlined his plans for the league. Fortune later called the reception a "splendid affair."[10]

In reviewing the convention for his newspaper, Fortune analyzed the different delegations. Of Illinois, he wrote that it was divided in to three factions; "one led by Mr. R. M. Mitchell, the other by Mr. E. H. Morris, and the third led itself." What the differences were between the three factions is not known. Fortune, perhaps diplomatically, praised both Mitchell and Morris as very able and influential men. He further praised Thomas and wrote, "I hope to see both of them [Mitchell and Morris] and the honorable J. W. E. Thomas, an able man of few words, working together for the success of the League." What faction of the Illinois delegation Thomas supported, or if he was a part of the third faction, is not known. Still, it is apparent that Fortune recognized that Thomas was someone the league needed.[11]

In the pages of the *New York Age*, Fortune, not surprisingly declared his convention a success. Other African American papers did too, as well as some of the daily Republican papers, including the *Inter-Ocean*. The *Tribune* opposed the convention from the beginning, seeing it as a threat to the Republican Party. Perhaps the best analysis came from the *Chicago Conservator*, one of Chicago's African American newspapers, which wrote, "The Afro-American League was a success so far as the planning is concerned. Now comes the test—the execution of the plans."[12]

Soon after the Afro-American League formed, the two other conventions met. The convention called for by Perry Carson met in Washington D.C. in February. It was well-attended and had some notable African American leaders such as John M. Langston, Blanche Bruce, and P. B. S. Pinchback. The convention formed the American Citizens Civil Rights Association of the United States. There were calls for the Afro-American League and the Association to unite, but the two organizations went their separate ways. As noted above, the convention called by Jones was a dismal failure.[13]

The Afro-American League, despite its promising start, had only a short life. The League held its 1891 convention in Knoxville, Tennessee, where only seven states had delegates. Illinois was not one of them. By 1893, Fortune declared the league dead. The Illinois branch of the league lasted somewhat longer, although by 1895 leading African Americans in the state, including Thomas, felt compelled to organize a new state league, named the Afro-American Citizen's Protective League.[14] Thomas does not appear to have taken a leading role in either state league, but his presence at the founding of the national Afro-American League demonstrates his support for its ideals.

Historians have debated the long-term importance of the Afro-American League. Bess Beatty called it "one of the most ambitious racial self-help efforts of the late nineteenth century." Emma Lou Thornbrough saw it as having a lasting significance, in that it represented a vision that would influence later civil rights organizations. Historian Albert Lee Kreiling said it could be seen as either the last gasp of the "colored convention" movement that had begun before the Civil War, or as the beginnings of the Niagara movement and NAACP of the twentieth century. However, Leslie Fishel would argue that it was doomed to failure because its aims were political, but it sought to achieve its aims outside the existing political structure.[15]

Although these interpretations are diverse, they are all consistent with Thomas's career. His activity as a teacher at his school for African Americans and his membership in African American fraternal organizations and churches demonstrate his support of self-help efforts. His work in the legislature to pass his civil rights bill shows a commitment to working with all groups to achieve equality. His attendance at the two state "colored conventions" and at the Louisville National Colored Convention show he was part and parcel of the convention movement. And Thomas could support the efforts of the Afro-American League as long as it sought to achieve its aims outside the existing political structure. In other words, by not attacking the Republican Party. But, as loyal as Thomas remained to the party, it would still cause him future disappointments.

The Election of 1892

Following the disappointing 1890 election, Thomas continued to play a role in local politics. He became an important part of the First Ward Republican organization, although there was never any hope at the time of Thomas, or any African American, becoming the leader of the ward. Thomas also continued to push to expand political opportunities for African Americans in Republican politics. Elective office served as an important symbol of African American progress. As an ambitious politician, Thomas had often promoted himself for elective office. However, he had also worked for other African Americans as well, and he continued to do so in the early 1890s working with three rising leaders of the African American community: Edward Morris, Edward Wright, and James Bish.

In the spring of 1891, Republicans nominated Hempstead Washburne, son of 1880 presidential hopeful Elihu B. Washburne, for mayor. The Democrats renominated incumbent mayor DeWitt Cregier. The year was fractured, as Republican Elmer Washburn ran as an independent candidate supported by the self-proclaimed "better element" of the city, and former mayor Carter Harrison ran as an independent Democrat after losing the party nomination to Cregier.[16]

Thomas, of course, supported Hempstead Washburne and was a delegate to the convention that nominated him. Thomas gave speeches for the Republican candidates, served as the First Ward representative on the Republican campaign committee, and also served as one of the vice presidents at a large preelection Republican rally. At a meeting in March, he criticized the supporters of Elmer Washburn, stating he was "opposed to a set of citizens who thought they were too good to be led by organized bodies." Thomas then described the grassroots work he and others in the First Ward did, including visiting boardinghouses to get out the vote and hiring persons to distribute ballots. Republican Hempstead Washburne won the election, as Cregier and Harrison split the Democratic vote and Elmer Washburn's candidacy failed to ignite.[17]

In the First Ward, Arthur Dixon did not run for reelection as alderman because he planned to move out of the ward. The First Ward Republicans nominated attorney William H. King, who lost to Democrat John R. Morris. Despite the loss, the Republican *Inter-Ocean* described Election Day in the First Ward as somewhat successful, as there was only one shooting at a polling place. The Republican paper was mistaken in viewing the election as a limited success. The loss of Dixon signaled the beginning of the end for the Republican First Ward machine that Thomas had so faithfully served. The next year, Taylor would fail in his bid to be renominated as congressman from the First Congressional District, losing to a Republican from the Thirty-second Ward.[18]

At the township level, four African Americans ran for the Republican nomination for South Town clerk. Before the South Town convention, the *Times*, in its bigoted reporting style, acknowledged the growing power of Edward H. Morris when discussing the clerk's position. It wrote, "The clerkship, as usual, will go to a colored brother, but who he will be no one, save Ed Morris, the disreputable 'coon' republican boss of the South Side, can tell. ... What he says is law, or will be when it comes to naming a candidate for clerk." That statement was not true. At the South Town Republican convention, Morris supported Franklin Denison for clerk, but the winning nominee was Canadian-born John W. Jones, described by the Democratic newspapers as a law clerk and by the Republican papers as an attorney. Although it is not known if Thomas was a delegate to the South Town convention, the First Ward supported G. H. Hutchinson, who resided in that ward and whose name was placed in nomination by Edward H. Wright. On the first, informal ballot, Hutchinson received 42 votes, to 28 for Jones, 10 for Ferdinand Barnett, and 4 for Denison. On the first formal ballot, the vote was Jones, 43, and Hutchinson, 41. The nomination was disputed due to a controversial decision by the chairman, so delegates took a second vote. Jones won again, this time by a margin of 44 to 40.[19]

Jones, however, ran into a unique situation that made him ineligible for the position. He was born in Canada in 1856, after his slave parents had escaped the South. In 1857 the Supreme Court ruled in the Dred Scott decision that African Americans were not citizens. This meant that, unlike children born overseas to American parents, Jones technically might not have been an American citizen. When he moved to the States, Jones assumed he was an American, so he never filed naturalization papers. The first public comment about the situation came at a First Ward Republican Club meeting, when Thomas announced that Jones was no longer a candidate due to the questions surrounding his citizenship. The South Town campaign committee replaced Jones with Hutchinson. Although the *Inter-Ocean* editorialized about the difficult decision that had to be made due to the lasting repercussions of the *Dred Scott* decision, the *Times* found the situation a little too convenient. It called the reasoning for Jones leaving the ticket a ruse designed to heal the rift caused by his controversial nomination. Whether there was a rift or not, the entire Republican South Town ticket lost the spring election.[20]

That fall, African Americans were again left off the Republican ticket. The Republicans created a plan in which the party chairman appointed a "Committee of Seven," consisting of upstanding businessmen charged with the responsibility of selecting the best possible candidates for the offices of judge, school superintendent, Cook County Board president, and the fifteen county board commissioners. The committee returned a list of candidates that delegates to the county convention then chose from. Only one African American, Dr. Daniel Hale Williams, made the list, and that was as a potential candidate for county board. Delegates, however, did not choose him, instead spending one of the three county board nominations from the South Town part of the city on a labor candidate, in an appeal to working men.[21]

The failure to nominate an African American to the ticket again caused some stir in the community. Although the *Inter-Ocean* editorialized that it was a shame that Williams was not nominated, it stated that he lost due to geographic considerations. A group calling itself the Independent Colored

Republican Committee disagreed. It wrote an unsigned appeal, printed in the Democratic papers, criticizing the Republicans for recognizing every ethnic group but African Americans. The appeal stated, "Among the names presented was that of Dr. Daniel Hale Williams, one of the leading colored citizens, but his name was entirely lost sight of by that body in the scramble to capture the Germans, Irish, Swedes, Bohemians and other nationalities, representatives of which were carefully selected and their names placed on the Republican ticket solely for the support they would bring that party in the campaign." The appeal caused some alarm in Republican circles, but Williams said that he was supporting the Republican candidates and was not offended about not being named to the ticket.

Still, Republicans realized they had made a mistake by not having an African American on the ticket. Former state senator George Gibbs successfully urged that the county central committee select an African American as an at-large member. The committee named Bish, who was becoming a power in the Second Ward. Bish earned his keep on the county central committee when, in a response to the Independent Colored Republican Committee, he strongly urged the community to support the entire Republican ticket. After having some difficult years, that fall the entire Republican ticket was elected, including all fifteen county board candidates.[22]

Thomas does not appear to have played a large role in that fall's election, but he was again active in the spring 1892 election, giving speeches on behalf of the Republican ticket. The South Town Republicans again nominated an African American for South Town clerk. This time, it was John R. Marshall, a bricklayer from the Fourth Ward. Republican Peter Laas was elected supervisor, but the Republican candidates for the three other offices, including Marshall, lost handily. In the First Ward, John Coughlin, the owner of a Turkish bathhouse, defeated two Republican candidates for alderman. "Bathhouse" Coughlin would serve forty-six years in the city council from the First Ward, and, with Michael "Hinky Dink" Kenna, would form one of the most famous and corrupt ward machines in Chicago history.[23]

Although he worked hard on behalf of the Republican ticket that spring, Thomas had his eye on another prize. Once again, he attempted to raise the ceiling for African Americans, choosing to seek nomination as a delegate-at-large to the Republican National Convention. It was a position he had tried for in 1884 but had been stopped by Reverend Smith. African American delegates were common at Republican National Conventions, but Illinois Republicans had never selected an African American to serve in this prestigious position.

Illinois Republicans would select eight at-large delegates at their state convention, held May 4–5 in Springfield. It was assumed that four of the at-large delegates would come from Cook County and four from downstate. The African American press supported Thomas early. On February 13, the *State Capital* newspaper of Springfield had a story stating that African Americans throughout Illinois were supporting Thomas for delegate. On February 27, the paper endorsed him for the position and displayed his picture. On March 5, an item appeared in the *Appeal* mentioning Thomas as a candidate for the position. Even the mainstream press recognized him as a candidate. On March 19, the *Chicago Inter-Ocean* wrote that the African American community wanted a delegate and supported either Thomas or Morris. The day before the state convention and on the convention's opening day, the *Springfield State Register* ran a front page picture of Thomas captioned "Candidate for Delegate-at-Large to the National Convention."[24]

The Cook County Republican Convention met April 29, five days before the state convention, and endorsed Joseph Fifer for reelection for governor and Henry Hertz for state treasurer. At the county convention, Edward H. Wright introduced a resolution calling for the state convention to select an African American as one of the eight at-large delegates. The resolution died in committee. The *Times* was able to write, not incorrectly, that "the joke of it is that while Mr. Wright's resolution was being consigned to the waste basket, a resolution endorsing Mr. Hertz, against whom the colored citizens cherish a long standing prejudice, was approved." The situation would repeat itself at the state convention.[25]

Thomas did not serve as a delegate to the Cook County Republican Convention, but both he and Wright served as First Ward delegates to the state convention. Morris, of the Third Ward, also served as a delegate, as did fifty-one other African Americans from throughout the state.[26]

The same day as the county convention, the First Congressional District Republican organization met. Thomas was a member of that convention, which selected J. Frank Aldrich as its candidate for Congress. Each congressional district received two delegates and two alternate delegates to the national convention. The First Congressional District caucus selected Morris as an alternate delegate to the national convention. While this was an honor for Morris and again demonstrated his growing political power, it also meant that Thomas was the only African American in the running for delegate-at-large.[27]

Republicans were in a festive mood for the state convention, which, with more than 1,200 delegates, was the largest in state party history. Thomas arrived in Springfield on May 3 on a train that had been reserved specifically to transport delegates from Chicago to Springfield. The rowdy trainload of delegates, supporters, well-wishers, and hangers-on made many stops along the route, including one in Dwight, Illinois. There the delegates, in various states of sobriety, visited the local attraction, which was the Keeley Institute, the first medical institution to treat alcoholism as a disease.[28]

The festivities continued in Springfield, where on the evening of the first day of the convention the city's African American citizens held a reception for the fifty-four African American delegates. The delegates assembled at the prestigious Leland Hotel, from where the local citizens and the Springfield Central Band escorted them to Armory Hall on Fourth Street for the 8:00 P.M. reception. There, the Springfieldians feted the delegates with songs, instrumental music, dramatic recitations, and speeches. Thomas delivered an address entitled "Needs of the Race," and Morris gave a speech entitled "The Political Necessities of the American People." The *Springfield State Journal* described the evening as "pleasant and successful."[29]

While the evening may have been pleasant, the opening day of the convention had not been for the African American delegates and especially for Thomas. A committee to select delegates-at-large and presidential electors-at-large had met that afternoon. The committee decided to select four delegate-at-large candidates from Cook County and four from downstate. For the downstate delegates, the committee named such luminaries as U.S. Senator Shelby Cullom, former governor Richard Oglesby, and future Speaker of the U.S. House Joseph Cannon. Because Cook County had four congressional districts, the committee decided to let the delegation from each district select a delegate. The First District, where Thomas resided, was being led by persons not aligned with the ever-weakening First Ward organization, so Thomas had no chance of being selected.[30]

Exactly how Thomas lost, however, is a matter of conjecture. The *Tribune* reported that the committee had made its selections and then a delegation of African Americans showed up to ask that Thomas be named as a delegate. According to the *Tribune*, some of the committee members said they weren't aware that the African American community wanted representation at the national convention, a rather disingenuous argument considering the publicity surrounding the Thomas candidacy. Also, it would seem unlikely that the delegation of African Americans who made the request would have shown up late to the committee meeting. The *Inter-Ocean* reported that the African American delegates asked that Thomas be made a presidential elector, as opposed to being named a delegate to the convention, but this story, too, seems incorrect.

More likely what happened is what was reported in the Democratic *Chicago Times* and the Republican *Springfield State Journal*. Both papers reported that the delegation that went before the committee consisted of Thomas, Morris, and Wright. They also reported that the committee debated the request at great length before offering a compromise, which was to have Thomas chosen as a presidential elector-at-large. Thomas accepted this compromise and in doing so became the first African American in Illinois history to run for presidential elector. The selection was an honor, but it was not what Thomas and the African American delegation wanted.[31]

Overall, African Americans were in an angry mood at the convention. George Hill of Bloomington voiced the sentiment of many of the African American delegates when, in learning of the compromise, he said, "the colored people ought to have more recognition of their claims upon the Republican Party than they have." There was still deep resentment at Hertz, and yet he was easily nominated for state treasurer. J. C. Buckner had organized a battalion of African American troops in Chicago and wanted it made a part of the Illinois National Guard. At a meeting with African American delegates held during the convention, however, Governor Fifer would not agree to Buckner's request. Fifer's record in office in appointing African Americans to patronage positions was considered poor as well.[32]

On the second day of the convention, delegates nominated the statewide candidates, including Fifer and Hertz. The convention also endorsed Harrison for reelection as president. Although no African Americans were considered for any of the statewide positions, the convention selected two African Americans, Morris and Hugh Singleton of downstate Decatur, as the two at-large members of the state central committee. The *Times* called this action an attempt to heal the wounds felt by the African American delegates. George Gibbs of Chicago attempted to prevent the selection of Morris, stating that Morris was currently "holding six offices now, while many Chicago people did not hold over two or three." Although delegates laughed at the truth behind the statement, they agreed with both Wright and James Porter, who informed the convention that Morris was the unanimous choice of the African American delegates. West Side political boss William Lorimer, who was beginning to reach out to African American voters, seconded the Morris nomination.[33]

After the convention, the Democrat *State Register* editorialized that "The colored Republican brother carries around 20,000 votes in his capacious pocket and can't get any office above a janitor." While African Americans did not achieve all they wished at the convention, overall they did well. Both at-large members of the state central committee and one of the four at-large presidential electors were African American. As *The State Capital* newspaper editorialized, "We Are Satisfied."[34]

Following the convention, more hardships awaited Thomas. On May 6, his infant son and namesake, John W. E. Thomas, died. His death meant that two of the three children Thomas's wife Crittie had borne him had died. Both of the daughters he had with his second wife, Justine, had also passed away. Only his adult daughter, Hester, and his three-year-old daughter, Ethel, survived of the six children he had had so far. At the time of son John's death, Crittie was again pregnant.

Still, Thomas continued his work in politics, and he entered the fall 1892 election committed to working for the party. In June he chaired a reception given by Chicago's African American community for African American delegates on their way to the Republican National Convention in Minneapolis. John M. Langston, the first African American congressman from Virginia, was the featured speaker, and Albion W. Tourgee, the leading white civil rights leader in the nation, also spoke. Thomas was still active in the First Ward Republican Club and served as one of three members from the First Ward on the county campaign ward committee. And, although probably not an active candidate, his name was again mentioned as a possible legislative candidate.[35]

In early September, Republicans in Cook County held their fall county convention. Thomas was as one of the sixteen delegate candidates for the First Ward slate. The slate was uncontested, and the *Inter-Ocean* said it was uninstructed as well. No other leading African American in the city appears as one of the delegates.

Despite the predictions of some of the newspapers, who saw a machine–antimachine fight developing, the convention was relatively harmonious. The *Times* would state that the Lorimer machine controlled the convention, although the Republican papers, some of which were anti-Lorimer, would state that the ticket selected was a compromise between all factions. Although Lorimer was allied with Hertz, Thomas had no problems in voting to nominate him for clerk of the Superior Court. For county board, the party once again allowed the delegates from the three different towns to select their own candidates. Only four persons sought the three positions given South Town, and none of them were African American. For Thomas, perhaps the only highlight of the otherwise dull convention was the selection of his legal mentor Kirk Hawes to run for another term as circuit court judge.[36]

The convention also chose one person from each ward and from county towns to serve on the county central campaign committee. J. R. R. Van Cleave was selected to serve on the committee from the First Ward. Two weeks later, the central committee created a subcommittee to perform grassroots political work such as registration and naturalization of voters. Each member of the central committee chose three persons to serve in his ward. Van Cleave chose Thomas as one of the three.[37]

As the county campaign plan was coming together, the battle for the leg-islature also was heating up. The legislature elected in 1892 would redraw the new legislative districts, meaning that the party in power could gerrymander them in its favor. Writing about Democratic control of the legislature in August, the *Tribune* warned that if the Democratic Party won the legislature, they would "gerrymander the state to hold the General Assembly for the next ten years, no matter what Republican popular majority there may be in the state." It was conceded that the senate would keep its Democratic majority so the house races were all the more important.[38]

In 1892, the odd-numbered districts did not have senators up for reelec-tion, so the Republicans of the Third District would only be nominating two house members. Edward H. Morris was up for renomination, and most of the Republican papers were satisfied with his first term in the house. The *Tribune* called him "one of the brightest and most attentive members of the last House on the Republican side," and the *Inter-Ocean* wrote that "he had an excellent record in the legislature." However, Morris came from the Third Ward, of which only a small part was in the Third District. In 1890, with two house nominations and a senate nomination to make, delegates selected one candidate from each ward. With only two house nominations to make in 1892, one ward would not receive a nomination. As the convention would consist of sixteen delegates each from the First and Second Wards and only four delegates from the Third Ward, this did not bode well for Morris. In addition, the community was divided over the position, as both J. E. Bish, who was president of the John A. Logan Second Ward (Colored) Republican Club, and Isaac Rivers both sought the nomination. Their candidacies cut any hope Morris might have had of running with the support of a unified African American community.[39]

The convention did not occur until October 4, but speculation on the can-didates for the two nominations began early. As in the past, it was assumed one nomination would go to an African American and one to a white can-didate, although at one point the *Inter-Ocean* did raise the possibility of two African American candidates being nominated. Republicans in other Chicago-based legislative districts were calling for their legislative conven-tions at this time, but the *Tribune* reported the Third District was being delayed due to "the conflicting claims of colored men for Representative." It listed Morris, Bish, and Rivers as candidates for what was now being termed "the colored seat." It also listed First Warders William H. King and Isaac N. Powell as probable candidates for the other nomination.[40] Speculation increased by late September, with the *Inter-Ocean* on September 21 add-ing Stephen A. Douglas Jr. as a possible candidate. Several other potential candidates emerged, including Robert M. Mitchell. As the convention neared, the newspapers began to list Thomas as a potential candidate.[41]

It is difficult to assess how much Thomas wanted the house nomination, if at all. The *Evening Journal* actively backed both Thomas and Douglas for the two nominations. Twice in late September it wrote that Thomas and Douglas would be the probable nominees. On October 1, it wrote that "the combination that appears to be the strongest is S. A. Douglas of the Second Ward and J. W. E. Thomas of the First." On October 3 it reported that in the First Ward, the race was between Thomas and King, implying Thomas was actively campaigning. It further wrote that Thomas would probably carry the ward.[42]

However the *Inter-Ocean* insisted that Thomas was not formally a candidate. Instead, it saw Thomas as a potential compromise candidate. The *Inter-Ocean* saw two scenarios that could lead to Thomas being chosen as a nominee. Under its first scenario, he would represent the First Ward as its nominee, if that ward could not agree to back either King or Powell. Under its second scenario, Thomas would be the choice of the African American community, if the increasingly bitter fight between Morris and Rivers led to division in naming a candidate for the African American nomination. In reviewing the potential for splits in both the First Ward and in the African American community, the *Inter-Ocean* editorialized that the best way to restore harmony in the district would be to select Thomas and Douglas for the two nominations.[43]

Any hopes Thomas had for the nomination may have been hurt by an article that appeared in the *Inter-Ocean* and other newspapers questioning whether he could be a candidate for both the house and presidential elector at the same time. The article said it was feared that if he was selected as a candidate for the house, he would have to resign as a presidential elector candidate. Although, in fact, he could have run for both offices, the article served as a reminder that in the limited world of political opportunity for African Americans, Thomas was already on the ballot.[44]

In the end, Thomas did not make the race. King easily defeated Powell in the First Ward, giving him 16 delegates. In the Second Ward, Bish won 10 delegates to Rivers's 6. Morris was the undisputed choice of the Third Ward, giving him 4 delegates to the convention. The primaries ensured King one of the nominations, for with 19 votes needed to nominate, he could make an agreement with any of the other three candidates and be elected.[45]

At this point, if Thomas were to have a chance, his only hope would be as the compromise choice of the African American community. Abner Taylor served as chairman of the convention. Whether purposely or not, he dashed any hopes Thomas may have had for a nomination when he called for the nomination of the white candidate first. King was easily nominated on the first ballot, receiving 23 votes to 12 for Douglas and 1 for Rivers. King received 16 votes from the First Ward and 7 from the Second. Douglas won all 4 from the Third Ward and 8 votes from the Second. The one vote for Rivers came from the Second Ward. With a First Ward candidate nominated, delegates would not choose another First Ward resident.

Only one ballot was needed for the second nomination, which Bish won. He received 14 votes from the First Ward and 9 from the Second Ward. Morris received 2 votes from the First Ward, 6 from the Second Ward, and 4 votes from the Third Ward. Rivers again received 1 vote from the Second Ward.[46]

Coming into the convention, the *Tribune* wrote, the King and Bish forces had "made a combination," and this appears to be the case. Although a hard party worker, Rivers had a less than favorable reputation, as Thomas certainly knew from having supported Rivers for a patronage position in 1885. Rivers's reputation had not gotten any better since then. The *Inter-Ocean* wrote, "The *Inter-Ocean* has said some kind things about Rivers, and we now have no desire to abuse him, but everybody who knows anything about him knows he is entirely unfitted for the position of legislator." With this in mind, King would not have joined forces with Rivers. Morris was a Third Ward ally of Douglas, and that ward had unanimously opposed King. As such, Bish became the choice of King and the First Ward.[47]

Morris, like Thomas in 1886, had lost the renomination for three reasons. First, geography hurt his chances. Second, he was aligned with the weaker faction at the convention and didn't have the backing of the First Ward. Third, the smallness of the African American community dictated that only one of the two nominees for representative would be an African American, and enough divisions existed within that small community to prevent it from naming its own candidate. Instead, white political bosses made the decision.[48]

As in 1886, not all African Americans were pleased with the way the incumbent African American legislator had been treated by the Republican Party. This time, John G. Jones led the protest. He started a petition drive to run S. Laing Williams as an independent candidate for the legislature. Williams was a prominent attorney who, with his wife Fannie, was one of the social leaders of the African American community. Although Jones was a friend of Morris and would dedicate his book to him in 1899, his actions may have been less about the way Morris was treated and more about his dislike of Bish. The combative Jones was active in many secret and benevolent organizations and during the course of the campaign Bish would be charged with misappropriating funds while he was the grand master of the Illinois chapter of the United Brothers of Friendship in 1888.[49]

The seriousness of the Jones-led drive was not lost on the newspapers of the day. While the third-party activities of African Americans drew the ire of the white mainstream press, it also demonstrated their paternalistic, condescending attitude toward the community. The *Tribune* in August reminded voters that the independent Carter candidacy had cost the Republicans a seat in the house in 1890. It wrote, "That fellow has since flopped over to the Democrats, where he naturally belongs, and he would be a slave today had that party defeated the Republicans on the battlefields of the war for the union." The *Evening Journal*, in response to Jones's activities, reported that Republican Party managers would end the practice of nominating an African American for the legislature if they couldn't settle their differences among themselves.[50]

What these mainstream papers overlooked was that running as an independent candidate for office when angry over party policy was a common practice of both whites and African Americans. This made the *Tribune* and *Evening Journal*'s responses to the potential independent campaign uncalled for when they couched their responses in terms of race. In addition, they missed the fact that an independent candidacy was much different than switching to the Democratic Party, something that had been threatened during the "colored conventions" of the 1880s.

Williams, however, was not interested in running for the legislature, and he later expressed surprise that his friends tried to get him to run. If he were interested in running, having Jones on his side would be no help. While Jones spoke before African American groups and to individual voters on behalf of Williams, African American leaders such as Thomas, Robert Mitchell, and James Porter came out against the independent candidacy. Jones also could not convince Morris to join in the revolt against the party nominee. In addition, the Australian ballot law had just gone into effect in Illinois. Before the Australian ballot law, parties or candidates printed and distributed their own ballots, which only contained one set of names. Voters would take the ballots into the polling place and deposit them in the ballot box. Sometimes they would scratch out or paste over some of the names listed on the ballot and write in the name of other candidates. Under the new system, the government printed ballots with the names of all the candidates and parties on them. To get on the ballot, candidates either had to win a party nomination or petition the election authorities. Jones had problems filing petitions on behalf of Williams with the proper election authorities in Springfield.[51]

In any event, within a week of the Third District Republican convention, the revolt began to fade. It ended in late October when Williams wrote a letter to his supporters declining to run. He wrote, "I can not consent to make the canvass when the only reason for my candidacy seems to be the comparative merits between some other candidates and myself." With the split in the African American community resolved, the election of both Bish and King was assured in the heavily Republican Third District.[52]

However, within the African American community there still burned resentment against Hertz, who was now running for state treasurer. Democrats tried to exploit that resentment, although their efforts seemed bizarre at times. In September in Alton, a circular addressed to African American voters reminded them about Hertz's role in the Zephyr Davis case. One of the two signers of the circular denied he had signed it and declared the circular a forgery. In October, another downstate circular stated that Hertz was a member of the Danish Brotherhood, a secret organization "sworn to keep the colored man down."[53]

Perhaps more seriously for Hertz and the Republican Party as a whole, however, was an address to Chicago's African American voters that appeared in the *Chicago Times*. Signed by some of the leading members of the African American community, including Lloyd G. Wheeler, Dr. C. E. Bentley, future state representative Louis Anderson, and Hannibal Carter, the address stated that Hertz was "a man who has proven himself a positive enemy to the colored race." The address stated, "we are confronted with the declaration that we must vote for him. How long are we to tolerate such political dictation? The clock has struck the hour when the black man must assert himself politically and resent the insults heaped upon him by the present representatives of the republican party." Although the signers declared that they had always voted the Republican ticket in the past, that was certainly not the case with Wheeler and Carter, two men who had run as independents for office in 1890. While Carter was a political dilettante who was always looking out for his own best interests, Wheeler, to his credit, was a Democrat based on more than just race issues. In 1892, he was a strong opponent of the Republican Party plank of supporting Congressman William McKinley's high, strong national tariff.[54]

Opposition to the McKinley tariff helped lead to landslide Democratic victories in Illinois and across the nation in 1892.[55] Democrats in Illinois ended thirty-six years of Republican rule in Springfield by electing John Peter Altgeld as governor. Altgeld and the Democrats also were helped by their opposition to the 1889 Edwards compulsory education bill that had proven unpopular with immigrants and some ethnic groups, especially Germans. The entire Republican state ticket lost, including Hertz, whose defeat the African American newspaper *The Appeal* wrote should serve as a lesson to the Republican Party to not nominate someone so strongly opposed by the African American community. Although both King and Bish won, Democrats won both houses of the General Assembly. Locally, Democrats won control of the county board and most county offices. Nationally, Grover Cleveland was elected to his second, nonconsecutive term as president. Cleveland won in Illinois, meaning that Thomas lost in his bid to be the first African American presidential elector from the state. His name never again appeared on a ballot.[56]

The Election of 1894

Politically, the year 1893 began like many of the previous springs in Chicago. However, it would be wild year for the city. It would also be a year of change for Thomas, who began to draw back from politics and focus more on his family and business. For African Americans, 1893 would be a divisive year, but the community's political leaders would work together in 1894 to achieve a long sought after goal. In doing so, they validated much of what Thomas had stood for in his career.

In March 1893, South Town Republicans nominated Edward H. Wright for South Town clerk. Thomas served on the South Town Republican Campaign Committee, most likely at Wright's request. It was the tenth consecutive time South Town Republicans had nominated an African American for the position, but in April the Democrats won three of the four South Town positions, with Republicans winning only the assessor's office.[57]

The town elections were low-key that year, in large measure because of the mayor's race. The World's Columbian Exposition was scheduled to open on May 1, so the new mayor would have the honor of being known as the world's fair mayor. Democrats nominated former mayor Carter Harrison for the position. Republicans approached several possible candidates, all of whom turned down the opportunity. Finally, the party nominated businessman Samuel W. Allerton. Former Democrat mayor DeWitt Cregier ran as a third-party candidate, but Harrison had no troubles winning the election.[58]

Thomas played an active role in the city election. He served as First Ward delegate to the convention that nominated Allerton. Missing from the First Ward delegation were party stalwarts Taylor and Dixon, with the latter serving as a delegate from his new home in the Third Ward. Thomas also served on the Republican city campaign committee, which consisted of about four hundred of the leading Republicans of the city. He was one of ten people who sat on the stage when Allerton spoke at a citywide rally of African American citizens on March 29, and he presided over a large meeting of First Ward African American voters that Allerton spoke to on April 1. The Logan Hall Association, which Thomas helped found as an organization supporting

Republican candidates, endorsed Harrison, but Thomas's name was not to be found on the endorsement, and, in fact, the only African American of note who did sign the endorsement was Hannibal Carter, who had long since left the Republican Party.[59]

Just after the election, Thomas followed Dixon in moving out of the First Ward. On April 21, he bought a house at 3308 South Indiana Avenue for $11,000 from Abraham Mendelsohn. Edward H. Morris notarized the sale. Mendelsohn had purchased the house the previous day for $10,000 from the home's original owner, Amos H. Hale. Hale and his wife had hired architect S. M. Randolph to design and build the home in 1884 at a cost of $6,000. The location of the house was much more suitable for a man of Thomas's stature and wealth than his previous home on Clark Street in the levee. However, the increasing industrialization and growth of downtown made land near the train station valuable. On March 1, 1893, Thomas had sold his old house at 198 Fourth Avenue across from Dearborn Station to the Chicago and Western Railroad Company for $51,250. His new home was located in the Douglas/Grand Boulevard residential neighborhood in the Fourth Ward. The two-story, red brick house was located across the street from the K.A.M. Synagogue, which had been designed by famous architects Louis Sullivan and Dankmar Adler and built in 1891. The Thomas family appears to have been the first African American family to live on the street, in what forty years later would be the heart of Chicago's black belt.[60]

The move distanced Thomas from Chicago politics. The Fourth Ward was under the firm control of Republican alderman and future congressman Martin Madden. Although Madden was a supporter of African American political rights, the move meant that Thomas would have to start all over to become active in ward politics. The African American population in the ward was smaller than the population had been in the First Ward, and there were already established African American leaders, such as J. C. Buckner, living there.[61] In addition, in 1893 the Democratic-controlled state legislature redistricted the legislative districts. The new map placed the First Ward and most of the Second Ward in the First Legislative District, and placed the Fourth Ward in the Fifth Legislative District. The Fifth District was the only district that would send an African American to the state legislature during the 1890s, but because it did not include the First Ward, Thomas was separated from many of his allies, both African American and white.

Thomas did not take an active role in the fall 1893 election campaign. That election, which followed the beginning of the 1893 recession, resulted in a landslide victory for Republicans in both Cook County and the nation. Chicago's South Side Republicans received their customary three nominations for county commissioner, but it appears that no African American sought one of these positions. J. E. Bish served as one of the political leaders of the Second Ward, but no African American served on the county campaign committee.[62]

One week before the fall election, an assassin shot and killed Mayor Harrison, who was just six months into his fifth term as mayor. The assassination cast a pall over the last week of the November campaign. The city called a special election for December to replace the mayor, and Democrat John Hopkins defeated Republican George Swift in an election the Republican press declared was stolen. Again, it does not appear that Thomas was very active in the campaign. He did not serve as a Fourth Ward delegate to the convention that nominated Swift. He did give at least one speech during the campaign, appearing at a campaign rally that also featured candidate Swift.[63]

While African Americans did not participate as candidates in the fall campaigns, that did not mean their leaders and the community were not active that year. In 1893 Chicago hosted the World's Columbian Exhibition, a world's fair so large that one historian called it "a defining moment in American history."[64] The fair ran from May 1 to October 30. Along with the rides, food, exhibitions, and festivities normally associated with carnivals, the fair featured academic conferences and attractions from all over the world designed to educate and inform the populace. Fair organizers denied African Americans the opportunity to participate in the organizing of the fair and placed restrictions on what exhibits African Americans could display. They also followed racist practices in the hiring of workers at the fair.[65] Still, as historian Christopher Reed has noted, there was a noticeable African American presence at the world's fair. National African American leaders such as Frederick Douglass, George Washington Carver, Booker T. Washington, and Ida B. Wells all came to Chicago for the fair. And, because the fair was held in Chicago, African Americans from the city played an active role in organizing events.[66]

The National Colored Men's Protective Association moved its annual convention to Chicago during the fair. Morris and Wright played significant roles at the gathering. At a symposium entitled the "Congress on Africa," African American leaders debated their role in the United States and the issue of emigrating to Africa. Ferdinand Barnett read a paper at the congress. Fannie Barrier Williams addressed both the World's Congress of Representative Women and the Parliament of Religions. Lloyd G. Wheeler spoke at the Congress on Labor. Daniel Hale Williams and Charles E. Bentley participated in medical congresses.[67] With the fair located five miles from his new home, there is no doubt that Thomas attended many of its activities. However, he does not appear to have participated in a major role at the fair.

While Thomas may have ceded the national stage to other Chicago African Americans and may have no longer had the base with which to run for political office, he still could get involved in politics, especially on behalf of his community. It was with that last issue in mind that Thomas worked in 1894 to expand the opportunities for African Americans to hold elective office.

The political season began with two African Americans competing for the Republican South Town nomination. W. L. Martin, a former Pullman Porter and future state representative, defeated future state senator Adelbert Roberts of the Third Ward for the nomination. Martin was defeated in the April election. Thomas again played no part in the campaign.[68]

In June, Thomas called a mass meeting of all African American voters. The purpose of the meeting was to demand that Cook County Republicans select an African American to run as one of the county commissioner candidates from the South Side. Possible candidates for the position included Bish, Wright, Phillips, and Theodore Jones. Along with advocating for a county commissioner spot, delegates at the meeting formed a Colored Men's Central Republican League of Cook County, whose purpose was to promote the interests of the Republican Party. The meeting was described as "contentious" by one newspaper, leading one to believe that either Thomas had to work to keep the meeting under Republican auspices or, more likely, that the various candidates for the commissionership nomination had disagreements.[69]

Bish supporters, mainly located in the Second Ward, advocated his nomination as commissioner, but Bish wanted to return to the legislature. As such, Edward H. Wright of the First Ward received the early support from the African American community. In the days leading to the June 22 Republican county convention, Wright was endorsed by both the Eighteenth Ward Colored Republican Club and the Thirtieth Ward Colored Republican Club. On June 19, two days before the convention, the executive committee of the Colored Central Republican League of Cook County endorsed him. The executive committee consisted of two delegates from each city ward and county township, although some wards had more than two delegates, and other wards and most of the townships had no representatives. Thomas was one of the two delegates from the Fourth Ward, joined by his old nemesis John G. Jones. Other well-known African Americans at the convention were Wright, Bish, Rivers, Morris, Buckner, S. B. Turner, and Theodore Jones.[70]

This meeting represented the cream of Chicago's African American politicians. Six former or future state representatives, plus two future county board members, participated in the meeting. The social elites of Chicago's African American community, such as Wheeler, Barnett, and S. Laing Williams, were not in attendance, but the growing political class was. And a Thomas ally and the man who would be the most successful African American political leader in Chicago for the next twenty-five years, Edward H. Wright, walked away with the endorsement.[71]

However, just as a nomination is not the equivalent of an election, an endorsement is not the equivalent of a nomination. At the Republican County Convention, African Americans were able to have one of their own nominated for county commissioner, but it was not to be Wright.

William Lorimer, Henry Hertz, Thomas Jamieson, and their allies were in firm control of the convention and had little difficulty in naming the slate of candidates to run countywide. The First Ward, now led by J. R. B. Van Cleave, had allied with the Lorimer machine, and the ward sought two of the three South Side nominations for county commissioner. Thomas was not a delegate to the convention, and so Morris led the fight for the African American community.

As had become the norm, the county commissioner nominations for the part of Cook County that was in the City of Chicago were selected by the delegates from Chicago's three towns. The convention voted to give West Town five slots for commissioner, North Town two, and South Town three. While in theory only the delegates from the South Town selected the city nominees for that area, in actuality the Lorimer machine, based in West Town, had a preselected slate of candidates. An African American was not on the slate.

In response, Morris made a motion to give the South Side four commissionerships. He argued that the African American population deserved a place on the county board but said if the South Side was limited to just three candidates, it would be impossible for them to do so. The delegates at the convention defeated his motion. Morris then proposed a motion that one of the commissioner candidates named from the South Side be an African American, stating that he wanted the party to be on record supporting African Americans. By a voice vote, the convention voted down his motion, and the chairman suggested that Morris's goal could be accomplished if he just nominated an African American for a spot.[72]

It is probable that Morris sought a guarantee that one of the South Side commissioner candidates would be an African American because he knew the Lorimer machine had preselected a slate of candidates. It is also possible that his efforts were due to a possible split in the African American community as to who should be nominated. Despite the endorsement of Wright by the executive committee of Colored Central Republican League, the *Times* reported that both Wright and Theodore Jones were placed in nomination for a commissionership. If that was the case, the two would have been rivals at a time when the community could only press its claim for a commissionership if it was united behind one candidate.[73]

None of the Republican papers reported that Wright was even nominated. Wright must have seen that his candidacy wasn't viable and so he switched his support to Jones. Three First Ward residents ran for a nomination, and the machine had wanted two of them to be chosen. So, the chances of Wright, who also resided in the First Ward and was an active member of the ward organization, would have been poor.

In all, the South Side delegates placed nine candidates in nomination for the three positions. As noted, three of the candidates placed in nomination came from the First Ward. The *Times* would charge that the slate makers had arranged that two of them, John Ritter and August Lundberg, were to be selected. The Second Ward nominated Theodore Jones, a good sign of his support among the African American community, as he was a resident of the Thirty-first Ward. The Thirty-third Ward nominated a white candidate named John H. Jones, and for a while there was confusion among the delegates between the two Joneses. Theodore Jones had the united support of the African American community, which had made a good case for having a representative on the ticket. Jones also could probably rely on strong support from the Second Ward delegation, which had nominated him, and the Thirty-first Ward, where he lived. In addition, if the *Times* claim that the First Ward was looking to have two of the three nominees were true, Jones offered South Side delegates the chance to prevent this.

With 280 votes needed for a nomination, Jones received 325, more than enough to be selected as a commissioner candidate. John Ritter of the First Ward and David Martin of the Fourth Ward received 372 and 375 votes, respectively, and also were nominated. The *Herald* noted that the Jones nomination represented the only time the slate put together by the Lorimer machine was broken. The paper also charged that Hertz got his revenge on the African American community for its efforts against him in the past when he cast all 16 votes of the Fourteenth Ward for three white candidates. More likely, however, was that Hertz, who was part of the Lorimer machine, was voting for the machine slate and not against an African American candidate.[74]

African American delegates to the convention were ecstatic over the nomination. It was another step for the community, which now boasted more than 7,000 voters in the county. The *Tribune* editorialized that "the convention acted wisely in giving the colored people representation in the person of Theodore W. Jones, nominated for county commissioner." While Thomas's role was minor, he had organized the community so that it could lay an early claim to one of the commissionership nominations.[75]

Thomas played a minor role in the rest of the campaign as well. The Democrats had redistricted the state legislature in 1893, and Thomas lived in the Fifth Senatorial District. The district included part of the Second Ward, plus the Third, Fourth and Thirty-second Wards. In July, the Republican senatorial committee met and selected J. C. Buckner, a caterer and resident of the Fourth Ward, as one of its two house candidates. Buckner was an ally of Fourth Ward alderman M. B. Madden. Although Buckner was easily nominated, African American delegates from the Second and Third Wards were split into two factions, with Morris leading one and James Porter leading the other. The split was not due to race but to the two factions supporting different candidates for the senate nomination. None of the newspapers listed Thomas as a potential candidate.[76]

Other events of importance to Chicago's African American community also passed Thomas by. He did not attend the Republican state convention in July, where Morris and Singleton were again elected to the state central committee. In October, the First Senatorial District convention met amidst much controversy and in-fighting. The district selected only one candidate for the house, William E. Kent, a member of the Lorimer-Hertz machine and former deputy coroner. J. E. Bish sought renomination to the house but was rebuffed. Had the Republicans nominated two candidates in the district, both might have been elected. Kent was the deputy coroner who had participated in the Zephyr Davis case in 1888, and Chicago's African Americans had not forgotten the issue. Bish would run for the house as an independent Republican. The *Inter*-Ocean supported him, arguing that both Kent and Bish were Republicans and both could be elected. The *Tribune* opposed Bish, arguing that his candidacy had the potential to cause Kent to lose to a Populist candidate. The *Tribune* urged African American voters to "forget their personal grievances in contemplating the greater grievances they have suffered at the hands of the Democrats and the irreparable harm they will do to their party if they give the Democrats the Speaker and the Senate."[77]

Thomas limited his campaign role to a few minor speaking engagements in October on behalf of the Republican ticket. At one event, he joined Aldermen Madden in speaking to a small group of the sixth precinct of the Fourth Ward. He also spoke to a meeting of First Ward Republicans, along with Theodore Jones, W. L. Martin, S. B. Turner, James Porter, and Adelbert Roberts. He also served as a vice president at a large African American Republican meeting held just before the election.[78]

On Election Day, Republicans swept to office after two straight even-numbered years of losses. The Republican Party won all ten city commissioners spots, which were now two-year terms, and all the county offices.

The victory made Theodore Jones the second African American to serve as Cook County commissioner and the first since John Jones more than two decades earlier. Buckner was one of two Republicans elected to the house in the Fifth District, but Bish lost his Independent bid for the house in the First District, meaning that only one African American would serve in the house.[79]

The election of an African American to the county board represented another electoral gain by the community. To achieve it, the community had to be united. Thomas began the process with calling a citywide meeting of African Americans. Morris, the leading African American attorney in the city, took command at the county convention. Wright withdrew his candidacy in the name of unity. Bish used his leadership position in the Second Ward to nominate Jones for the commissionership. Even Bish's independent candidacy for the house kept the community united, as African Americans in the First District rallied behind his candidacy and in opposition to Kent, who they believed to be an enemy of the race. As a county board candidate, Jones, a successful businessman, was well qualified. The top leaders overcame personal differences and ambitions and came together within the Republican Party to achieve a major accomplishment. It was validation for everything Thomas had stood for during his twenty-year political career. Despite this, with his removal to the Fourth Ward and with the needs of his growing family, Thomas's political career was winding down.

Conclusion: "Leader of the Colored Race Is Dead"

After almost twenty years as the political leader of Chicago's African Americans, Thomas in the mid-1890s sharply curtailed his role and ceded leadership to others. He became involved in issues that affected the community, but even here he generally let others take the lead.

In 1895, Edward H. Wright won the nomination and election as South Town clerk. Wright was nominated with no opposition, although at one time W. L. Martin, the nominee in 1894, was mentioned as a potential candidate. Thomas played a limited role in the campaign, most notably giving a speech on behalf of Alderman Madden's reelection efforts at a Fourth Ward meeting. Both Wright and Madden easily won election in a strong Republican year.[1]

By 1896, Thomas had all but dropped out of politics. The 1896 election saw the Cook County Republican Party under the firm control of the Lorimer machine. There was disagreement over whom to support for the presidential nomination, but overall harmony reigned throughout the county party. At the county convention, called for the early date of February 15 in an attempt to influence the presidential nomination, the party endorsed Lorimer stalwarts John Tanner for governor, Henry Hertz for state treasurer, T. N. Jamieson for clerk of the appellate court, and Charles S. Deneen for state's attorney.[2]

The general state of harmony bode well for African American Republicans. In 1894, the only time the Republican machine was defeated at the county convention was when Theodore Jones was nominated for county commissioner. By 1896, it was assumed that the South Town Republicans would again nominate an African American for one of the commissioner spots. The *Inter-Ocean* wrote at least two articles recommending that Jones be renominated and also had a story that a group of leading African Americans, including James Porter and Rev. J. F. Thomas, supported Dr. J. Norman Croker for the nomination.[3] However, at the convention delegates unanimously voted for a preselected slate of candidates for commissionerships. That slate included

Wright, meaning he must have cut a deal with the Lorimer machine. In January, Wright had led a group of African Americans in endorsing Hertz for state treasurer, and that may have helped Wright's cause with Lorimer. At the Fifth District senatorial convention, held the same day as the county convention, J. C. Buckner had no problem being renominated for the house in a meeting that lasted approximately twenty minutes. In the Republican landslide year of 1896, Wright and Buckner were elected that fall.[4]

There were some failures for the community, however. James Bish failed again to be nominated for the legislature in the divided First District, and Ida B. Wells-Barnett was apparently snubbed at the Republican county convention when she wished to address the delegates. At the state party convention in May, Illinois African Americans were also unable to have an African American selected to serve as a delegate to the national convention.[5]

Chicago held its city and town elections in April. For the first time, the nominations for these offices followed the nominations for the November elections. The success of African Americans in getting both a Republican county commissionership and a legislative nomination led the *Inter-Ocean* to write that with respect to the town positions "it is now probable that the colored people will receive no further nominations."[6]

The paper underestimated the growing strength of African Americans in the party and their unwillingness to give up any of the symbolic gains it made electorally. Although no African Americans competed for nomination to either a citywide or aldermanic office, once again the position of South Town clerk seems to have been reserved for an African American. The *Inter-Ocean* acknowledged this fact in the days leading up to the South Town Convention when it wrote, "In the South Town, the probable nominees are J. W. Hepburn of the Fourth Ward, assessor; Charles Wathier, First Ward, collector; James Hogan, Sixth Ward, supervisor; and some colored man for clerk."[7] That man was W. L. Martin who, with the support of Stephen A. Douglas Jr., had no problem being nominated. All four of the Republican candidates for South Town office won that April, although Martin's margin of victory was by far the closest. The *Inter-Ocean* would say the closeness of Martin's race was because "a vicious and persistent attack was made on him because of his color."[8]

African Americans were a solid part of the 1896 Republican campaign, providing almost complete loyalty to the party. In the spring, before the Republican state convention, rumors had been spread that Illinois African Americans would oppose Hertz's nomination for state treasurer. As early as January, the *Tribune* ran a story entitled "Why They Hate Hertz." The story gave a history of the Zephyr Davis case and questioned the wisdom of nominating someone who was opposed by such a large base of the party. The fears about African Americans deserting Hertz that year proved to be unfounded. Just before a meeting of the statewide Afro-American League was to convene in Galesburg, Reverend Jesse Woods of Peoria attempted to have the convention single out Hertz as an enemy of the race. However, S. B. Turner, Edward H. Wright, and Dr. J. H. Magee quickly denounced Woods. In letters and interviews to newspapers, they stated that Woods's opposition to Hertz was based on his support of a Peoria candidate for treasurer and that Woods was trying to use the African American voters as a tool to aid in that candidate's nomination. The convention, which Thomas did not attend, took no action against Hertz. Ferdinand Barnett, who received an appointment in 1896 as an assistant state's attorney, served as chief of the Colored Republican Bureau out of an office in Chicago. John G. Jones sat on the platform at a large McKinley-Tanner meeting and also was listed as one of the leading African American Republicans who supported Hertz. Even Reverend C. S. Smith, having failed to reap any rewards under the Cleveland administration and perhaps confident of Republican success and still hopeful for a possible patronage position, campaigned for the Republican ticket that year.[9]

The Chicago campaign, due in part to the efforts of Barnett, brought in several nationally known African American speakers to rally Chicago's African American community. In September, John L. Waller, ex-consul of the United States to Madagascar, came to Chicago for a series of speeches. In mid-October, Charles Anderson of New York spoke before a large meeting held under the auspices of the African American hotel and restaurant employees of Chicago and the next night spoke before a smaller banquet consisting of forty guests. Near the end of October, Bishop Benjamin Arnett, a prominent African American minister from Ohio, and J. Madison Vance, an African American attorney from Louisiana, spoke before a large meeting of African American voters, with estimates of the crowd size ranging from two thousand to eight thousand. The meeting, held at the ten-thousand-seat Tattersall Hall on the near South Side, followed an hour-long "Grand Republican Rally of the Colored Citizens of Chicago" torchlight parade through South Side neighborhoods.[10]

Thomas attended many of these events. Consul Waller's first speech was at a large, nonpartisan meeting chaired by John G. Jones and held at Quinn Church. Four days later, Waller addressed a large African American Republican rally where Thomas served as chairman of the meeting. Thomas served as a vice president for Arnett's talk at Tattersall Hall and for a large Fourth Ward Republican Club torchlight parade and rally held just two blocks south of his home.[11]

Thomas was now the elder statesman in Chicago's African American political community. With the birth of his daughter, Grace, in 1898, the Thomas household consisted of his wife Crittie, four children under the age of eleven, and a housekeeper. Thomas appears to have begun to choose his causes more selectively. In 1897, he participated with longtime rival John G. Jones in an indignation meeting protesting the treatment of African Americans by the Cook County sheriff, the county jailer, and the superintendent of the Post Office. Thomas served with George Ecton and Theodore Jones to deliver the complaints of the meeting to the Cook County Board and the authorities in Washington, D.C.[12] In November 1898, he joined several prominent African Americans in serving as a vice president of a meeting held to protest crimes against African Americans in South Carolina. He also served on the banking committee of a national association whose object was to secure funds for erecting monuments in some of the larger cities of the country in memory of the African American soldiers and sailors who died in the Civil War and the Spanish-American War. George Ecton also served on that committee, and John G. Jones served as president of the organization.[13]

In 1898 Thomas helped form the Sumner Club, a Republican political and social organization for African Americans designed to rival similar white clubs. The *Appeal* described it as being "founded upon the principles that govern the Hamilton and Marquette clubs," two all-white political and social clubs. The Sumner Club supported Republican candidates but differed from previous African American political clubs in that it met its own expenses. This meant that it did not have to rely on the regular party organization. Thomas served as the president of the club, with J. Gray Lucas serving as vice-president, Edward H. Morris serving as treasurer, and Edward H. Wright serving as chairman of the executive committee. The club was active in working campaigns. It also sponsored speakers to Chicago, including Booker T. Washington.[14]

Thomas served as a vice president at two large rallies sponsored by the African American Republicans during the spring 1897 elections, but almost every prominent African American in the city other than Democrat Lloyd G. Wheeler served at these.[15] The Republicans had nominated Judge N. C. Sears for mayor, but he lost the election to Carter Harrison II, son of the mayor assassinated in 1893. Like his father, the second Mayor Harrison would use patronage to make some inroads among African American voters. The spring election was a Democratic landslide, meaning that rising African American attorney Adelbert Roberts, who had been nominated for South Town clerk by the Republicans, lost in his first bid for office. Roberts would eventually be elected a state representative and in 1924 was elected as the first African American state senator in Illinois.[16]

The year 1898 was a mixed one politically for African Americans. That spring, Republicans nominated African American businessman F. W. Rollins for South Town clerk. Two days later, Rollins turned down the nomination and a campaign committee replaced him on the ticket with African American attorney M. A. Mardis. The entire South Town Republican ticket would lose in the April election. In June, Edward H. Wright had no trouble being renominated for the county board as one of the three Republican candidates from South Town. The names of eight men were placed in nomination, including future African American leader Daniel M. Jackson. Republicans in the Fifth Senatorial District did not renominate Buckner to a third term in the house, but they did nominate another African American, W. L. Martin. Buckner's efforts for renomination were hurt by a very public feud he had with Republican governor John Tanner and by his vote as a legislator in favor of the Allen Bill, a controversial measure that would permit the Chicago City Council to grant fifty-year franchises to streetcar companies. Such a measure seemed rife with corruption possibilities, and eighteen of the twenty-four Republican state legislators who voted for the bill were not renominated.[17]

Efforts by leading African Americans to have a representative of their group named to a countywide position failed. Also, at the state Republican convention in June, the party eliminated the at-large positions to the state central committee. With committee members only coming from congressional districts, no African Americans served on the central committee. Buckner was nominated for delegate-at-large to the off-year National Republican Convention, but he turned down the nomination.[18]

In 1899, Buckner followed Thomas's footsteps and was nominated by the Republicans for South Town clerk. Thomas did not serve as a delegate to the Republican City Convention that spring, choosing instead to do his work through the newly created Sumner Club. The club had a large meeting in March to ratify the Republican ticket and plan strategy for the spring campaign. However, it was the Afro-American League and the African American churches that took the lead in protesting the brutal beating of an African American political worker at the hands of First Ward alderman John "Bathhouse" Coughlin. The affair united the community, but even a united African American community couldn't stop the Democratic landslide that spring, as Carter Harrison II was easily reelected mayor and the entire Republican South Town ticket, including Buckner, lost.[19]

By the late 1890s, Chicago's African Americans were solidly in the Republican camp. As in the 1880s, there were Democratic African American clubs, but they were small and featured the same speakers: Hannibal Carter, attorney R. A. Dawson, and alienated Republican Stephen A. Douglas Jr. Under

Carter Harrison II, African Americans received some patronage positions, most notably Robert M. Mitchell as assistant prosecuting attorney, but African Americans were nowhere to be found as candidates or party decision makers.[20]

In the Republican Party, African Americans fared better. The community was a part of the Republican political fabric enough so that an African American was almost assured of receiving a party nomination for South Town clerk, county board commissioner, or state representative. However, in an era of ethnic politics, the community's numbers needed to grow for African Americans to be considered for higher positions, such as alderman or judge, or for countywide or statewide offices. Elected Republican officials routinely gave patronage jobs to African Americans, although here too, there was a limit to how high a position an African American could hold. Similarly, African Americans played a role in Republican Party leadership and decision-making circles, but again, this role was limited, with the true leaders of the party being ward committeemen and aldermen, none of whom were African American in 1899.

Thomas had greatly assisted in advancing the community in the political world. He began his political activity at the same time African Americans first received the vote in Illinois. Over the course of his career, he had served in two of the three elective positions that had been held by an African American in Chicago and had run for the third. He also had served in several Republican Party positions and had even received a federal patronage position in the early 1880s, when he was appointed to the federal treasury department. He had continually organized the community in political ways.

But while Thomas had taken the community through its initial stage of political activity, moving on to a higher stage of political power and decision making would only come about through an increase in the number of African American voters, something that would not occur until the great migration of the early twentieth century. In a world of ethnic politics, numbers mattered most.

Thomas would not live to see that next stage. He developed chronic interstitial nephritis, a kidney disease that to this day has no known cure. In late 1898 or early 1899, his health began to fail. By the fall of 1899 he was unable to work. In early December, his illness worsened and by the middle of the month he fell unconscious. On Monday, December 18, 1899, he died at his home, attended by Daniel Hale Williams, the nation's leading African American physician.[21]

All of Chicago's daily newspapers wrote lengthy obituaries of Thomas. Some, like the *Tribune* and the *Evening Journal*, focused on his wealth when he died, estimating his estate to be worth $100,000. The *Inter-Ocean*'s five stacked headlines focused on his being the first African American in the state legislature and his establishing the first school for African Americans in Chicago. The *Chicago Chronicle*'s headline merely stated, "Leader of Colored Race Is Dead."[22]

On Thursday, December 22, his funeral was held at Olivet Baptist Church. Reverend Richard DeBaptiste, although no longer associated with Olivet, officiated. Two of the leading African American ministers in Chicago at that time, Reverend A. J. Carey and Reverend J. F. Thomas, assisted him. Among the ten active pallbearers were Edward H. Wright, Edward H. Morris, and J. Gray Lucas. There were also eight honorary pallbearers, including Judge Orrin N. Carter, who at the time was a candidate for the Republican nomination for governor, former aldermen Arthur Dixon and Martin Madden, First Ward politician Isaac N. Powell, and African American politicians John C. Buckner, Theodore Jones, and Franklin Dennison. Dr. George C. Hall also served as a pallbearer. Thomas was buried at Oak Woods Cemetery, where his parents, second wife Justine, and four deceased children had also been laid to rest, although in a separate plot.[23]

On December 31, 1899, the Sumner Club paid tribute to Thomas with a memorial service at Bethel A.M.E. Church. A large crowd attended the service. J. Gray Lucas, Arthur Dixon, Edward H. Morris, and Reverend R. C. Ransom all spoke. Edward H. Wright told the story of Thomas's life. Presumably the tributes were similar to those expressed in the *Legal News* article on his death, which stated that "He was regarded by all who knew him as a man of honor and integrity."[24]

Taking advantage of the post–Civil War opportunities the city offered to African Americans, limited though they were, Thomas had become a successful teacher, businessman, attorney, real estate investor, and politician. Indeed, politically speaking, his personal successes are clear. In the course of his career, he met presidents, presidential candidates, governors, senators, and the leading African Americans in the nation. For fifteen years, from 1876 to 1890, he was the political leader of Chicago's African American community, a difficult task given the fractious nature of any small community and one made more so by the need to leverage the small numbers into a working relationship with the large white majority. He was the only African American to serve three terms in the Illinois House of Representatives until the 1920s. His political allies and supporters, such as Edward H. Morris, Edward H. Wright, and J. C. Buckner, went on to serve as the next generation of African American leaders, having learned their political skills while working with Thomas.

But while Thomas profited on a personal level from his activities, he always sought to help Chicago's African American community. His founding of a school for African Americans, his participation in fraternal organizations and his church, and his willingness to live in the levee district until long after most other successful African Americans had left the neighborhood demonstrate a commitment to the community that went beyond personal political success. He was a fierce defender of African American rights and equality, as seen by his successful sponsorship of the state's first civil rights act, his support of T. Thomas Fortune's Afro-American League, his work at the 1883 and 1885 Illinois Colored Conventions, and his participation in numerous protests by the African American community. Indeed, his protests due to the Zephyr Davis case probably cost him a county board nomination.

The post–Civil War years for Chicago's African American community represented a coming to terms with newfound freedoms and opportunities, and with the limits placed upon them. Thomas's life reflects those opportunities and those limitations. More importantly, as the community's political leader, his work increased those opportunities for other African Americans.

Appendixes

Notes

Bibliography

Index

Appendix A: Illinois' Leading African American Politicians, 1870–99

With the exception of Dr. Daniel Hale Williams and John Jones, full-scale biographies do not exist for the leaders of the African American community in post–Civil War Illinois. They are, like John W. E. Thomas, little known today. Below is a quick reference guide to African American leaders mentioned in this book as they and their careers relate to the life and times of John W. E. Thomas.

Baker, William. A community activist both before and after the Civil War, Baker served as a doorman in the Illinois House in 1877. He ran and lost against Thomas for the Republican nomination for state representative in both 1882 and 1884 and also lost the Republican nomination for South Town clerk to Thomas in 1887.

Barnett, Ferdinand L. Attorney and founder of Chicago's first African American newspaper, the *Conservator*. In the 1880s, he was a supporter of a more independent political course for African Americans. In 1885, he and Thomas were at odds when Thomas supported Isaac Rivers over Barnett for a patronage position. Barnett was a leading activist in the early 1900s. In 1895, he married noted antilynching crusader Ida B. Wells in a wedding ceremony Thomas attended.

Barnett, Ida B. Wells. Leading antilynching crusader who came to Chicago from Memphis, Tennessee, in the mid-1890s. In 1895 she married Ferdinand L. Barnett at a wedding Thomas attended. Her career as a civil rights and women's rights activist extended into the 1930s. Overall, she and Thomas do not appear to have crossed paths much.

Bird, John J. Republican leader from Cairo, Illinois. Bird was elected justice of the peace in 1873. He and Thomas were allies at the 1883 and 1885 colored conventions.

Bish, James. Chicago Republican politician, he served one term in the General Assembly. He was one of the protesters when Thomas failed to receive a Senate nomination in 1890. He and Thomas appear to have been allies.

Buckner, John C. As a politician, Buckner spent much of his time working with an Illinois African American militia unit but a dispute with Illinois governor John Tanner meant that he was not called to service in the Spanish-American War when the unit was. A member of Martin Madden's Fourth Ward organization, Buckner served two terms in the Illinois House. Appearing on the political scene as Thomas was leaving it, he and Thomas appear to have been friends.

Carter, Hannibal. Originally from Louisiana, Carter joined with Thomas to form the Logan Hall Association, an African American Republican political organization, and also served as president of the 1888 John W. E. Thomas First Ward Republican Club. However, in 1890, Carter ran as an independent for state representative and after that campaign left the Republican Party.

DeBaptiste, Richard. Nationally known Baptist religious leader, DeBaptiste was minister at Olivet Baptist Church when Thomas moved to Chicago. DeBaptiste officiated at Thomas's third wedding and at his funeral.

Ecton, George. The head waiter at the Woodruff House, Ecton replaced Thomas in the General Assembly, serving two terms. He was an extremely popular, outgoing person who appears to have had Thomas's support.

Howard, John. A political dilettante and perpetual office-seeker, Howard owned a cigar and liquor store. He was nicknamed "Senator" by the African American press, but he never won an elective office. He began his career as a Republican and eventually filtered over to the Democratic Party. He and Thomas were on-again, off-again allies.

Jones, John. Regarded as the first leader of Chicago's small African American community, Jones led the fight for the 1865 repeal of the Illinois Black laws. He was a friend of Frederick Douglass and John Brown, and his Chicago house was used as a stop on the underground railroad. In 1871 he became the first African American elected to the Board of County Commissioners and he was reelected in 1872. His career generally pre-dated that of Thomas, but Thomas did attend his funeral in 1879.

Jones, John G. Nicknamed "Indignation," Jones was an attorney and a leading Mason who was best known for never backing down from a fight. He earned his nickname by organizing numerous protests, known as indignation rallies, when he felt his community had been insulted. He was the leading organizer behind the Illinois colored conventions of the 1880s and strongly advocated a course more independent of the Republican Party.

He served one term as a state representative (1901–3) as a Republican. He and Thomas were bitter opponents throughout most of Thomas's career.

Jones, Theodore. In 1894, Jones became only the second African American elected to the Cook County Board and the first since John Jones in 1872. He served as an honorary pallbearer at Thomas's funeral.

Magee, James. Originally from downstate Metropolis, Illinois, Magee served as the first African American on the Republican State Central Committee and later moved to Chicago after receiving a patronage appointment from Illinois governor Richard Oglesby. Magee and Thomas both were in the pro-Republican camps at the 1883 and 1885 Illinois colored conventions.

McAllister, C. H. Elected South Town clerk after he defeated Thomas for the Republican nomination for the position in 1888, McAllister had his name placed in nomination for reelection at the 1889 South Town Republican Convention by Thomas, who also worked for his candidacy in 1890.

Mitchell, Henry J. Elected South Town clerk for two terms before Thomas, Mitchell generally appears to have been a friend and ally of Thomas. In 1885, Mitchell visited Thomas who was serving in the General Assembly in Springfield, and in 1888 they cofounded the Logan Hall Association, an African American political club.

Mitchell, Robert M. Republican politician who served as an assistant clerk of the criminal court. Mitchell ran and lost against Thomas for the Republican nomination for state representative in both 1882 and 1884, but remained active in ward politics and at one point was named president of the Second Ward Republican Club. He became an attorney later in his career.

Moore, Joseph. In 1880, Moore became the first African American in Cook County to be elected to a township position, when he was elected South Town clerk.

Morris, Edward. Chicago's leading African American attorney for most of the 1880s and 1890s, Morris was able to bridge most of the divisions in Chicago's African American community and be considered a friend by all. He served two separate terms as a Republican state representative (1891–93, 1903–5) and was a national leader on race issues. He represented Thomas in at least one law case, and they worked together on other legal issues. Morris spoke at a memorial service held for Thomas after his death.

Phillips, W. C. Thomas's closest friend and ally, Phillips was a carpenter by trade. He and Thomas both were active in Olivet Baptist Church and in local Republican politics. Phillips received a patronage appointment as a clerk in the Cook County Recorder of Deeds Office and worked there for several years. Republicans nominated him for the state legislature to succeed Thomas, but he failed to meet residency requirements for the district and had to step down as a candidate.

Rivers, Isaac "Ike." A political enforcer, Rivers worked the tough levee district on behalf of Republican causes. He failed in his few efforts for political office. In 1885, Thomas supported Rivers over Ferdinand Barnett for a state patronage position, an action that hurt Thomas politically. Despite this, Thomas and Rivers were, at best, on-again, off-again political allies.

Scott, William. A Democratic newspaper editor from downstate Cairo, Illinois, Scott was a member of the "mugwump" faction at the 1883 and 1885 Illinois colored conventions that sought a course more independent of the Republican Party.

Smith, C. S. A minister and resident of Bloomington, Illinois in the 1870s and 1880s, Smith was a leading member of the African Methodist Episcopal Church. A former member of the Alabama state legislature, Smith was a member of the independent "mugwump" faction at the 1883 and 1885 Illinois colored conventions. During the 1884 presidential election, he served as an alternate delegate to the Republican National Convention, supported Benjamin Butler's independent candidacy for the White House, and then endorsed Democrat Grover Cleveland's candidacy. He was instrumental in preventing Thomas from becoming a Republican delegate to the 1884 Republican National Convention and the two were bitter enemies.

Turner, S. B. As a resident of Springfield, Illinois, and a newspaper correspondent for the African American weekly the *Cleveland Gazette*, Turner was a defender of Thomas. He later moved to Chicago, where he founded his own newspaper and, after Thomas's death, became a state representative.

Waring, Robert. Served in the Cook County Clerk's office as deputy and generally appears to have been a Thomas ally at the Illinois colored conventions of the mid-1880s, although he lost the Republican nomination for South Town clerk to Thomas in 1887.

Wheeler, Lloyd G. Son-in-law of John Jones and the first African American attorney in Chicago. He inherited Jones's tailoring business and became one of Chicago's wealthiest African Americans. He was a leader of the independent movement in the 1880s and eventually settled in the Democratic Party. He and Thomas appear to have been fierce opponents.

White, Louis. White lived in the neighborhood where Thomas moved to when he settled in Chicago in 1869. A postal worker, White was active in Republican Party politics and Olivet Baptist Church and was mentioned as a possible candidate for the legislature in 1872 and for probate clerk in 1877.

Williams, Daniel Hale. The most famous African American physician of the nineteenth century, Williams performed the world's first open heart surgery in 1893 and founded Chicago's Provident Hospital. He was the Thomas family's physician, signing the death certificate of John W. E. Thomas and serving as Crittie Thomas's physician in the early 1900s.

Williams, S. Laing. Prominent attorney and leading socialite in Chicago's African American community in the 1890s. He was a friend and ally of Booker T. Washington. He and Thomas do not appear to have had much public interaction together.

Wright, Edward. Republican South Side politician and preeminent political strategist known as the Ironmaster, Wright and Thomas were friends and allies. He was elected South Town clerk in 1895 and to the Cook County Board in 1896. Wright served as a pallbearer at Thomas's funeral and spoke at a Sumner Club tribute to Thomas after his death. In 1920, he became the first African American ward committeeman in Chicago.

Appendix B: Illinois Civil Rights Act of 1885

An Act *to protect all citizens in their civil and legal rights and fixing a penalty for violation of the same.*

SECTION 1. *Be it enacted by the People of the State of Illinois, represented in the General Assembly*: That all persons within the jurisdiction of said state shall be entitled to the full and equal enjoyment of the accommodations, advantages, facilities and privileges of inns, restaurants, eating houses, barber shops, public conveyances on land or water, theaters, and all other places of public accommodation and amusement, subject only to the conditions and limitations established by law, and applicable alike to all citizens.

SECTION 2. That any person who shall violate any of the provisions of the foregoing section by denying to any citizen, except for reasons applicable alike to all citizens of every race and color, and regardless of color or race, the full enjoyment of any accommodations, advantages, facilities, or privileges in said section enumerated, or by aiding or inciting such denial, shall, for every such offense, forfeit and pay a sum not less than twenty-five (25) dollars nor more than five hundred (500) dollars to the person aggrieved thereby, to be recovered in any court of competent jurisdiction, in the county where said offense was committed; and shall also, for every such offense, be deemed guilty of a misdemeanor, and upon conviction thereof, shall be fined not to exceed five hundred (500) dollars, or shall be imprisoned not more than one year, or both: *And, provided further*, that a judgment in favor of the party aggrieved, or punishment upon an indictment, shall be a bar to either prosecution respectively.
Approved June 10, 1885

(*Laws of the State of Illinois Enacted by the Thirty-Fourth General Assembly*, 64–65)

Notes

Introduction: "A Representative of Its Colored Citizens"

1. *Springfield State Journal*, January 4, 1877, 4.
2. Illinois General Assembly, *Journal of the House: 30th General Assembly*, 11.
3. Ibid.
4. Keiser, *Building for the Centuries*, 180–214, 336–43.
5. Walch, "Construction of the Capitol of Illinois," 11–13.
6. For a full discussion on Chicago's African American community and its fight for political, social, and economic equality in post–Civil War society, see Drake and Cayton, *Black Metropolis*.
7. Branham, "Black Chicago," 363.
8. Drake and Cayton, *Black Metropolis*, 45.
9. Kogan, *First Century*, 202–4.
10. Ibid., 201.
11. Reed, *Black Chicago's First Century*, 264, 267–84, 382–90; Gatewood, *Aristocrats of Color*, 121–27; Drake, *Churches and Voluntary Associations*, 10.
12. 1873 Articles of Incorporation, Cook County Building Loan and Homestead Association, Record Series 103.112, Dissolved Domestic Corporation Charters (1849–1979), Illinois State Archives.
13. Drake and Cayton, *Black Metropolis*, 46–56. Twelfth Census of the United States (1900), Chicago, Ward 4, Vol. 17, E.D. 83. Sheet 2, Line 1.
14. See, for example, Gosnell, *Negro Politicians*; Drake and Cayton, *Black Metropolis*; Spear, *Black Chicago*.
15. Biographies do exist for Dr. Daniel Hale Williams, Dr. Charles Edwin Bentley, and socialite Fannie Barrier Williams. There are also biographies and an autobiography of black activist Ida B. Wells-Barnett, although her career began in the South and she did not arrive in Chicago to stay until 1895. There are no published biographies of Chicago African American politicians of the era, although there have been unpublished biographies and short articles on John Jones (1818–79), widely considered to be Chicago's first African American political leader.
16. Spear, *Black Chicago*, x.; Reed, *Black Chicago's First Century*, 479; Katznelson, *Black Men, White Cities*, 86.
17. L. Grossman, *Democratic Party and the Negro*, xi. See Thornbrough, *Negro in Indiana*, for a comparison of the African American experience in a state similar to Illinois.

1. "Let Us Come Out Like Men": The Historic Election of 1876

1. Various sources place his birth anywhere from 1842 to 1849. The 1877 *Illinois Legislative Manual*, a privately published book, lists his birth date as 1842, but obituaries in both the *Chicago Tribune* and the *Chicago Inter-Ocean* list it as 1847. Thomas's death certificate places his age at time of death on December 18, 1899, at 54, which would place his birth in 1845. The 1880 census places his age at 35, which also would make his year of birth 1845. However, the census record for 1870 places his age at 27, meaning he would have been born in 1843. There are no records for the 1890 census. Thomas's 1887 marriage certificate from his third marriage lists his age as 38, meaning he would have been born in 1849.

2. Phillips, *Biographies of State Officers*, 229.

3. Death Certificates of Edinboro Thomas, April 16, 1881, and Martha Thomas, March 10, 1881, Cook County Clerk's Office; Probate Records for Edinboro Thomas, General Number 4–1563, filed April 1881, Cook County Circuit Clerk's Office; Bailey, *Chicago City Directory, 1865–1866*, Halpin, *Directory*, 1867–1868, Edwards, *Annual Directory* for the years 1868, 1870, 1871. John W. E. Thomas's entry in the 1883 *United States Biographical Dictionary* lists Edinburgh Thomas's birthplace as North Carolina.

4. *Chicago Tribune*, October 16, 1876, 2. According to the Cook County records, Edinboro Thomas purchased the lot on December 18, 1865 for $1,250; see Cook County Recorder of Deeds, bk. 468, pp. 44–45, School Section Add'n. Sec. 16.39.14, block 127, lot 41).

5. City of Chicago Permit Reports, Book A (February 21, 1872–July 20, 1875), p. 68, line 2489.

6. *Chicago Tribune*, October 16, 1876, 2 and December 19, 1899; 7; *Chicago Inter-Ocean*, December 19, 1899, 7.

7. Eighth Census of the United States (1860), Mobile, Ala., Ward 3, Roll M653-17, p. 305. Ibid., slave schedule, p. 42. Some in the Thomas family believe Dr. McCleskey may have been John W. E. Thomas's natural father, due to Thomas's light complexion and Dr. McCleskey's interest in his advancement. Author's interview with Jackie Rhodes, great-granddaughter of John W. E. Thomas. July 14, 2006.

8. *Chicago Tribune*, October 16, 1876, 2.

9. Author's interview with Jackie Rhodes, July 14, 2006; *Chicago Tribune*, December 19, 1899, 7; Ninth Census of the United States (1870), Chicago, Ill., Ward 3, Roll M593-199, p. 336.

10. *Report of the Board of Police*, 140.

11. Gordon and Paulett, *Printers Row Chicago*, 11.

12. *Chicago Tribune*, October 9, 1874, 3; *Chicago by Day and Night*, 201–2; Gordon and Paulett, *Printers Row Chicago*, 12.

13. Ninth Census, Chicago, Ward 3, Roll M593-199, p. 336. Edinboro Thomas is not listed in the census.

14. Einhorn. *Property Rules*, 264–65.

15. Fisher, "History of the Olivet Baptist Church," 24–32. For DeBaptiste's biography, see Simmons, *Men of Mark*, 352–57; Fisher, "History of the Olivet Baptist Church," 46 n 2, appendix E, 102, and appendix F, 103. See also Drake, *Churches and Voluntary Associations* 46, 53–59; and Gatewood, *Aristocrats of Color*, 281.

16. *Minutes of the Twenty-fourth Annual Meeting.* See also the minutes of the Thirty-fifth, Thirty-eighth, and Forty-first annual meetings of the Wood River Baptist Association.

17. *Edwards' Annual Directory for the City of Chicago, 1871,* 884; *Chicago Tribune,* May 3, 1870, 4; *Lakeside Annual Directory,* 1871–80.

18. *Chicago Inter-Ocean,* December 19, 1899, 7; *Chicago Chronicle,* December 19, 1899, 4.

19. Keiser, *Building for the Centuries,* 262–63.

20. *Chicago Tribune,* December 8, 1872, 2; Articles of Incorporation, Cook County Building Loan and Homestead Association, Illinois State Archives. The fact that the association organized at a church demonstrates the importance of the African American church as an institution in the community.

21. *Report of the Board of Police,* 140.

22. *Robinson's Atlas;* Record of Building Permits Issued by the Board of Public Works, Item 2489, August 22, 1874, Richard J. Daley Library, University of Illinois–Chicago.

23. *Chicago Tribune,* October 21, 1877, 8.

24. *Chicago Tribune,* September 21, 1875, 8.

25. *Chicago Tribune,* October 26, 1870, 4.

26. *Chicago Inter-Ocean,* September 5, 1872, 6; *Chicago Tribune,* September 7, 1872, 4. For more on Jones, see Gliozzo, "John Jones."

27. *Chicago Inter-Ocean,* March 24, 1879, 4.

28. *Chicago Inter-Ocean,* November 2, 1875, 5; *Chicago Tribune,* November 1, 1875, 1.

29. Spear, *Black Chicago,* 12.

30. *Chicago Inter-Ocean,* October 15, 1874, 8; Reed, *Black Chicago's First Century,* 69, 180.

31. *Chicago Tribune,* June 14, 1874, 4.

32. *Chicago Tribune,* October 15, 1874, 2 and October 17, 1874, 1; *Chicago Inter-Ocean,* October 15, 1874, 8.

33. *Chicago Tribune,* October 8, 1874, 2, and October 18, 1874, 1.

34. *Chicago Tribune,* November 5, 1874, 1.

35. *Chicago Tribune,* September 1, 1875, 2; *Chicago Inter-Ocean,* September 1, 1875, 8, and September 22, 1875, 8; *Chicago Times,* September 1, 1875, 2, and September 22, 1875, 2.

36. *Chicago Tribune,* September 23, 1875, 4, and September 26, 1875, 4.

37. *Chicago Inter-Ocean,* October 20, 1875, 1 and 2; *Chicago Times,* October 20, 1875, 1.

38. *Chicago Tribune,* September 1, 1875, 2; *Chicago Inter-Ocean,* September 1, 1875, 8; *Chicago Times,* September 1, 1875, 2.

39. *Chicago Times,* October 3, 1875, 3; *Chicago Tribune,* October 3, 1875, 9.

40. *Chicago Inter-Ocean,* October 4, 1875, 3, October 18, 1875, 2, October 20, 1875, 1, October 26, 1875, 1 , and November 1, 1875, 1; *Chicago Times,* October 20, 1875, 1.

41. *Chicago Tribune,* November 1, 1875, 1; *Chicago Inter-Ocean,* November 2, 1875, 5.

42. Styx, *Chicago Ward Maps,* 21–25.

43. *Chicago Inter-Ocean*, March 11, 1876, 8.

44. *Chicago Evening Journal*, October 1, 1880, 4; *Chicago Times-Herald*, March 24, 1898, 12.

45. *Chicago Inter-Ocean*, March 18, 1876, 8, and March 25, 1876, 8; *Chicago Tribune*, March 18, 1876, 2.

46. *Chicago Tribune*, April 6, 1876, 4, and April 16, 1876, 4.

47. *Chicago Inter-Ocean*, March 1, 1876, 2; *Chicago Tribune*, March 1, 1876, 1 and March 2, 1876, 4.

48. *Chicago Tribune*, March 5, 1876, 12.

49. *Chicago Inter-Ocean*, March 28, 1876, 5; *Chicago Tribune*, April 6, 1876, 4, and May 10, 1876, 7; Reed, *Black Chicago's First Century*, 139–40.

50. *Chicago Tribune*, April 16, 1876, 3.

51. *Chicago Tribune*, May 19, 1876, 2; *Springfield State Journal*, May 24, 1876, 4.

52. *Chicago Inter-Ocean*, April 11, 1876, 8.

53. For more information about cumulative voting in Illinois, see *Illinois Legislative Manual*, 137–38; and Blair, *Cumulative Voting.*

54. *Chicago Tribune*, October 7, 1870, 3, and October 17, 1870, 4.

55. *Chicago Inter-Ocean*, September 4, 1872, 6, and September 10, 1872, 6.

56. *Chicago Inter-Ocean*, July 11, 1876, 8; *Chicago Times*, July 11, 1876, 2; *Chicago Tribune*, July 11, 1876, 1.

57. *Chicago Tribune*, August 9, 1876, 2, and August 15, 1876, 1.

58. *Chicago Times*, September 15, 1876, 1; *Chicago Tribune*, September 17, 1876, 1.

59. *Chicago Times*, September 24, 1876, 3, and October 8, 1876, 3; *Chicago Tribune*, September 24, 1876, 2, and October 8, 1876, 2.

60. *Chicago Tribune*, September 28, 1876, 1.

61. *Chicago Tribune*, September 29, 1876, 1; *Chicago Evening Journal*, October 9, 1876, 4.

62. *Chicago Inter-Ocean*, October 13, 1876, 5.

63. *Chicago Inter-Ocean*, October 13, 1876, 5; *Chicago Tribune*, October 13, 1876, 1; *Chicago Times*, October 13, 1876, 1.

64. *Chicago Inter-Ocean*, July 11, 1876, 8.

65. The *Chicago Evening Journal* of October 17, 1876, 3, reports a ratification meeting scheduled for that evening; however, the *Chicago Inter-Ocean* on October 24, 1876, 5, reports a ratification meeting of African American voters, which Thomas addressed, as occurring at Olivet on October 23.

66. *Chicago Evening Journal*, October 13, 1876, 1; *Chicago Inter-Ocean*, October 13, 1876, 5; *Chicago Tribune*, October 13, 1876, 1.

67. *Chicago Inter-Ocean*, October 16, 1876, 5; *Chicago Times*, October 24, 1876, 1.

68. *Chicago Evening Journal*, October 21, 1876, 2 and 6, and October 26, 1876, 4; *Chicago Tribune*, October 21, 1876, 2.

69. *Chicago Times*, October 15, 1876, 3; *Chicago Tribune*, October 29, 1876, 3.

70. *Chicago Inter-Ocean*, April 17, 1876, 8.

71. *Chicago Evening Journal*, October 25, 1876, 3, October 26, 1876, 4, and October 31, 1876, 4; *Chicago Times*, October 28, 1876, 3.

72. Jackson that night was attending the same Second Ward Republican meeting that Thomas spoke to. *Chicago Tribune*, October 31, 1876, 2.

73. Ibid.; *Chicago Times,* October 31, 1876, 2.

74. *Chicago Tribune*, November 1, 1876, 2; *Chicago Evening Journal*, November 1, 1876, 4, and November 2, 1876, 4.

75. *Chicago Times*, November 3, 1876, 1.

76. Ibid., 2; *Chicago Times*, November 3, 1876, 1; *Chicago Evening Journal*, November 6, 1876, 4.

77. *Chicago Inter-Ocean*, November 6, 1876, 5.

78. *Chicago Times*, September 15, 1876, 1. *Abstract of Votes*.

79. Massachusetts elected its first African American to the state legislature in 1867. Ohio followed in 1880, Indiana in 1881, Rhode Island in 1885, Kansas in 1889, Michigan in 1893, Minnesota in 1898, Wisconsin in 1906, Pennsylvania in 1911, New York in 1917, and New Jersey in 1921. Jones, *Some Foot-Steps of Progress*, 39.

80. *Chicago Evening Journal*, October 8, 1878, 3.

2. "An Able, Attentive, and Sensible Representative": The First Term and a Failed Reelection Bid

1. Temple, "Alfred Henry Piquenard," 22, 25.

2. Bunting, *Ulysses S. Grant*, 129–39.

3. *Chicago Tribune*, November 26, 1876, 4, and December 4, 1876, 4; *Chicago Inter-Ocean*, April 14, 1877, 5, and November 11, 1877, 4; Pierce, *History of Chicago*, 349.

4. *Springfield State Journal*, March 29, 1877, 4.

5. Campbell, *Representative Democracy* 31–32; Keiser, *Building for the Centuries*, 44; *Illinois Legislative Manual*, 119–33; *Springfield State Journal*, January 10, 1877, 2.

6. *Chicago Inter-Ocean*, January 6, 1877, 5.

7. White, *Illinois Blue Book*, 466–67, 475–76; Moses, *Illinois Historical and Statistical*, 821, 828, 845, 855; Church, *History of the Republican Party*, 129.

8. Illinois General Assembly, *Journal of the House: Thirtieth General Assembly*, 6–8; *Springfield State Journal*, January 4, 1877, 4.

9. Illinois General Assembly, *Journal of the House: Thirtieth General Assembly*, 10.

10. *Chicago Inter-Ocean*, January 6, 1877, 5; *Illinois Legislative Manual*, plate F.

11. Moses, *Illinois Historical and Statistical*, 845; Campbell, 31–32.

12. Illinois General Assembly, *Journal of the House: Thirtieth General Assembly*, 80–83.

13. Moses, *Illinois Historical and Statistical*, 957.

14. James Pickett Jones, *John A. Logan Stalwart Republican from Illinois* (Tallahassee: University Press of Florida, 1982; reprint, Carbondale: Southern Illinois University Press. 2001), xi, 1–2; *Chicago Inter-Ocean*, January 6, 1877, 1.

15. *Springfield State Journal*, January 6, 1877, 4.

16. Moses, *Illinois Historical and Statistical*, 848–49; Church, 130- 131; Illinois General Assembly, *Journal of the House: Thirtieth General Assembly*, 85, 89–95, 99–104, 106–11, 113–17, 121–26, 130–37, 140–45, 149–50. The choice of Davis also affected the presidential contest, as it had been thought that he might be appointed to the electoral commission created by Congress and serve as the swing vote on the commission. See William H. Rehnquist, *Centennial Crisis: The Disputed Election of 1876* (New York: Alfred A. Knopf, 2004), 118–119, 132–142, 157–160, 180, 185, 221.

17. *Chicago Tribune*, February 28, 1877, 5.

18. *Chicago Tribune*, Dec. 17, 1876, 4, December 19, 1876, 3–4; *Chicago Inter-Ocean*, October 19, 1877, 3.

19. *Chicago Tribune*, December 17, 1876, 4.

20. Illinois General Assembly, *Journal of the House: Thirtieth General Assembly*, 483, 794, 803, 836, 846–47; *Springfield State Journal*, May 25, 1877, 4.

21. *Chicago Tribune*, December 17, 1877, 4; Illinois General Assembly, *Journal of the House: Thirtieth General Assembly*, 300.

22. *Chicago Inter-Ocean*, March 31, 1877, 2, and May 2, 1877, 5.

23. *Chicago Tribune*, December 8, 1877, 4; Illinois General Assembly, *Journal of the House: Thirtieth General Assembly*, 458, 698, 633–34; Illinois General Assembly, *Journal of the Senate: Thirtieth General Assembly*, 980.

24. Illinois General Assembly, *Journal of the House: Thirtieth General Assembly*, 159, 508–9; *Springfield State Journal*, April 12, 1877, 4.

25. Illinois General Assembly, *Journal of the House: Thirtieth General Assembly*, pp. III–V and IX–XVIII.

26. *Springfield State Register*, May 25, 1877, 2.

27. Illinois General Assembly, *Journal of the House: Thirtieth General Assembly*, 42, 640.

28. *Chicago Inter-Ocean*, February 8, 1877, 2; *Springfield State Register*, February 7, 1877, 1.

29. For a discussion on the conflicting roles minority representatives faced in the legislature, see Haynie, *African American Legislators*, 1–13.

30. *Chicago Inter-Ocean*, May 5, 1877, 5; *Chicago Times*, May 5, 1877, 10; *Chicago Tribune*, May 5, 1887, 9.

31. Illinois General Assembly, *Journal of the House: Thirtieth General Assembly*, p. XIX.

32. *Springfield State Journal*, February 5, 1877, 5; *Chicago Tribune*, February 5, 1877, 9; *Chicago Inter-Ocean*, February 5, 1877, 5; Illinois General Assembly, *Journal of the House: Thirtieth General Assembly*, p. XIX.

33. *Illinois Legislative Manual*, 176.

34. *Minutes of the Twenty-Fourth Annual Meeting*, 18.

35. Justine Thomas birth certificate, on file with the Sangamon County Clerk's office.

36. *Springfield State Journal*, January 24, 1877, 4.

37. *Springfield State Journal*, March 14, 1877, 4; Illinois General Assembly, *Journal of the House: Thirtieth General Assembly*, 349. Thomas served on a three-person temperance committee at the 1872 Wood River Baptist Association meeting in Chicago, but the committee's report merely endorsed recently passed legislation that placed stricter controls on the sale of liquor in Illinois. *Minutes of the Twenty-Fourth Annual Meeting*, 9.

38. *Springfield State Register*, March 29, 1877, 1, and April 12, 1877, 1.

39. *Springfield State Journal*, May 18, 1877, 4, and May 21, 1877, 4; *Springfield State Register*, May 17, 1877, 4, and May 21, 1877, 4.

40. *Springfield State Register*, May 21, 1877, 1.

41. *Springfield State Journal*, May 7, 1877, 2; Hill, "Hyers Sisters,"115–30.

42. *Springfield State Journal*, May 4, 1877, 4.

43. *Chicago Inter-Ocean*, April 23, 1877, 4; *Springfield State Register*, May 2, 1877, 2; *Chicago Tribune*, April 24, 1877, 4.

44. Illinois General Assembly, *Journal of the House: Thirtieth General Assembly*, 583; *Chicago Inter-Ocean*, April 25, 1877, 5.

45. *Chicago Tribune*, April 27, 1877, 5; *Cleveland Gazette*, May 2, 1885, 2.

46. *Chicago Tribune*, April 27, 1877, 5.

47. *Chicago Inter-Ocean*, March 26, 1877, 8.

48. *Chicago Inter-Ocean*, March 27, 1877, 2, March 30, 1877, 2, March 31, 1877, 2, and April 2, 1877, 3.

49. *Chicago Tribune*, March 19, 1877, 7.

50. *Chicago Inter-Ocean*, March 20, 1877, 4.

51. *Chicago Inter-Ocean*, March 26, 1877, 8.

52. *Chicago Inter-Ocean*, March 26, 1877, 4.

53. Miller, *City of the Century*, 451–52, 466.

54. *Chicago Tribune*, March 19, 1877, 7.

55. Illinois General Assembly, *Journal of the House: Thirtieth General Assembly*, 268.

56. *Chicago Tribune*, May 25, 1877, 4; *Chicago Times*, May 24, 1877, 4.

57. Illinois General Assembly, *Journal of the House: Thirtieth General Assembly*, 635–36, 796, 845–46; Moses, *Illinois Historical and Statistical*, 1014–15.

58. Moses, *Illinois Historical and Statistical*, 851–52.

59. Illinois General Assembly, *Journal of the House: Thirtieth General Assembly*, 518, 822; Moses, *Illinois Historical and Statistical*, 851.

60. Illinois General Assembly, *Journal of the House: Thirtieth General Assembly*, 399–400, 646, 740.

61. Ibid., 810–11, 581–82, 348, 801, 241, 818–19.

62. Ibid., 754–55.

63. *Chicago Times*, May 21, 1877, 6.

64. *Chicago Tribune*, December 17, 1876, 4, and April 24, 1877, 4.

65. Illinois General Assembly, *Journal of the House: Thirtieth General Assembly*, 266–68; *Chicago Inter-Ocean*, February 21, 1877, 2, and February 28, 1877, 4; *Springfield State Journal*, February 21, 1877, 4, and February 28, 1877, 4.

66. Illinois General Assembly, *Journal of the Senate: Thirtieth General Assembly*, 908–78; *Chicago Inter-Ocean*, May 16, 1877, 4 and May 17, 1877, 4.

67. *Chicago Times*, May 25, 1877, 5; *Chicago Inter-Ocean*, May 25, 1877, 5; Illinois General Assembly, *Journal of the House: Thirtieth General Assembly*, 854–55, Public Laws, 6.

68. *Springfield State Journal*, May 4, 1877, 4.

69. *Chicago Evening Journal*, October 8, 1878, 3.

70. *Lakeside Annual Directory, 1878–1879*, 1022; *Lakeside Annual Directory, 1879–1880*, 1062.

71. *Chicago Inter-Ocean*, October 17, 1877, 3.

72. *Chicago Inter-Ocean*, October 16, 1877, 2, October 19, 1877, 5, and October 24, 1877, 2; *Chicago Tribune*, October 16, 1877, 3, October 19, 1877, 5, and October 23, 1877, 5.

73. *Chicago Tribune*, September 5, 1877, 2, and November 2, 1877, 2; *Chicago Inter-Ocean*, October 17, 1877, 3, October 22, 1877, 8 and November 8, 1877, 1.

74. *Chicago Tribune*, November 21, 1877, 8, and November 22, 1877, 8.

75. *Chicago Inter-Ocean*, March 12, 1878, 5, March 26, 1878, 4, and April 3, 1878, 5; *Chicago Times*, March 12, 1878, 3, March 29, 1878, 4, April 2, 1878, 2, and April 3, 1878, 2; *Chicago Tribune*, March 24, 1878, 5, and March 31, 1878, 4.

76. *Chicago Inter-Ocean*, March 20, 1878, 5, and March 22, 1878, 2.

77. *Chicago Inter-Ocean*, March 27, 1878, 5, and March 28, 1878, 2; *Chicago Times*, March 27, 1878, 4; *Chicago Tribune*, March 27, 1878, 7, and April 4, 1878, 7.

78. *Chicago Tribune*, June 25, 1878, 2, and June 27, 1878, 1.

79. *Chicago Inter-Ocean*, August 22, 1878, 8; *Chicago Evening Journal*, August 24, 1878, 1.

80. *Chicago Inter-Ocean*, August 23, 1878, 8.

81. *Chicago Tribune*, August 28, 1878, 8.

82. *Chicago Tribune*, September 3, 1878, 8; *Chicago Inter-Ocean*, September 3, 1878, 2.

83. *Chicago Evening Journal*, September 6, 1878, 4.

84. *Chicago Inter-Ocean*, September 30, 1878, 3.

85. *Chicago Evening Journal*, October 8, 1878, 3.

86. *Chicago Tribune*, October 15, 1878, 5.

87. *Chicago Times,* October 16, 1878, 2; *Chicago Evening Journal*, October 15, 1878, 4.

88. *Chicago Inter-Ocean*, October 16, 1878, 289. Kogan, *First Century*, 26–27, 200; Wheaton, *Myra Bradwell*, 30–41.

90. *Chicago Inter-Ocean*, October 7, 1878, 1; *Chicago Times*, October 6, 1878, 4; *Chicago Tribune*, October 6, 1878, 5.

91. *Chicago Inter-Ocean*, October 16, 1878, 2.

92. *Chicago Inter-Ocean*, October 22, 1878, 2; *Chicago Tribune*, October 22, 1878, 5; *Chicago Times*, October 22, 1878, 2.

93. *Chicago Tribune*, October 22, 1878, 5; *Chicago Inter-Ocean*, October 25, 1878, 3.

94. *Chicago Tribune*, October 18, 1878, 7, October 22, 1878, 5, October 24, 1878, 5, and October 26, 1878, 3; *Chicago Inter-Ocean*, October 26, 1878, 3.

95. *Chicago Tribune*, October 29, 3, and October 30, 1878, 3; *Chicago Daily News*, October 29, 1878, 1; *Chicago Evening Journal*, October 28, 1878, 4.

96. *Chicago Tribune*, October 25, 1878, 5.

97. *Chicago Inter-Ocean*, October 26, 1878, 3; *Chicago Times*, November 2, 1878, 2.

98. *Chicago Times*, October 28, 1878, 4.

99. *Abstract of Votes for Representatives, 1878,* Illinois State Archives, Record Series 103.032.

3. "Justly Entitled to Representation": The Long Road Back to the Legislature

1. *Chicago Tribune*, May 22, 1879, 7.

2. *Lakeside Annual Directory for the City of Chicago*, 1875–81.

3. *Chicago Chronicle*, December 19, 1899, 4; *Lakeside Annual Directory of the City of Chicago 1879*, 508; Ward, *History of the Republican Party*, 93–94; *Chicago Legal News*, December 23, 1899, 151, and October 31, 1896, 75–78; Kogan, *First Century*, 200.

4. Kogan, *First Century*, 200–204; Jones, *Some Foot-Steps*, 73; *Chicago Legal News*, October 31, 1896, 75–78.

5. *Chicago Legal News*, December 23, 1899, 151; *Chicago Chronicle*, December 19, 1899, 4; *Chicago Inter-Ocean*, December 19, 1899, 7.

6. Willrich, *City of Courts*, 11; Haines, *Practical Treatise*, 40.

7. Willrich, *City of Courts*, 3–28; Haines, *Practical Treatise*, 39–78.

8. *Chicago Times*, March 26, 1879, 4.

9. Willrich, *City of Courts*, 24.

10. *Chicago Evening Journal*, September 4, 1890, 4.

11. Willrich, *City of Courts*, 3, 10, 25–40.

12. Stead, *If Christ Came to Chicago*, 18.

13. *Chicago Tribune*, August 1, 1896, 5.

14. *Chicago Inter-Ocean*, March 26, 1891, 7; *Chicago Tribune*, April 6, 1891, 3, and May 17, 1881, 6.

15. *Chicago Tribune*, December 11, 1887, 25.

16. *Chicago Tribune*, November 18, 1891, 9, and February 13, 1892, 3.

17. Michael B. Leavitt vs. John W. E. Thomas and W. W. Charles, Case no. 91C88323, Clerk of the Circuit Court of Cook County; *Chicago Tribune*, January 28, 1891, 3.

18. *Chicago Legal News*, October 31, 1896, 75–78; *Chicago Tribune*, December 11, 1887, 25.

19. Harris, *Colored Man's Business and Professional Directory*, 10; Will, Bond, and Letter Files of John W. Thomas, General Number 5–7094, Docket 58, Page 108, Circuit Court of Cook County; *Chicago Tribune*, December 19, 1899, 7; *Chicago Evening Journal*, December 19, 1899, 3.

20. Tenth Census of the United States (1880), Chicago, Cook County, Ill., Roll T9–184, p. 232D, Enumeration District 9.

21. Marriage License of John W. E. Thomas and Justine E. C. Latcher, April 29, 1880, no. 46.112, Cook County Clerk's Office; Death Certificate of Joseph Benjamin Latcher, April 19, 1879, no. 2182, Cook County Clerk's Office.

22. *Chicago Inter-Ocean*, April 26, 1880, 6.

23. *Chicago Inter-Ocean*, May 14, 1880, 8 and May 18, 1880, 8.

24. Graham, *Senator and the Socialite*, 7.

25. *Chicago Evening Journal*, May 5, 1880, 4; *Chicago Inter-Ocean*, May 5, 1880, 8; *Chicago Tribune*, May 5, 1880, 6 and 8.

26. *Chicago Inter-Ocean*, March 4, 1879, 4; *Chicago Tribune*, April 27, 1879, 11.

27. *Chicago Inter-Ocean*, March 24, 1879, 3; *Chicago Tribune*, March 26, 1879, 8, March 27, 1879, 8, and May 11, 1879, 8.

28. *Chicago Times*, March 26, 1879, 4; *Chicago Tribune*, March 22, 1879, 8.

29. *Chicago Inter-Ocean*, March 11, 1879, 3, March 12, 1879, 3, March 24, 1879, 3, March 25, 1879, 2, March 28, 1879, 3; *Chicago Times*, March 11, 1879, 11, March 12, 1879, 10, March 25, 1879, 2 and March 28, 1879, 5.

30. *Chicago Times*, March 26, 1879, 5, and March 27, 1879, 5.

31. Johnson, *Carter Henry Harrison*, 188–200.

32. Gliozzo, "John Jones"; *Chicago Evening Journal*, May 23, 1879, 4; *Chicago Times*, May 22, 1879, 3; *Chicago Tribune*, May 24, 1879, 8.

33. *Chicago Legal News*, October 31, 1896, 75–78.

34. *Chicago Inter-Ocean*, October 7, 1879, 2, October 15, 1879, 2, October 21, 1879, 8, October 22, 1879, 5, and November 3, 1879, 3; *Chicago Times*, October 7, 1879, 1, October 24, 1879, 5, and October 29, 1879, 5; *Chicago Tribune*, October 24, 1879, 4, and October 26, 1879, 2; *Lakeside Annual Directory of the City of Chicago 1879*, 651; ibid. (1880), 667.

35. *Chicago Inter-Ocean*, March 9, 1880, 3; *Chicago Times*, April 7, 1880, 2, and April 8, 1880, 2.

36. *Chicago Tribune*, March 28, 1880, 7.

37. Joens, "Ulysses S. Grant."

38. Moses, *Illinois Historical and Statistical*, 836.

39. *Chicago Times*, June 1, 1880, 3; *Chicago Inter-Ocean*, May 7, 1880, 2, and May 4, 1880, 5; *Chicago Times*, March 2, 1880, 3; *Chicago Tribune*, February 22, 1880, 2.

40. *Chicago Times*, May 9, 1880, 2; *Chicago Inter-Ocean*, May 10, 1880, 1.

41. *Chicago Tribune*, May 11, 1880, 2; *Chicago Times*, May 11, 1880, 1.

42. *Chicago Times*, May 26, 1880, 2; *Chicago Tribune*, May 26, 1880, 2, and May 27, 1880, 1.

43. For an account of the role Cook County and Illinois played in the 1880 Republican presidential nomination, see Joens, "Ulysses S. Grant." See also *History of the Illinois Republican State Convention*.

44. *Chicago Tribune*, August 6, 1880, 5.

45. *Chicago Inter-Ocean*, September 6, 1880, 2.

46. *Chicago Inter-Ocean*, September 7, 1880, 2.

47. *Chicago Evening Journal*, September 13, 4; *Chicago Times*, September 14, 1880, 2; *Chicago Tribune*, September 14, 1880, 6; *Chicago Inter-Ocean*, September 14, 1880, 6.

48. *Chicago Inter-Ocean*, September 29, 1880, 3, October 18, 1880, 5, and October 20, 1880, 5.

49. *Chicago Inter-Ocean*, October 6, 1880, 3; *Chicago Tribune*, October 6, 1880, 6; *Chicago Times*, October 6, 1880, 1–2, and October 7, 1880, 4.

50. *Chicago Inter-Ocean*, September 28, 1880, 2 and October. 6, 1880, 3; *Chicago Times*, October 2, 1880, 3, and October 5, 1880, 2.

51. Branham, citing arguments offered by political scientists Ira Katznelson and Martin Kilson, sees this as the development of a "patron-client" nexus that carried over well into the next century. He sees it as a negative development, resulting in African American political leaders who sold out their community interests to white power-brokers for self-serving interests. Branham, "Black Chicago."

52. *Official Register of the United States*, 1: 67–68.

53. Boyd, *Boyd's Directory* (1882), 676; ibid. (1883), 803; Birth Certificate of Blanche Thomas, September 18, 1881, Government of the District of Columbia, Department of Health, Vital Records Division.

54. John A. Logan Papers, Correspondence, 1879, Abraham Lincoln Presidential Library; *Chicago Times*, October 15, 1882, 6.

55. Death Certificate of Martha Thomas, March 10, 1881; Cook County Clerk's Office, no. 2699; Death Certificate of Edinburgh Thomas, April 16, 1881, Cook County Clerk's Office, no. 3735; Estate of Edinboro Thomas, Probate Court of Cook County, Case no. 4–1563.

56. *Chicago Tribune*, February 8, 1881, 8, March 12, 1881, 6, and March 17, 1881, 3; *Chicago Times*, April 7, 1881, 6; *Chicago Inter-Ocean*, March 24, 1881, 2, and March 28, 1881, 8.

57. *Chicago Times*, March 9, 1881, 6, March 22, 1881, 6, April 3, 1881, 9, and April 7, 1881, 6; *Chicago Inter-Ocean*, March 22, 1881, 8, and March 29, 1881, 3.

58. *Chicago Tribune*, April 2, 1882, 7; Death Certificate of Blanche D. L. Thomas, June 16, 1882, Cook County Clerk's Office, no. 6321.

59. *Chicago Times*, August 27, 1882, 8.

60. *Chicago Times*, September 17, 1882, 6; *Lakeside Annual Directory, 1881*, 954, 1008; *Chicago Tribune*, September 27, 1882, 6; *Chicago Times*, November 2, 1882, 2.

61. Harris, *Colored Men's Professional and Business Directory*, 36.

62. *Springfield State Register*, July 2, 1880, 4, and July 22, 1880, 4; *Springfield State Journal*, July 21, 1880, 5, and July 22, 1880, 3.

63. *Chicago Times*, August 22, 1882, 4; *Chicago Tribune*, October 4, 1882, 2.

64. *Chicago Times*, October 13, 1882, 1; *Chicago Tribune*, September 19, 1882, 3.

65. *Chicago Times*, September 12, 1882, 2, September 19, 1882, 3, and September 26, 1882, 2; *Chicago Herald*, September 26, 1882, 1; *Chicago Tribune*, September 16, 1882, 6, September 19, 1882, 3, September 24, 1882, 10, and September 26, 1882, 6.

66. *Chicago Times*, September 30, 1882, 5; *Chicago Tribune*, September 30, 1882, 6.

67. *Chicago Herald*, September 30, 1882, 1.

68. *Chicago Tribune*, October 3, 1882, 3, and October 9, 1882, 3.

69. *Chicago Tribune*, October 6, 1882, 6, and October 8, 1882, 10; *Chicago Times*, October 7, 1882, 6, and October 8, 1882, 5.

70. *Chicago Tribune*, October 6, 1882, 6, October 7, 1882, 6, October 10, 1882, 6, October 11, 1882, 6, October 13, 1882, 6, and October 14, 1882, 4; *Chicago Times*, October 13, 1882, 1.

71. *Chicago Tribune*, October 13, 1882, 6, and October 14, 1882, 7.

72. *Chicago Times*, October 14, 1882, 5.

73. *Chicago Inter-Ocean*, October 16, 1882, 5; *Chicago Daily News*, October 14, 1882, 1; *Chicago Evening Journal*, October 14, 1882, 6; *Chicago Times*, October 15, 1882, 6; *Chicago Herald*, October 15, 1882, 1.

74. *Chicago Tribune*, October 13, 1882, 6, and October 14, 1882, 7.

75. *Chicago Times*, October 15, 1882, 6; *Chicago Daily News*, November 2, 1882, 1.

76. *Chicago Inter-Ocean*, October 16, 1882, 4; *Chicago Tribune*, October 15, 1882, 10.

77. *Chicago Tribune*, October 14, 1882, 4, and October 22, 1882, 10; *Chicago Evening Journal*, October 16, 1882, 2.

78. *Chicago Inter-Ocean*, October 24, 1882, 3.

79. *Chicago Times*, October 22, 1882, 6; *Chicago Herald*, October 22, 1882, 1; *Chicago Tribune*, October 22, 1882, 10.

80. *Chicago Tribune*, October 23, 1882, 8; *Chicago Times*, October 23, 1882, 3.

81. *Chicago Times*, October 24, 1882, 2.

82. *Chicago Times*, November 1, 1882, 3, and November 2, 1882, 2.

83. *The Times* said this was a meeting of the First Ward Republican Club and happened to have a large African American audience. The *Tribune* said it was a meeting of the African American Republicans of the First Ward. The *Tribune* is probably correct. *Chicago Times*, November 2, 1882, 2 and 3; *Chicago Tribune*, November 2, 1882, 7.

84. *Chicago Tribune*, November 7, 1882, 6, and November 3, 1882, 12; *Chicago Herald*, November 7, 1882, 1.

85. Before the state switched to the Australian ballot in the 1890s, voting was done by voters submitting a list of names and offices at the ballot box. In other words, the government did not issue a ballot and anyone could submit a list of candidates. The political parties printed up ballots, but names could be scratched off or replaced by voters who did not endorse the entire ticket. Similarly, outside organizations and individuals could submit their own lists. The system was replaced due to the obvious fraud that could, and did, occur. For an explanation about the Australian Ballot and attempts to reform it, see Reynolds and McCormick, "Outlawing 'Treachery.'"

86. *Chicago Times*, November 8, 1882, 3.

87. *Chicago Tribune*, November 8, 1882, 5.

88. *Abstract of Votes, 1882*, Illinois State Archives, Record Group 103.032.

89. *Chicago Times*, November 9, 1882, 2.

4. "Advising Moderation in All Things": The 1883 Legislative Session and Colored Convention

1. *Morgan County Register of Death* (May 8, 1883) vol. 1, p. 121; Birth Certificate for (unnamed female) Thomas, dated April 24, 1883, Sangamon County Clerk's Office; Death certificate of Blanche D. L. Thomas, June 16, 1882, no. 6321, Cook County Clerk's Office.

2. *Chicago Evening Journal*, January 2, 1883, 1.

3. *Springfield State Journal*, January 3, 1883, 7, and January 2, 1883, 2.

4. Illinois General Assembly, *Journal of the House: Thirty-third General Assembly*, 11–12.

5. *Chicago Tribune*, November 14, 1882, 6.

6. 1870 Illinois State Constitution, Article V.

7. *Chicago Evening Journal*, January 11, 1883, 1; *Springfield State Journal*, January 12, 1883, 1.

8. *Springfield State Journal*, January 13, 1883, 1.

9. *Springfield State Journal*, January 18, 1883, 1.

10. *Springfield State Journal*, January 24, 1883, 1; Illinois General Assembly, *Journal of the House: Thirty-third General Assembly*, LI (index).

11. *Springfield State Journal*, January 4, 1883, 4.

12. Illinois General Assembly, *Journal of the House: Thirty-third General Assembly*, 92, 140, and 572; *Springfield State Journal*, April 12, 1883, 2.

13. Howard, *Illinois: A History*, 411; *Springfield State Journal*, February 20, 1883, 5; February 24, 1883, 4; March 6, 1883, 1; March 7, 1883, 5; March 9, 1883, 5; March 10, 1883, 4; and March 26, 1883, 4.

14. *Springfield State Journal*, January 30, 1883, 1.

15. *Springfield State Journal*, March 22, 1883, 6.

16. *Springfield State Journal*, February 23, 1883, 4, and March 3, 1883, 1; *Chicago Evening Journal*, March 16, 1883, 2, and March 19, 1883, 2.

17. HB 228, 33rd Session, Illinois General Assembly; *Springfield State Journal*, March 2, 1883, 2; SB 153, 33rd Session, Illinois General Assembly.

18. The bills were HB 120, 197, 213, 286, and 656 and SB 126 and 129.

19. Illinois General Assembly, *Journal of the House: Thirty-third General Assembly*, 173, 476, 623, 866, 965–66.

20. Ibid., 12.

21. Ibid., 589–608.

22. *Springfield State Journal*, April 18, 1883, 4, April 19, 1883, 4, April 20, 1883, 2, April 21, 1883, 2 and 4, and April 23, 1883, 2.

23. Birth Certificate for (unnamed female) Thomas, dated April 24, 1883, Sangamon County Clerk's Office.

24. *Illinois State Register*, April 22, 1883, 3.

25. *Morgan County Register of Death*, dated May 8, 1883, 1:121; *Chicago Inter-Ocean*, May 9, 1883, 8.

26. *Chicago Evening Journal*, May 21, 1883, 4; *Chicago Tribune*, May 22, 1883.

27. *Springfield State Journal*, May 9, 1883, 2; Illinois General Assembly, *Journal of the House: Thirty-third General Assembly*, 488–99, 611–788, 795–96, 797–820, 867–900.

28. Illinois General Assembly, *Journal of the House: Thirty-third General Assembly*, 432, 995–96; *Chicago Evening Journal*, June 8, 1883, 1.

29. Illinois General Assembly, *Journal of the House: Thirty-third General Assembly*, 1195.

30. Ibid., 752–53, 897, 971, 1003, 1013, 1036, 1039; Moses, *Illinois Historical and Statistical*, 893.

31. *Chicago Evening Journal*, June 19, 1883, 2; Illinois General Assembly, *Journal of the House: Thirty-third General Assembly*, p. III.

32. Litwack and Meier, *Black Leaders of the Nineteenth Century*, xi; Foner and Walker, *Proceedings, 1865–1900*, xix–xxvi and 246–83; Foner and Walker, *Proceedings, 1840–1865*, 52–83; *Chicago Tribune*, December 3, 1873, 4; *Chicago Times*, December 3, 1873, 7.

33. *Chicago Inter-Ocean*, April 3, 1888, 3; Reed, *Black Chicago's First Century*, 265.

34. Grossman, *Democratic Party and the Negro*, 60–61. See also Meier, "Negro and the Democratic Party."

35. *Chicago Times*, July 19, 1880, 1.

36. *Springfield State Journal*, July 20, 1880, 2; *Chicago Inter-Ocean*, July 9, 1880, 6.

37. *Springfield State Journal*, July 20, 1880, 2, and July 21, 1880, 5.

38. *Chicago Times*, July 21, 1880, 1 and 2; *Chicago Tribune*, July 23, 1880, 4; *Chicago Inter-Ocean*, July 9, 1880, 6.

39. *Chicago Times*, July 22, 1880, 1 and 2.

40. *Springfield State Journal*, July 21, 1880, 2 and 5.

41. Grossman, *Democratic Party and the Negro*, 61, 95; Meier, "Negro and the Democratic Party," 175; Beatty, *Revolution Gone Backward*, 45–59; *Chicago Tribune*, October 19, 1883, 4.

42. Grossman, *Democratic Party and the Negro*, 60–63; Beatty, *Revolution Gone Backward*, 45–59; *Chicago Inter-Ocean*, September 20, 1883, 2; *Cleveland Gazette*, September 15, 1883, 4, September 22, 1883, 2, and September 29, 1883, 3; Martin, *Mind of Frederick Douglass*, 84; Blassingame and McKivigan, *Frederick Douglass Papers*, 80–111.

43. *Chicago Evening Journal*, May 9, 1883, 5; *Chicago Inter-Ocean*, September 21, 1883, 2; *Chicago Evening Journal*, September 21, 1883, 4; *Chicago Tribune*, September 21, 1883, 7; *Cleveland Gazette*, March 22, 1883, 1.

44. *Springfield State Register*, Oct. 16, 1883, 3; *Chicago Evening Journal*, October 16, 1883, 1. For information on Bird and Scott, see Portwood, "African-American Politics," 13–21.

45. *Chicago Evening Journal*, October 16, 1883, 1; *Chicago Times*, October 16, 1883, 8; *Springfield State Register*, Oct. 16, 1883, 3; *Springfield State Journal*, October 16, 1883, 7.

46. *Chicago Evening Journal*, October 16, 1883, 1; *Chicago Inter-Ocean*, October 16, 1883, 3; *Springfield State Register*, Oct. 16, 1883, 3.

47. *Springfield State Register*, October 16, 1883, 3; *Chicago Times*, October 16, 1883, 8.

48. *Springfield State Register*, October 16, 1883, 3; *Springfield State Journal*, October 16, 1883, 7.

49. *Chicago Tribune*, October 16, 1883, 1; Beatty, *Revolution Gone Backward*, 56–58; Blight, *Race and Reunion*, 309.

50. *Chicago Times*, October 19, 1883, 3.

51. *Chicago Times*, October 17, 1883, 3.

52. *Chicago Evening Journal*, October 17, 1883, 1 and October 18, 1883, 1; *Chicago Inter-Ocean*, October 17, 1883, 2; *Chicago Times*, October 17, 1883, 3; *Chicago Tribune*, October 17, 1883, 2; *Springfield State Register*, Oct. 17 1883, 3; *Springfield State Journal*, October 18, 1883, 4 and 7.

53. *Chicago Evening Journal*, October 17, 1883, 1, and October 18, 1883, 1; *Springfield State Register*, October 17, 1883, 3.

54. *Springfield State Register*, October 17, 1883, 3; Beatty, *Revolution Gone Backward*, 51–54.

55. *Chicago Times*, January 30, 1884, 3, and January 31, 1884, 2; Beatty, *Revolution Gone Backward*, 65; Call for a Conference of Representative Colored Men, C. S. Smith Papers, Reel 1, Bentley Historical Library, University of Michigan, Ann Arbor.

56. *Chicago Inter-Ocean*, March 19, 1884, 6; *Chicago Tribune*, March 19, 1884, 6; *Cleveland Gazette*, March 22, 1884, 1, and March 29, 1884, 2.

57. *Cleveland Gazette*, May 3, 1884, 3, and May 10, 1884, 1; *Chicago Tribune*, April 30, 1884, 5, and May 1, 1884, 5; *Chicago Times*, April 30, 1884, 5, and May 1, 1884, 7; Beatty, *Revolution Gone Backward*, 65.

58. *Chicago Tribune*, December 9, 1884, 6, and December 10, 1884, 6, and December 14, 1884, 12.

59. *Chicago Inter-Ocean*, March 8, 1884, 12.

60. *Chicago Inter-Ocean*, February 1, 1884, 5; *Cleveland Gazette*, April 12, 1884, 1, and April 26, 1884, 1; *Chicago Evening Journal*, April 15, 1884, 1; *Chicago Inter-Ocean*, April 13, 1884, 5, April 16, 1884, 2; *Chicago Tribune*, April 15, 1884, 1.

61. *Chicago Inter-Ocean*, April 17, 1884, 1; *Chicago Times*, April 17, 1884, 1 and 2; *Springfield State Journal*, April 17, 1884, 1 and 4; *Chicago Tribune*, April 18, 1884, 1.

62. *Cleveland Gazette*, April 26, 1884, 1.

63. *Chicago Inter-Ocean*, March 20, 1885, 1; *Springfield State Journal*, March 25, 1885, 4.

5. "We Are Here as Citizens": Reelection, the Civil Rights Bill, and Another Colored Convention

1. *Chicago Times*, March 22, 1883, 3, and March 24, 1883, 4; *Chicago Inter-Ocean*, May 22, 1883, 3, and March 24, 1883, 8; *Chicago Times*, March 27, 1884, 3; *Chicago Inter-Ocean*, March 27, 1884, 3.

2. *Chicago Inter-Ocean*, November 1, 1883, 2.

3. *Chicago Inter-Ocean*, March 30, 1884, 8, April 3, 1884, 3, and April 5, 1884, 5; *Chicago Times*, April 3, 1884, 3, and April 5, 1883, 6.

4. *Cleveland Gazette*, June 21, 1884, 2, and November 1, 1884, 1; *Chicago Times*, October 1, 1884, 2, and November 2, 1884, 6; Campaign literature, 1884, Democratic Party, Illinois, Chicago Historical Museum.

5. *Cleveland Gazette*, August 2, 1884, 1; *Chicago Inter-Ocean*, April 19, 1884, 6.

6. *Chicago Inter-Ocean*, August 28, 1884, 4.

7. *Cleveland Gazette*, April 26, 1884, 1, May 10, 1884, 1, May 17, 1884, 1, September 13, 1884, 2 and September 20, 1884, 1; *Chicago Times*, September 12, 1884, 5; *Chicago Tribune*, September 16, 1884, 9, and September 18, 1884, 6.

8. *Chicago Inter-Ocean*, September 20, 1884, 3.

9. *Chicago Inter-Ocean*, September 18, 1884, 2.

10. *Chicago Inter-Ocean*, September 20, 1884, 3; *Chicago Tribune*, September 20, 1884, 12.

11. *Chicago Evening Journal*, September 20, 1884, 6; *Chicago Tribune*, September 21, 1884, 3; *Chicago Inter-Ocean*, September 21, 1884, 3.

12. *Chicago Evening Journal*, September 20, 1884, 1; *Cleveland Gazette*, October 4, 1884, 1.

13. *Chicago Times*, September 21, 1884, 3, and September 23, 1884, 2.

14. *Chicago Inter-Ocean*, September 23, 1884, 3; *Chicago Times*, September 23, 1884, 2, and September 30, 1884, 2.

15. *Chicago Times*, September 23, 1884, 2; *Chicago Inter-Ocean*, September 24, 1884, 3.

16. *Chicago Inter-Ocean*, September 23, 1884, 3; *Chicago Herald*, September 24, 1884, 2; *Chicago Times*, September 24, 1884, 2.

17. *Chicago Herald*, September 21, 1884, 5; *Chicago Inter-Ocean*, September 21, 1884, 3.

18. *Chicago Inter-Ocean*, September 23, 1884, 3; *Chicago Tribune*, September 30, 1884, 10.

19. *Chicago Times*, October 1, 1884, 2; Campaign literature, 1884, Democratic Party, Illinois, Chicago Historical Museum.

20. *Chicago Herald*, September 24, 1884, 2; *Chicago Evening Journal*, November 2, 1884, 4; *Chicago Times*, September 1, 1884, 6.

21. *Chicago Inter-Ocean*, October 19, 1884, 3, and October 25, 1884, 3.

22. *Abstract of Votes, 1884*, Illinois State Archives, Record Series 103.032; *Chicago Inter-Ocean*, November 6, 1884, 3.

23. *Chicago Inter-Ocean*, November 6, 1888, 6.

24. *Chicago Inter-Ocean*, May 1, 1885, 5.

25. *Chicago Inter-Ocean*, March 5, 1885, 3, March 6, 1885, 1, June 23, 1885, 1, and June 24, 1885, 2; *Springfield State Journal*, April 1, 1885, and June 29, 1885, 8; Moses, *Illinois Historical and Statistical*, 907–8.

26. *Chicago Inter-Ocean*, January 6, 1885, 4; Moses, *Illinois Historical and Statistical*, 901.

27. Merriner, *Grafters and Goo Goos*, 44–45; *Chicago Inter-Ocean*, June 27, 1885, 12.

28. *Chicago Inter-Ocean*, January 3, 1885, 3.

29. *Chicago Inter-Ocean*, January 7, 1885, 2; *Springfield State Journal*, January 7, 1885, 8.

30. *Chicago Inter-Ocean*, January 8, 1885, 2.

31. Illinois General Assembly, *Journal of the House: Thirty-fourth General Assembly*, 9–10 and 16–17; *Chicago Inter-Ocean*, January 10, 1885, 2.

32. *Chicago Inter-Ocean*, January 13, 1885, 4, January 13, 1885, 2, January 17, 1885, 2, January 19, 1885, 4, January 22, 1885, 2, January 26, 1885, 4, and January 30, 1885, 2 and 4.

33. *Chicago Inter-Ocean*, February 6, 1885, 2; J. P. Jones, *John A. Logan*, 201.

34. Illinois General Assembly, *Journal of the House: Thirty-fourth General Assembly*, 169–70.

35. Church, 156–158; Jones, *John A. Logan*, 198–210; Moses, 903–907; *Chicago Inter-Ocean*, May 20, 1885, 2.

36. *Chicago Inter-Ocean*, May 20, 1885, 2 and May 24, 1885, 2.

37. *The State Capital*, February 27, 1892, 1.

38. *Cleveland Gazette*, March 14, 1885, 1; *Illinois State Journal*, June 17, 1885, 8.

39. *Illinois State Journal*, May 7, 1885, 2.

40. Illinois General Assembly, *Journal of the House: Thirty-fourth General Assembly*, p. LIV.

41. Ibid., 113, 127, 594, 650, 710. Copies of House Bills 46, 85, and 599 and Senate Bill 69 are in the Illinois State Archives, Record Group 600.001; Illinois General Assembly, *Thirty-fourth General Assembly*, Laws, 138.

42. Illinois General Assembly, *Journal of the House: Thirty-fourth General Assembly*, 441 and 587; *Springfield State Journal*, April 2, 1885, 2, and April 25, 1885, 2.

43. Howard, *Mostly Good and Competent Men*, 138.

44. Richard J. Oglesby, Correspondence (third term), Record Series 101.020, Illinois State Archives, Springfield.

45. *Chicago Tribune*, November 8, 1883, 8, December 26, 1886, 4, and July 22, 1900, 35.

46. Copy of petition in Oglesby Correspondence (third term), Illinois State Archives.

47. *Cleveland Gazette*, November 17, 1883, 3; *Chicago Tribune*, December 26, 1886, 9; Oglesby Correspondence (third term), Illinois State Archives.

48. Oglesby Correspondence (third term), Illinois State Archives.

49. *Cleveland Gazette*, June 13, 1885, 4, and February 28, 1885, 1.

50. *Cleveland Gazette*, February 14, 1885, 1, February 21, 1885, 1, and March 28, 1885, 1.

51. *Chicago Inter-Ocean*, Feb. 4, 1885, 3; *Chicago Tribune*, February 4, 1885, 2; Oglesby Correspondence (third term), Illinois State Archives.

52. Oglesby Correspondence (third term), Illinois State Archives.

53. Ibid.

54. Ibid.

55. Konvitz, *Century of Civil Rights Cases*, 103–5.

56. Dale, " 'Social Equality Does Not Exist,' " 326; *Chicago Tribune*, March 4, 1885, 3.

57. *Cleveland Gazette*, November 22, 1884, 1.

58. *Cleveland Gazette*, February 7, 1885, 1; *Chicago Tribune*, January 6, 1885, 6, *Chicago Defender*, May 3, 1930, 6, and February 20, 1943, 4.

59. Massachusetts, New York, and Kansas passed civil rights laws before the 1875 Civil Rights Act was declared unconstitutional. Connecticut, Iowa, New Jersey and Ohio passed civil rights law in 1884 and Colorado, Illinois, Indiana, Michigan, Minnesota, Nebraska, and Rhode Island passed civil rights laws in 1885. Konvitz, *Century of Civil Rights Cases*, 57; Dale, "Social Equality Does Not Exist," 324.

60. *Enrolled Acts of the General Assembly*, Illinois State Archives, Record Group 103.030. For an interpretation of the effect of the legislation on civil rights in Illinois, see Dale, "Social Equality Does Not Exist," in which the author argues that the integrationist idealism behind the law was removed through the years by judges and attorneys.

61. *Springfield State Journal*, February 21, 1885, 7; *Cleveland Gazette*, February 7, 1885, 1, and February 14, 1885, 1; *Chicago Inter-Ocean*, February 21, 1885, 4.

62. *Chicago Inter-Ocean*, March 13, 1885, 1.

63. *Chicago Inter-Ocean*, March 26, 1885, 2.

64. Grossman, *Democratic Party and the Negro*, 94.

65. *Chicago Inter-Ocean*, April 3, 1885, 3; Illinois General Assembly, *Journal of the House: Thirty-fourth General Assembly*, 447: Grossman, *Democratic Party and the Negro*, 93–94.

66. Illinois General Assembly, *Journal of the Senate: Thirty-fourth General Assembly*, 587 and 631; Illinois General Assembly *Journal of the House: Thirty-fourth General Assembly*, 1888.

67. *Springfield State Journal*, June 19, 1885, 8.

68. *Chicago Tribune*, June 19, 1885, 8.

69. Illinois General Assembly, *Journal of the House: Thirty-fourth General Assembly*, p. LXXXV; Illinois General Assembly, *Journal of the Senate: Thirty-fourth General Assembly*, p. LXIII.

70. Illinois General Assembly, *Journal of the House: Thirty-fourth General Assembly*, 913, 916, and 1084; *Laws Enacted by the Thirty-fourth General Assembly*, 139, 187, 188, and 193; *Chicago Inter-Ocean*, June 27, 1885, 4.

71. Illinois General Assembly, *Journal of the House: Thirty-fourth General Assembly*, 770, 863, 922, 982, 1075, 1080, and 1081; *Laws Enacted by the Thirty-fourth General Assembly*, 16, 200, 252, 256, and 265; *Chicago Inter-Ocean*, June 27, 1885, 4 and 12; Moses, *Illinois Historical and Statistical*, 907–9.

72. *Chicago Evening Journal*, June 27, 1885, 2; *Chicago Times*, June 27, 1885, 4; *Chicago Inter-Ocean*, June 27, 1885, 12.

73. *Chicago Inter-Ocean*, June 28, 1885, 12.

74. Illinois General Assembly, *Journal of the House: Thirty-fourth General Assembly*, p. III.

75. *Cleveland Gazette*, April 11, 1885, 2, June 6, 1885, 2, June 13, 1885, 1, June 20, 1885, 1, and June 27, 1885, 2.

76. *Cleveland Gazette*, August 15, 1885, 1, August 29, 1885, 1, September 5, 1885, 1.

77. *Chicago Evening Journal*, October 16, 1885, 2; *Chicago Times*, October 15, 1885, 3.

78. *Chicago Times*, October 16, 1885, 1 and 2; *Chicago Inter-Ocean*, October 16, 1885, 1; *Chicago Tribune*, October 16, 1885, 2.

79. *Chicago Times*, September 15, 1885, 5, September 29, 1885, 3; *Chicago Inter-Ocean*, September 29, 1885, 3.

80. *Chicago Inter-Ocean*, October 16, 1885, 1; *Chicago Tribune*, October 16, 1885, 2; *Springfield State Journal*, 4; Bridges, "James H. Magee," 36–47.

81. *Chicago Tribune*, October 16, 1885, 2; *Chicago Herald*, October 16, 1885, 1; *Chicago Inter-Ocean*, October 16, 1885, 1; *Chicago Times*, October 16, 1885, 1 and 2; *Springfield State Journal*, October 16, 1885, 4.

82. *Chicago Inter-Ocean*, October 16, 1885, 1; *Springfield State Journal*, October 16, 1885, 4.

83. *Springfield State Journal*, October 17, 1885, 4; *Chicago Times*, October 18, 1885, 6.

84. *Chicago Times*, October 17, 1885, 5.

85. Accounts of the second day of the 1885 colored convention are taken from *Chicago Herald*, October 17, 1885, 1; *Chicago Inter-Ocean*, October 17, 1885, 2; *Chicago Times*, October 17, 1885, 5, and October 18, 1885, 6; *Chicago Tribune*, October 17, 1885, 6; *Springfield State Journal*, October 17, 1885, 4 and 5. In 1886, Ferdinand Barnett formed a Cook County Colored League, but Wheeler's and Smith's names do not appear on its incorporation papers. Cook County Colored League Incorporation Papers, dated June 25, 1886, Illinois State Archives.

86. *Appeal*, October 12, 1889, 1; *Springfield State Journal*, October 8, 1889, 4, and October 9, 1889, 4; *Springfield State Register*, October 8, 1889, 3; *Chicago Inter-Ocean*, October 9, 1889, 1; *Chicago Times*, October 9, 1889, 2.

87. Grossman, *Democratic Party and the Negro*, 61.

88. Harris, *Colored Men's Professional and Business Directory*, 24.

6. "By No Means an Unimportant Position": Election to the Office of South Town Clerk in 1887

1. *Cleveland Gazette*, August 15, 1885, 1; Branham, "Black Chicago," 354.

2. For analyses on Chicago's political system of the late nineteenth century, see Merriner, *Grafters and Goo Goos*, 41; Simpson, *Rogues, Rebels, and Rubber Stamps*, 46–50.

3. *Chicago Inter-Ocean*, March 8, 1885, 6; *Chicago Times*, March 5, 1886, 5; *Chicago Times*, October 21, 1885, 2; *Chicago Tribune*, April 5, 1885, 11; *Chicago Inter-Ocean*, April 3, 1885, 3; *Chicago Times*, March 30, 1886, 5.

4. *Chicago Inter-Ocean*, April 4, 1885, 3, October 21, 1885, 6, and October 22, 1885, 3.

5. *Chicago Evening Journal*, September 17, 1886, 1; *Chicago Times*, September 18, 1886, 2.

6. *Chicago Times*, September 11, 1886, 2.

7. *Chicago Herald*, September 18, 1886, 1; *Chicago Times*, September 18, 1886, 2; *Chicago Tribune*, September 18, 1886, 1; *Chicago Evening Journal*, September 18, 1886, 3.

8. *Chicago Times*, September 18, 1886, 2; *Chicago Herald*, September 18, 1886, 1; *Chicago Tribune*, September 18, 1886, 1.

9. *Chicago Evening Journal*, September 18, 1886, 3, and September, 20, 1886, 2; *Chicago Tribune*, September 18, 1886, 1.

10. *Chicago Herald*, September 19, 1886, 1.

11. *Chicago Times*, September 19, 1886, 8; *Chicago Tribune*, September 19, 1886, 10.

12. *Chicago Herald*, March 19, 1887, 1; *Chicago Tribune*, September 20, 1886, 2, and September 21, 1886, 4; *Chicago Daily News*, September 21, 1886, 1; *Chicago Times*, September 22, 1886, 5.

13. *Chicago Daily News*, September 20, 1886, 1; *Chicago Evening Journal*, September 20, 1886, 1; *Chicago Times*, September 21, 1886, 5; *Chicago Tribune*, September 20, 1886, 4.

14. *Chicago Tribune*, September 21, 1886, 4; *Chicago Times*, September 21, 1886, 5.

15. *Chicago Times*, October 5, 1886, 6; *Chicago Inter-Ocean*, October 10, 1886, 7.

16. *Chicago Times*, September 28, 1886, 2; *Chicago Inter-Ocean*, September 29, 1886, 6; *Chicago Tribune*, October 5, 1886, 1.

17. *Chicago Evening Journal*, September 29, 1886, 6; *Chicago Times*, September 30, 1886, 2, and September 22, 1886, 5; *Chicago Tribune*, October 13, 1886, 1, and October 15, 1886, 5; *Chicago Evening Journal*, October 13, 1886, 3.

18. *Chicago Tribune*, October 13, 1886, 1, and October 15, 1886, 5; *Chicago Times*, October 12, 1886, 5, and October 13, 1886, 5.

19. *Chicago Times*, October 28, 1886, 2.

20. *Chicago Inter-Ocean*, October 20, 1886, 6; *Chicago Tribune*, October 30, 1886, 12.

21. *Chicago Inter-Ocean*, October 25, 1886, 8; *Chicago Tribune*, October 23, 1886, 2; *Chicago Evening Journal*, October 26, 1886, 3.

22. *Chicago Times*, October 28, 1886, 2.

23. *Abstract of Votes, 1886*, Illinois State Archives, Record Series 103.032; *Chicago Times*, November 4, 1886, 5; *Chicago Tribune*, November 4, 1886, 6.

24. Drake and Cayton, *Black Metropolis*, 50.

25. Grossman, Keating, and Reiff, *Encyclopedia of Chicago*, 375–77; Howard, *Illinois: A History*, 379–82.

26. *Chicago Inter-Ocean*, April 3, 1887, 12.

27. *Chicago Tribune*, March 20, 1887, 10; *Chicago Inter-Ocean*, April 3, 1887, 12.

28. *Chicago Times*, February 27, 1887, 3; *Chicago Herald*, February 27, 1887, 1.

29. *Chicago Times*, March 1, 1887, 5.

30. *Chicago Herald*, March 10, 1887, 1; *Chicago Times*, March 10, 1887, 6; *Chicago Inter-Ocean*, March 13, 1887, 7.

31. *Chicago Inter-Ocean*, March 12, 1887, 5; *Chicago Tribune*, March 11, 1887, 7, and March 17, 1887, 5.

32. *Chicago Herald*, February 26, 1887, 2, and March 20, 1887, 1; *Chicago Inter-Ocean*, March 15, 1887, 6, and March 17, 1887, 6; *Chicago Evening Journal*, March 17, 1887, 3; *Chicago Times*, March 13, 1887, 2.

33. *Chicago Herald*, March 19, 1887, 1; *Chicago Inter-Ocean*, March 19, 1887, 2; *Chicago Times*, March 19, 1887, 2.

34. *Chicago Times*, March 19, 1887, 2; *Chicago Tribune*, March 18, 1887, 5.

35. *Chicago Herald*, March 19, 1887, 1, and March 20, 1887, 1; *Chicago Times*, March 20, 1887, 2; *Chicago Inter-Ocean*, March 20, 1887, 9; *Chicago Tribune*, March 20, 1887, 10.

36. *Chicago Tribune*, March 20, 1887, 10, and April 5, 1887, 2; *Chicago Inter-Ocean*, March 22, 1887, 4.

37. Crawford, *Civil Government of Illinois*, 73–86.

38. *Chicago Tribune*, March 20, 1887, 10; *Chicago Inter-Ocean*, March 25, 1887, 3.

39. *Chicago Inter-Ocean*, March 23, 1887, 6, and March 24, 1887, 7.

40. *Chicago Times*, March 29, 1887, 1; *Chicago Inter-Ocean*, March 26, 1887, 12, and March 27, 1887, 12; *Chicago Herald*, April 2, 1887, 1.

41. *Chicago Times*, March 26, 1887, 1; *Chicago Inter-Ocean*, March 27, 1887, 12, and April 3, 1887, 6.

42. *Chicago Times*, April 5, 1887, 1 and 4; *Chicago Tribune*, March 27, 1887.

43. *Chicago Tribune*, April 6, 1887, 3; *Cleveland Gazette*, May 21, 1887, 1, and July 23, 1887, 1.

44. *Chicago Times*, April 6, 1887, 1 and 2; *Chicago Evening Journal*, April 6, 1887, 1 and 2.

45. Marriage License of Edward R. Morrison and Hester V. Thomas, dated April 4, 1887, Cook County Clerk's office; Marriage License of John W. E. Thomas and Crittie Marshall, dated July 12, 1887, Cook County Clerk's office; *Western Appeal*, August 6, 1887, 1.

46. *Cleveland Gazette*, May 30, 1885, 1; Reed, *Black Chicago's First Century*, 238–40.

47. *Lakeside Annual Directory, 1887.*

48. *Cleveland Gazette*, February 16, 1884, 2.

49. *Lakeside Annual Directory, 1885*, 1357; *Lakeside Annual Directory, 1886*, 1459; *Lakeside Annual Directory, 1887*, 1536; *Lakeside Annual Directory 1888*, 1668; *Lakeside Annual Directory, 1889*, 2189; *Lakeside Annual Directory 1890*, 2667; *Robinson's Atlas of Chicago*, vol. 1, map 100; Cook County Recorder's Office, School Section Add'n., bk. 468, pp. 44–45.

50. *Western Appeal*, August 6, 1887, 1, and April 28, 1888, 1.

51. *Western Appeal*, January 7, 1888, 1, February 4, 1888, 4, February 18, 1888, 1, February 25, 1888, 1, and July 25, 1891, 1; Reed, *Black Chicago's First Century*, 264. One exception to Thomas not being a part of Chicago's African American social elite occurred in 1895, when he attended the wedding of Barnett to activist Ida B. Wells in what was called the social event of the season in the African American community. *Chicago Inter-Ocean*, June 28, 1895, 3.

52. *Western Appeal*, October 22, 1887, 1, March 16, 1889, 1, March 23, 1889, 2, and May 11, 1889, 1; *Chicago Times*, March 7, 1888, 1.

53. *Appeal*, May 4, 1889, 1.

54. *Chicago Inter-Ocean*, October 21, 1887, 7, and November 3, 1887, 4.

55. *Chicago Times*, October 27, 1887, 1 and 2; *Chicago Inter-Ocean*, October 27, 1887, 3.

56. *Chicago Times*, October 30, 1887, 5, November 2, 1887, 2.

57. *Chicago Times*, November 3, 1887, 4, and November 9, 1887, 1; *Chicago Inter-Ocean*, November 6, 1887, 11, and November 9, 1887, 4.

58. *Chicago Inter-Ocean*, November 1, 1887, 2.

59. *Chicago Evening Journal*, October 1, 1880, 4; *Chicago Inter-Ocean*, November 3, 1887, 4; Travis, *Autobiography of Black Chicago*, 11.

60. *Chicago Inter-Ocean*, March 22, 1888, 7, and April 4, 1888, 6; *Chicago Times*, March 22, 1888, 5, and April 4, 1888, 5; *Chicago Tribune*, March 22, 1888, 3.

61. *Chicago Times*, March 14, 1888, 2, and March 21, 1888, 2.

62. *Chicago Times*, March 29, 1888, 2, and April 1, 1888, 6.

7. "You Ought Not to Insult the Colored People!": Final Bids for Office

1. *Chicago Times*, March 7, 1888, 1, March 9, 1888, 1, and March 10, 1888, 2.

2. *Chicago Inter-Ocean*, April 28, 1888, 6, and April 29, 1888, 9.

3. *Chicago Inter-Ocean*, April 24, 1888, 6.

4. *Springfield State Journal*, May 2, 1888, 1 and 4; *Chicago Times*, May 2, 1888, 1, and May 3, 1888, 1.

5. *Chicago Inter-Ocean*, May 3, 1888, 2.

6. *Chicago Inter-Ocean*, June 10, 1888, 1 and 4, June 12, 1888, 4 and 9; *Chicago Times*, June 12, 1888, 8; *Chicago Tribune*, June 12, 1888, 3.

7. *Chicago Inter-Ocean*, June 19, 1888, 3; *Chicago Tribune*, June 19, 1888, 6.

8. *Chicago Times*, October 8, 1888, 5.

9. Merriner, *Grafters and Goo Goos*, 50–53.

10. *Chicago Tribune*, September 9, 1888, 4.

11. *Chicago Times*, September 2, 1888, 3; *Western Appeal*, September 29, 1888, 2.

12. *Chicago Times*, April 24, 1888, 4, and August 31, 1888, 5; *Chicago Tribune*, June 10, 1888, 9.

13. *Chicago Tribune*, September 1, 1888, 3.

14. *Chicago Inter-Ocean*, September 8, 1888, 6; *Chicago Times*, September 8, 1888, 2, and September 11, 1888, 5; *Chicago Tribune*, September 8, 1888, 5.

15. *Chicago Tribune*, September 9, 1888, 9–10.

16. *Chicago Tribune*, September 7, 1888, 3, and September 9, 1888, 10; *Chicago Inter-Ocean*, September 9, 1888, 9.

17. For a complete account of the trial, the role race played in it, and the response to the Zephyr Davis case by Chicago's African American elite, see Dale, *Rule of Justice; Chicago Times*, September 11, 1888, 5; *Chicago Tribune*, September 12, 1888, 2.

18. Dale, *Rule of Justice*, 48; *Chicago Tribune*, March 7, 1888, 1; *Chicago Herald*, March 7, 1888, 3; *Chicago Tribune*, September 12, 1888, 2.

19. Dale, *Rule of Justice*, 84. Dale reports that John G. Jones was on the jury and was the only African American who served on it. However, she also lists H. J. Mitchel as a member, and this probably was H. J. Mitchell, the former South Town clerk.

20. For the African American perspective on the Hertz situation and the convention, see "To the Colored Voters of the City of Chicago and County of Cook," in Fifer, Correspondence, Record Series 101.021, Illinois State Archives, Springfield.

21. *Chicago Inter-Ocean*, September 9, 1888, 4; *Chicago Times*, September 9, 1888, 9; *Chicago Tribune*, September 9, 1888, 9 and 10.

22. *Chicago Tribune*, September 9, 1888, 10; *Chicago Inter-Ocean*, September 9, 1888, 4.

23. *Chicago Times*, September 11, 1888, 5, and September 14, 5; *Chicago Tribune*, September 20, 1888, 5.

24. *Chicago Times*, September 14, 1888, 5, and September 15, 1888, 3; *Chicago Inter-Ocean*, September 12, 1888, 2 and 4; *Chicago Tribune*, September 16, 1888, 10, and September 26, 1888, 2.

25. *Chicago Times*, October 3, 1888, 5, October 11, 1888, 5, and October 28, 1888, 16; *Chicago Tribune*, October 4, 1888, 2, October 5, 1888, 3, October 7, 1888, 10, and October 28, 1888, 11.

26. *Chicago Tribune*, October 8, 1888, 2, and October 16, 1888, 3; *Chicago Inter-Ocean*, October 16, 1888, 3; *Western Appeal*, October 20, 1888, 1.

27. *Abstract of Votes for Cook County, 1888*, Record Series 103.032, Illinois State Archives; *Western Appeal*, September 29, 1888, 2; *Chicago Times*, November 8, 1888, 3.

28. *Chicago Tribune*, November 4, 1888, 12; *Chicago Inter-Ocean*, November 4, 1888, 2.

29. *Chicago Tribune*, November 8, 1888, 2; *Abstract for Votes, 1888*, Record Series 103.032, Illinois State Archives.

30. *Chicago Inter-Ocean*, March 10, 1889, 6, March 16, 1889, 2, March 17, 1889, 2, March 21, 1889, 3, and March 24, 1889, 3; *Chicago Times*, March 9, 1889, 5, March 10, 1889, 6, and March 16, 1889, 1.

31. *Chicago Inter-Ocean*, March 17, 1889, 2; *Chicago Tribune*, March 17, 1889, 9; *Chicago Times*, March 9, 1889, 5, and March 17, 1889, 2; *Chicago Daily News*, March 20, 1889, 1.

32. *Chicago Inter-Ocean*, March 17, 1889, 2; *Chicago Tribune*, March 17, 1889, 9.

33. Incorporation papers, Logan Hall Association of Cook County, Illinois, Illinois State Archives; *Chicago Tribune*, March 12, 1888, 7; *Chicago Times*, March 13, 1889, 1; *Chicago Inter-Ocean*, March 21, 1889, 3.

34. *Chicago Inter-Ocean*, April 3, 1889, 4, and April 4, 1889, 4; *Chicago Times*, April 3, 1889, 1.

35. *Chicago Inter-Ocean*, November 6, 1889, 3.

36. Travis, *Autobiography of Black Chicago*, 11.

37. *Chicago Inter-Ocean*, October 26, 1889, 3, and October 27, 1889, 14; *Chicago Times*, October 26, 1889, 6; *Chicago Herald*, October 27, 1889, 12; *Chicago Tribune*, October 27, 1889, 4.

38. *Chicago Inter-Ocean*, March 9, 1890, 3, March 23, 1890, 2, and March 26, 1890, 3; *Chicago Times*, April 2, 1890, 1.

39. *Chicago Inter-Ocean*, March 25, 1890, 6, and March 26, 1890, 3; *Chicago Times*, March 25, 1890, 1.

40. *Chicago Inter-Ocean*, June 21, 1890, 6, and June 25, 1890, 1; *Chicago Times*, June 21, 1890, 6, and June 25, 1890, 1; *Chicago Tribune*, June 25, 1890, 1 and 2.

41. Death Certificate of Martha Minerva Thomas, dated July 19, 1890, Cook County Clerk's Office.

42. *Chicago Times*, October 19, 1890, 7; *Appeal*, August 17, 1889, 1.

43. *Chicago Times*, October 19, 1890, 7.

44. *Chicago Inter-Ocean*, September 4, 1890, 3 and September 8, 1890, 4.

45. *Chicago Inter-Ocean*, September 7, 1890, 6.

46. *Chicago Inter-Ocean*, September 13, 1890, 1, and September 14, 1890, 2; Tarr, *Study in Boss Politics*, 30.

47. *Chicago Inter-Ocean*, September 14, 1890, 2.

48. *Chicago Tribune*, September 23, 1890, 3, and October 18, 1890, 8; *Chicago Inter-Ocean*, October 17, 1890, 5; *Chicago Evening Journal*, October 18, 1890, 1; *Chicago Times*, October 19, 1890, 7; *Chicago Post*, October 21, 1890, 1.

49. *Chicago Evening Journal*, October 9, 1890, 1, and October 10, 1890, 1 and 2; *Chicago Times*, October 10, 1890, 1; *Chicago Tribune*, October 10, 1890, 2.

50. *Chicago Times*, October 10, 1890, 1, October 11, 1890, 1, and November 1, 1890, 3.

51. *Chicago Tribune*, October 18, 1890, 2.

52. *Chicago Inter-Ocean*, October 21, 1890, 3; *Chicago Times*, October 21, 1890, 2; *Chicago Tribune*, October 21, 1890, 2.

53. *Chicago Evening Journal*, October 21, 1890, 1; *Chicago Inter-Ocean*, October 22, 1890, 5; *Chicago Times*, October 22, 1890, 3; *Chicago Tribune*, October 22, 1890, 5.

54. *Chicago Inter-Ocean*, October 29, 1890, 2; *Chicago Evening Journal*, October 29, 1890, 2; *Chicago Tribune*, November 1, 1890, 2.

55. *Chicago Tribune*, October 31, 1890, 2.

56. *Chicago Evening Journal*, October 31, 1890, 4; *Chicago Times*, October 22, 1890, 3; *Chicago Tribune*, October 23, 1890, 5; *Chicago Evening Post*, October 22, 1890, 4.

57. *Chicago Evening Journal*, October 22, 1890, 4, and November 1, 1890, 4; *Chicago Inter-Ocean*, October 22, 1890, 5, and November 3, 1890, 4.

58. *Chicago Times*, October 22, 1890, 3; *Chicago Tribune*, October 22, 1890, 5, and October 24, 1890, 7; *Chicago Evening Journal*, October 23, 1890, 1; *Chicago Inter-Ocean*, October 24, 1890, 2, and October 26, 1890, 2; *Chicago Times*, November 1, 1890, 3, and November 2, 1890, 2; *Appeal*, October 18, 1890, 2.

59. *Abstract of Votes, 1890*, Record Series 103.032, Illinois State Archives.

60. Church, *History of the Republican Party*, 164–70.

61. *Chicago Inter-Ocean*, September 14, 1890, 4; *Chicago Tribune*, November 1, 1890, 2; *Chicago Post*, October 31, 1890, 2.

8. "Forget Personal Grievances": Uniting the Community as Elder Statesman

1. Grossman, *Democratic Party and the Negro*, 60–63.

2. Thornbrough, *T. Thomas Fortune*, 2.

3. *Chicago Tribune*, January 12, 1890, 11; *Chicago Inter-Ocean*, January 5, 1890, 7.

4. *Chicago Tribune*, January 12, 1890, 11; *Birth of the Afro-American League*, 15–16.

5. *Chicago Tribune*, January 12, 1890, 11; *Chicago Inter-Ocean*, January 5, 1890, 7; *Birth of the Afro-American League*, 5, 19; *New York Age*, January 18, 1890, 2.

6. *New York Age*, January 18, 1890, 2, July 12, 1890, 2; *Chicago Tribune*, June 24, 1890, 2.

7. *New York Age*, November 30, 1889, 1, January 4, 1890, 1, January 11, 1890, 1, January 18, 1890, 1, and February 1, 1890, 2.

8. *Cleveland Gazette*, January 18, 1890, 1; *Birth of the Afro-American League*, 20, 28, 35, 36.

9. *New York Age*, February 1, 1890, 2.

10. *Chicago Inter-Ocean*, January 16, 1890, 8; *Chicago Tribune*, January 16, 1890, 6; *New York Age*, February 1, 1890, 2.

11. *New York Age*, February 1, 1890, 2.

12. *New York Age*, February 1, 1890, 1, and February 8, 1890, 2; *Chicago Inter-Ocean*, January 17, 1890, 4.

13. Thornbrough, *T. Thomas Fortune*, 116–17; *New York Age*, February 15, 1890, 1.

14. Thornbrough, *T. Thomas Fortune*, 119–22; *New York Age*, July 25, 1891, 1. For the Illinois Afro-American League, see *Joliet Record and Sun*, July 10, 1891, 2; *Joliet News*, July 6, 1891, 3; *Springfield State Capital*, August 8, 1891, 1; *Chicago Tribune*, October 21, 1895, 5, and July 10, 1896, 14. For the Afro-American Citizen's Protective League, see the *Springfield Evening Telegraph*, September 24, 1895, 8; *Chicago Times-Herald*, September 25, 1895, 10; *Springfield State Journal*, September 24, 1895, 5, and September 25, 1895, 1; *Springfield State Register*, September 24, 1895, 5, and September 25, 1895, 5; and *Rockford Register- Gazette*, July 9, 1896, 7, and July 10, 1896, 6. For more on the national Afro-American League, see Thornbrough, *T. Thomas Fortune*, 105–22.

15. Beatty, *Revolution Gone Backward*, 90; Thornbrough, *T. Thomas Fortune*, 134–35; Kreiling, "Making of Racial Identities,"12; Fishel, "Negro in Northern Politics."

16. *Chicago Inter-Ocean*, March 15, 1891, 1, and April 9, 1891, 2.

17. *Chicago Tribune*, March 14, 1891, 1; *Chicago Inter-Ocean*, March 20, 1891, 2, April 1, 1891, 2, April 3, 1891, 2, and April 5, 1891, 2; *Chicago Times*, March 20, 1891, 2.

18. *Chicago Tribune*, March 10, 1891, 4; *Chicago Inter-Ocean*, April 8, 1891, 1, April 9, 1891, 2, and April 30, 1892, 1.

19. *Chicago Times*, March 8, 1891, 2, and March 15, 1891, 3; *Chicago Inter-Ocean*, March 15, 1891, 2; *Chicago Tribune*, March 15, 1891, 3.

20. *Chicago Inter-Ocean*, March 20, 1891, 2, March 24, 1891, 4, and March 25, 1891, 2; *Chicago Times*, March 16, 1891, 2, March 24, 1891, 2, and April 9, 1891, 2.

21. *Chicago Tribune*, September 20, 1891, 6, September 25, 1891, 4, and September 30, 1891, 1; *Chicago Inter-Ocean*, September 30, 1891, 3, October 2, 1891, 14.

22. *Chicago Inter-Ocean*, October 2, 1891, 1, October 7, 1891, 6, November 2, 1891, 1 and 2, and November 5, 1891, 1; *Chicago Times*, October 7, 1891, 1, and October 31, 1891, 1.

23. *Chicago Inter-Ocean*, March 10, 1892, 6, March 29, 1892, 6, March 30, 1892, 2, March 31, 1892, 2, April 1, 1892, 2 and 5, and April 7, 1892, 1; Grossman, Keating, and Reiff, *Encyclopedia of Chicago*, 963, 976.

24. *State Capital*, February 13, 1892, 1, and February 27, 182, 1; *Appeal*, March 19, 1892, 1; *Chicago Inter-Ocean*, March 19, 1892, 6; *Springfield State Register*, May 4, 1892, 1, and May 5, 1892, 1.

25. *Chicago Times*, April 30, 1892, 1.

26. Ibid., 2; *Chicago Inter-Ocean*, April 30, 1892, 3; *Springfield State Register*, May 5, 1892, 1. The *State Capital* newspaper stated that there were 42 African American delegates at the convention. *State Capital*, April 30, 1892, 1.

27. *Chicago Times*, April 30, 1892, 2; *Chicago Inter-Ocean*, April 30, 1892, 1.

28. *Chicago Inter-Ocean*, May 4, 1892, 1; *Chicago Times*, May 4, 1892, 2.

29. *Springfield State Journal*, May 3, 1892, 1, and May 5, 1892, 1; *Springfield State Register*, May 5, 1892, 1.

30. *Chicago Inter-Ocean*, May 5, 1892, 2.

31. *Chicago Tribune*, May 5, 1892, 2; *Chicago Inter-Ocean*, May 5, 1892, 2; *Chicago Times*, May 5, 1892, 2; *Springfield State Journal*, May 5, 1892, 1.

32. *Chicago Times*, May 5, 1892, 2; *Springfield State Register*, May 4, 1892, 1, and May 5, 1892, 1; *Chicago Tribune*, May 3, 1892, 1; *Appeal*, November 12, 1892, 2; *Chicago Times*, April 30, 1892, 2.

33. *Chicago Times*, May 6, 1892, 2; *Springfield State Register*, May 6, 1892, 1; *Springfield State Journal*, May 6, 1892, 4.

34. *Springfield State Register*, May 6, 1892, 4; *State Capital*, May 14, 1892, 1.

35. *Chicago Inter-Ocean*, June 4, 1892, 3; *Chicago Tribune*, June 4, 1892, 3; *Chicago Inter-Ocean*, May 8, 1892, 2.

36. *Chicago Inter-Ocean*, September 7, 1892, 3, and September 8, 1892, 1 and 3; *Chicago Times*, September 8, 1892, 1 and 2; *Chicago Tribune*, September 8, 1892, 5.

37. *Chicago Inter-Ocean*, September 22, 1892, 7; *Chicago Tribune*, September 22, 1892, 6.

38. *Chicago Tribune*, August 30, 1892, 4.

39. *Chicago Tribune*, August 27, 1892, 8; *Chicago Inter-Ocean*, September 21, 1892, 9.

40. *Chicago Inter-Ocean*, September 27, 1892, 3; *Chicago Tribune*, August 26, 1892, 9, August 27, 1892, 8, and August 28, 1892, 3.

41. *Chicago Inter-Ocean*, September 21, 1892, 9, and September 23, 1892, 3; *Chicago Tribune*, September 25, 1892, 2.

42. Chicago Evening Journal, September 24, 1892, 4, September 26, 1892, 2, October 1, 1892, 4, and October 3, 1892, 2.

43. *Chicago Inter-Ocean*, September 27, 1892, 3, October 3, 1892, 3, and October 4, 1892, 3.

44. *Chicago Inter-Ocean*, October 1, 1892, 3.

45. *Chicago Tribune*, October 4, 1892, 3.

46. *Chicago Evening Journal*, October 4, 1892, 2; *Chicago Inter-Ocean*, October 5, 1892, 3; *Chicago Tribune*, October 5, 1892, 3. For a campaign biography of Bish, see *Chicago Inter-Ocean*, October 28, 1892, 3.

47. *Chicago Tribune*, October 4, 1892, 3; *Chicago Inter-Ocean*, October 3, 1892, 4.

48. *Chicago Tribune*, October 2, 1890, 4, and October 4, 1892, 3; *Chicago Times*, October 5, 1892, 5.

49. J. G. Jones, *Some Foot-Steps*, Dedication page; *Chicago Tribune*, October 5, 1892, 3, and October 14, 1892, 8; *Chicago Times*, October 5, 1892, 5.

50. *Chicago Tribune*, August 30, 1892, 4. For Carter's response to the *Tribune*, see *Chicago Times*, September 11, 1892, 5; *Chicago Evening Journal*, October 12, 1892, 7.

51. *Chicago Inter-Ocean*, October 12, 1892, 3; *Chicago Tribune*, October 12, 1892, 5, and October 1, 1892, 4.

52. *Chicago Tribune*, October 13, 1892, 6; *Chicago Inter-Ocean*, October 25, 1892, 8.

53. *Chicago Tribune*, October 2, 1892, 4; *Chicago Inter-Ocean*, November 4, 1892, 3.

54. *Chicago Times*, November 5, 1892, 5, and September 30, 1892, 5.

55. Historian Lawrence Grossman also credits the Democrats' skillful handling of the race issue, where they practiced race baiting and white supremacy in the South and racial moderation in the North, with contributing to their national victory. Grossman, *Democratic Party and the Negro*, 156–71.

56. *Chicago Tribune*, November 10, 1892, 6; Howard, *Mostly Good and Competent Men*, 191–92; Jensen, *Winning of the Midwest*, 122–53, 160–61; Church, *History of the Republican Party*, 173; *Appeal*, November 12, 1892, 1 and 2.

57. *Chicago Inter-Ocean*, March 17, 1893, 1, and April 6, 1893, 1; *Chicago Tribune*, March 19, 1893, 2.

58. *Chicago Times*, March 8, 1893, 1, and April 2, 1893, 20; *Chicago Inter-Ocean*, March 16, 1893, 1, and April 5, 1893, 1.

59. *Chicago Inter-Ocean*, March 15, 1893, 2, March 18, 1893, 1, March 30, 1893, 2, and April 2, 1893, 2; *Chicago Times*, March 15, 1893, 2, March 18, 1893, 2, and April 3, 1893, 3.

60. Cook County Recorder of Deeds Office, Plat Book 531A, Deed Book 4185, p. 515, and Deed Book 4180, p. 362; Permit Ledger, Records of Building Permits for Permanent Structures Issued by the Commissioner of Buildings, Book D, January 1, 1882 to September 17, 1885; 1900 Census, City of Chicago, Fourth Ward, SD 1, ED 83, Sheet 2; *Chicago Tribune*, April 23, 1893, 30; *Chicago Inter-Ocean*, January 3, 1885, 7.

61. Historian Charles Branham would term Buckner "Madden's most trusted black lieutenant." Branham, "Black Chicago," 355.

62. *Chicago Herald*, October 7, 1893, 1; *Chicago Inter-Ocean*, October 7, 1893, 1, October 28, 1893, 4, and November 9, 1893, 2; *Chicago Times*, October 7, 1893, 9; *Chicago Tribune*, October 7, 1893, 9.

63. *Chicago Tribune*, December 2, 1893, 2, and December 16, 1893, 3.

64. Reed, *"All the World Is Here,"* xxi.

65. Grossman, Keating, and Reiff, *Encyclopedia of Chicago*, 898–902; Wells et al., *Reason Why*, xi–xii.

66. Reed, *Black Chicago's First Century*, 362–64. For a detailed account of African American participation at the fair, see Reed, *"All the World Is Here."*

67. Reed, *Black Chicago's First Century*, 362–77.

68. *Chicago Herald*, March 17, 1894, 2; *Chicago Inter-Ocean*, March 17, 1894, 2; *Chicago Times*, March 17, 1894, 1; *Chicago Tribune*, March 17, 1894, 2.

69. *Chicago Inter-Ocean*, June 8, 1894, 7, and June 12, 1894, 2; *Chicago Tribune*, June 10, 1894, 3.

70. *Chicago Inter-Ocean*, June 10, 1894, 14, June 16, 1894, 2, June 18, 1894, 4, and June 20, 1894, 2; *Chicago Tribune*, June 16, 1894, 2, and June 19, 1894, 2; *Chicago Herald*, June 19, 1894, 7.

71. *Chicago Tribune*, June 19, 1894, 2; *Chicago Herald*, June 19, 1894, 7.

72. *Chicago Tribune*, June 23, 1894, 2 and 12; *Chicago Times*, June 22, 1894, 1 and 8.

73. *Chicago Times*, June 23, 1894, 8.

74. *Chicago Herald*, June 23, 1894, 1 and 2.

75. *Chicago Tribune*, June 23, 1894, 12.

76. *Chicago Evening Post*, July 12, 1894, 1; *Chicago Herald*, July 12, 1894, 7, and July 13, 1894, 10; *Chicago Tribune*, July 13, 1894, 7; Branham, "Transformation of Black Political Leadership."

77. *Chicago Inter-Ocean*, September 25, 1894, 2, September 26, 1894, 3, September 27, 1894, 8, and September 29, 1894, 6; *Chicago Tribune*, October 3, 1894, 5, October 5, 1894, 2, and November 5, 1894, 6.

78. *Chicago Tribune*, October 11, 1894, 5; *Chicago Inter-Ocean*, October 19, 1894, 2, October 20, 1894, 2, and November 4, 1894, 3.

79. *Abstract of Votes, 1894*, Record Series 103.032, Illinois State Archives.

Conclusion: "Leader of the Colored Race Is Dead"

1. *Chicago Inter-Ocean*, March 15, 1895, 1, March 16, 1895, 1, March 26, 1895, 2; *Chicago Tribune*, March 26, 1895, 2.

2. *Chicago Inter-Ocean*, February 15, 1896, 1 and 12, and February 16, 1896, 1 and 28.

3. *Chicago Inter-Ocean*, February 2, 1896, 2, February 6, 1896, 7, and February 14, 1896, 2.

4. *Chicago Inter-Ocean*, January 28, 1896, 2, and February 15, 1896, 1 and 2.

5. *Chicago Inter-Ocean*, February 9, 1896, 2, and April 28, 1896, 1; *Chicago Times-Herald*, February 17, 1896, 2; *Springfield Journal*, April 28, 1896, 6.

6. *Chicago Inter-Ocean*, March 4, 1896, 2.

7. *Chicago Inter-Ocean*, February 25, 1896, 2.

8. *Chicago Inter-Ocean*, March 15, 1896, 2 and April 18, 1896, 4.

9. *Chicago Tribune*, January 27, 1896, 3; *Galesburg Evening Mail*, March 25, 1896, 1, March 26, 1896, 1, and March 27, 1896, 1 and 4; *Chicago Inter-Ocean*, March 27, 1896, 2, March 28, 1896, 3, September 28, 1896, 5, October 4, 1896, 3, October 22, 1896, 3, October 23, 1896, 3, and October 31, 1896, 5; *Chicago Times-Herald*, October 25, 1896, 9; J. C. Smith, *Emancipation*, 370.

10. *Chicago Inter-Ocean*, September 20, 1896, 17, cols. 1–2, September 22, 1896, 3, cols. 4–5, September 24, 1896, 3, October 15, 1896, 3, col. 2, October 25, 1896, 3, col. 3, October 30, 1896, 7, col. 7, October 31, 1896, 5, cols. 5–6; *Chicago Times-Herald*, October 29, 1896, 12, cols. 3–4 , and October 31, 1896, 6, col. 2; *Chicago Tribune*, October 31, 1896, 3, col. 5.

11. *Chicago Inter-Ocean*, September 22, 1896, 3, September 24, 1896, 3, October 28, 1896, 3, and October 31, 1896, 5; *Chicago Tribune*, September 27, 1896, 3.

12. *Chicago Tribune*, August 12, 1897, 2.

13. *Appeal*, November 26, 1898, 4; Jones, *Some Foot-Steps*, 73.

14. *Appeal*, November 26, 1898, 4; *Chicago Tribune*, June 27, 1897, 4; J. G. Jones, *Some Foot-Steps*, 49. See also, *Chicago Inter-Ocean*, January 14, 1900, 28.

15. *Chicago Inter-Ocean*, March 26, 1897, 2, and April 3, 1897, 2.

16. *Chicago Inter-Ocean*, April 8, 1897, 2.

17. *Chicago Inter-Ocean*, March 23, 1898, 8, and June 9, 1898, 3; *Chicago Tribune*, March 22, 1898, 7, March 23, 1898, 4, April 6, 1898, 10, May 21, 1898, 8, May 28, 1898, 6, June 9, 1898, 7, June 10, 1898, 4; Tarr, *Study in Boss Politics*, 85–86.

18. *Chicago Inter-Ocean*, May 29, 1898, 8, and June 15, 1898, 4.

19. *Chicago Times-Herald*, March 7, 1899, 3, March 9, 1899, 3; *Chicago Tribune*, April 5, 1899, 3; *Chicago Inter-Ocean*, March 7, 1899, 2, March 16, 1899, 3; March 31, 1899, April 1, 1899, 1, April 2, 1899, 1.

20. *Appeal*, May 8, 1897, 1.

21. Death Certificate for John W. E. Thomas, dated December 18, 1899, no. 19173, Cook County Clerk's Office.

22. *Chicago Tribune*, December 19, 1899, 7; *Chicago Evening Journal*, December 19, 1899, 3; *Chicago Inter-Ocean*, December 19, 1899, 7: *Chicago Chronicle*, December 19, 1899, 4.

23. *Chicago Legal News*, December 23, 1899, 151.

24. *Chicago Inter-Ocean*, January 1, 1900, 13; *Chicago Legal News*, December 23, 1899, 151.

Bibliography

Newspapers

Chicago Broad Ax
Chicago Chronicle
Chicago Conservator
Chicago Daily News
Chicago Defender
Chicago Evening Journal
Chicago Herald
Chicago Inter-Ocean
Chicago Post
Chicago Record
Chicago Times
Chicago Times-Herald
Chicago Tribune
Cleveland Gazette
Jacksonville Courier
Joliet News
Joliet Record & Sun
Legal News
New York Age
Rockford Register-Gazette
Springfield Evening Telegraph
Springfield State Capital
Springfield State Journal
Springfield State Register
St. Paul Western Appeal/St. Paul Appeal

Primary Sources

Abstract of Votes for State Senator and Representatives, 1876–1900. Record Series 103.032. Illinois State Archives, Springfield.

Bailey, J. C. W. *Chicago City Directory, 1865–1866.* Chicago: J. C. W. Bailey & Co., 1865.

The Birth of the Afro-American League Organized in Convention of Afro-Americans, held at Chicago, Ill., January 15, 16 & 17, 1890. Official Certified Compilation of Proceedings. Chicago: J. C. Battles and R. B. Cabbell, 1890.

Boyd, William. *Boyd's Directory of the District of Columbia 1882.* Washington, D.C., 1882.

———. *Boyd's Directory of the District of Columbia 1883*. Washington, D.C., 1883.

Chicago by Day and Night: The Pleasure Seeker's Guide to the Paris of America. Chicago: Thomson and Zimmerman, 1892.

Crawford, Edwin C. *Civil Government of Illinois and the U.S.: Special Chapters on Chicago and Cook County*. Chicago: Scott, Foreman and Co., 1890.

Edwards' Annual Directory for the City of Chicago. St. Louis: Richard Edwards, 1868–71.

Enrolled Acts of the General Assembly (1877–85). Record Series 103.030, Illinois State Archives, Springfield.

Fifer, Joseph Wilson. "To the Colored Voters of the City of Chicago and County of Cook." Fifer Papers. Correspondence file (1889–93). Record Series 101.021, Illinois State Archives, Springfield.

Haines, Elijah M. *A Practical Treatise of the Powers and Duties of Justices of the Peace and Police Magistrates; with a Summary of the Law Relating to the Duties of Constables, Coroners, and Notaries Public, in the State of Illinois*, 12th ed. Chicago: Legal Adviser Publishing Co., 1886.

Halpin, T. M. *Halpin's Chicago City Directory, 1867–1868*. Chicago: T. M. Halpin, 1867.

Harlow, George H. *Thirtieth General Assembly Official Directory*. Springfield: D. W. Lusk, State Printer and Binder, 1877.

Harris, I. C. *The Colored Men's Professional and Business Directory of Chicago and Valuable Information on the Race in General*. Chicago: I. C. Harris, 1885, 1886.

History of the Illinois Republican State Convention, Held at Springfield May 19, 1880. Chicago: Jno. B. Jeffrey "Old Reliable" Political Printing House, 1880.

Illinois General Assembly. *Journal of the House of Representatives: Thirtieth General Assembly*. Springfield: D. W. Lusk, 1877.

———. *Journal of the House of Representatives: Thirty-third General Assembly*. Springfield: H. W. Rokker, 1883.

———. *Journal of the House of Representatives: Thirty-fourth General Assembly*. Springfield: Journal Co., 1885.

———. *Journal of the Senate: Thirtieth General Assembly*. Springfield: D. W. Lusk, 1877.

———. *Journal of the Senate: Thirty-third General Assembly*. Springfield: H. W. Rokker, 1883.

———. *Journal of the Senate: Thirty-fourth General Assembly*. Springfield: Journal Co., 1885.

———. *Laws Enacted by the Thirtieth General Assembly*. Springfield: D. W. Lusk, 1877.

———. *Laws Enacted by the Thirty-third General Assembly*. Springfield: H. W. Rokker, 1883.

———. *Laws Enacted by the Thirty-fourth General Assembly*. Springfield: Journal Co., 1885.

———. *Legislative Manual for the Thirtieth General Assembly, 1877 and 1878*. Springfield: M. G. Tousley & Co., 1877.

———. *List of Members and Officers of the House of Representatives, Thirty-fourth General Assembly*. Springfield: H. W. Rokker, 1885.

———. *Rules of the Senate and House of Representatives: Thirty-third General Assembly*. Springfield: H. W. Rokker, 1883.

Jones, John G. *Some Foot-Steps of the Progress of the Colored Race*. Chicago: J. S. McCleland & Son, 1899.

Lakeside Annual Directory of the City of Chicago. Chicago: Chicago Directory Co., 1875–1900.

Logan, John A. Papers, Correspondence, 1879. Abraham Lincoln Presidential Library, Springfield, Ill.

Lusk, D. W. *History of the Contest for United States Senator before the Thirty-fourth General Assembly of Illinois, 1885.* Springfield: H. W. Rokker, 1885.

———. *Thirty-Fourth General Assembly Legislative Directory.* Springfield: D. W. Lusk, 1885.

Magee, James K. *Illinois Legislative Hand-Book.* Springfield: E. L. Merritt & Bros., 1877.

Minutes of the Twenty-Fourth Annual Meeting of the Wood River Baptist Association and Sunday School Convention, held with the Olivet Baptist Church, Chicago, Illinois. Chicago: J. J. Spalding & Co., 1872.

Morgan County Register of Death, bk. 1. Illinois Regional Archives Depository, University of Illinois at Springfield.

Official Register of the United States. Vol. 1: *Legislative, Executive, Judicial.* Washington, D.C.: Government Printing Office, 1881.

Oglesby, Richard J. Correspondence, Third Term (1885–89). Record Series 101.020, Illinois State Archives, Springfield.

Phillips, David Lyman. *Biographies of the State Officers and Thirty-Third General Assembly of Illinois.* Springfield: Biographical Publishing Co., 1883.

Pickering, J. L. *Official Directory of the Forty-first General Assembly of Illinois.* Springfield: Press of the Illinois State Register, 1899.

Record of Election Returns, 1818–1950. Record Series 103.033, Illinois State Archives, Springfield.

Record of the Proceedings of the Cook County Republican Convention, held at Farwell Hall, May 10, 1880. Pamphlet from the Republican National Convention File, Item JK2353, 1880Z. Chicago State History Museum.

Report of the Board of Police in the Fire Department to the Common Council of the City of Chicago, for the Year Ending March 31, 1875. Chicago: Hazlitt & Reed, 1875.

Robinson's Atlas of the City of Chicago, Illinois. Vol. 1. Nassau, N.Y.: E. Robinson, 1886.

Simmons, William J. *Men of Mark, Eminent, Progressive and Rising.* Cleveland: George M. Rewell & Co., 1887.

Smith, C. S. Papers. Bentley Historical Library. University of Michigan–Ann Arbor.

United States Biographical Dictionary and Portrait Gallery of Eminent and Self-Made Men, Illinois Volume, edited by H. C. Cooper. Chicago: H. C. Cooper Jr. & Co., 1883.

The War of the Rebellion: A Compilation of the Official Records of the Union and Confederate Armies. Ser. 1. Vol. 39. Pt. 1. Washington, D.C.: Government Printing Office, 1880–1901.

Wells, Ida B., Frederick Douglass, Irvine Garland Penn, and Ferdinand Barnett. *The Reason Why the Colored American is not in the World's Columbian Exposition.* Urbana: University of Illinois Press, 1993.

Secondary Sources

Asbury, Herbert. *The Gangs of Chicago: An Informal History of the Chicago Underworld.* New York: Thunder's Mouth, 1940.

Beatty, Bess. *A Revolution Gone Backward: The Black Response to National Politics, 1876–1896*. New York: Greenwood, 1987.

Blair, George S. *Cumulative Voting: An Effective Electoral Device in Illinois Politics*. Urbana: University of Illinois Press, 1960.

Blassingame, John W., and John R. McKivigan, eds. *The Frederick Douglass Papers, Series One: Speeches, Debates, and Interviews*. Vol. 5: 1881–95. New Haven: Yale University Press, 1992.

Blight, David W. *Race and Reunion: The Civil War in American Memory*. Cambridge, Mass.: Belknap Press of Harvard University Press, 2001.

Bogart, Ernest Ludlow, and Charles Manfred Thompson. *Centennial History of Illinois*. Vol. 4: *The Industrial State, 1870–1893*. Springfield: Illinois Centennial Commission, 1920.

Bracey, John H., August Meier, and Elliot Rudwick, eds. *Black Nationalism in America*. Indianapolis: Bobbs-Merrill, 1970.

Branham, Charles. "Black Chicago: Accommodationist Politics before the Great Migration." In *Ethnic Chicago*, ed. Melvin G. Holli and Peter d'A. Jones, 338–79. Grand Rapids, Mich.: Eerdman's, 1984.

———. "The Transformation of Black Political Leadership in Chicago, 1864–1942." PhD diss., University of Chicago, 1981.

Bridges, Roger D. "Equality Deferred: Civil Rights for Illinois Blacks, 1865–1885." *Journal of the Illinois State Historical Society* 74, no. 2 (Summer 1981): 82–108.

———. "James H. Magee: Triumph over Adversity." *Illinois History Teacher* 10, no. 1, (2003): 36–47.

Broderick, Francis L. "The Gnawing Dilemma: Separatism and Integration, 1865–1925." In *Key Issues in the Afro-American Experience*, edited by Nathan I. Higgins, Martin Kilson, and Daniel M. Fox, 93–104. New York: Harcourt Brace Jovanovich, 1971.

Buckler, Helen. *Doctor Dan: Pioneer in American Surgery*. Boston: Little, Brown, 1954.

Bunting III, Josiah. *Ulysses S. Grant*. New York: Times Books, 2004.

Calhoun, Charles W. *Conceiving a New Republic: The Republican Party and the Southern Question, 1869–1900*. Lawrence: University of Kansas Press, 2006.

Campbell, Ballard C. *Representative Democracy: Public Opinion and Midwestern Legislatures in the Late Nineteenth Century*. Cambridge, Mass.: Harvard University Press, 1980.

Cherny, Robert W. *American Politics in the Gilded Age, 1868–1900*. Wheeling, Ill.: Harlan Davidson, 1997.

Church, C. A. *History of the Republican Party in Illinois, 1854–1912*. Rockford, Ill.: Wilson Brothers, 1912.

Dale, Elizabeth. *The Rule of Justice: The People of Chicago versus Zephyr Davis*. Columbus: Ohio State University Press, 2001.

———. "'Social Equality Does Not Exist among Themselves, nor among Us': *Baylies vs. Curry* and Civil Rights in Chicago, 1888." *American Historical Review* 102, no. 2 (April 1997): 311–39.

Dillard, Irving. "Civil Liberties of Negroes in Illinois since 1865." *Journal of the Illinois State Historical Society* 41, no. 3 (Autumn 1963): 592–624.

Drake, St. Clair. *Churches and Voluntary Associations in the Chicago Negro Community*. Chicago: Works Projects Administration, 1940.

Drake, St. Clair, and Horace R. Cayton. *Black Metropolis: A Study of Negro Life in a Northern City*. New York: Harcourt, Brace, 1945.

Dummett, Clifton O., and Lois Doyle Dummett. *Charles Edwin Bentley: A Model for All Times.* St. Paul, Minn.: North Central Publishing, 1982.

Ecelbarger, Gary. *Black Jack Logan: An Extraordinary Life in Peace and War.* Guilford, Conn.: Lyons, 2005.

Einhorn, Robin. *Property Rules: Political Economy of Chicago, 1833–1872.* Chicago: University of Chicago Press, 1991.

Fishel, Leslie H. "The Negro in Northern Politics, 1870–1900." *Mississippi Valley Historical Review* 42 (1955): 466–89.

Fisher, Miles Mark. "The History of the Olivet Baptist Church of Chicago." Master's thesis, University of Chicago, June 1922.

Foner, Phillip S., and George E. Walker. *Proceedings of the Black National and State Conventions, 1865–1900.* Vol. 1. Philadelphia: Temple University Press, 1986.

———. *Proceedings of the Black State Conventions, 1840–1865.* Vol. 2. Philadelphia: Temple University Press, 1980.

Gatewood, Willard B. *Aristocrats of Color: The Black Elites, 1880–1920.* Fayetteville: University of Arkansas Press, 2000.

Gliozzo, John. "John Jones: A Study of a Black Chicagoan." *Illinois Historical Journal* 80, no. 3 (Autumn 1987): 177–88.

Goff, John S. *Robert Todd Lincoln: A Man in His Own Right.* Norman: University of Oklahoma Press, 1969.

Gordon, Ron, and John Paulett. *Printers Row Chicago.* Charleston, S.C.: Arcadia, 2003.

Gosnell, Harold F. *Negro Politicians: The Rise of Negro Politics in Chicago.* 3rd ed. Chicago: University of Chicago Press, 1969. Originally published in 1935.

Graham, Lawrence Otis. *The Senator and the Socialite: The True Story of America's First Black Dynasty.* New York: HarperCollins, 2006.

Grant, Bruce. *Fight for a City: The Story of the Union League Club of Chicago and Its Times, 1880–1955.* Chicago: John S. Swift, 1955.

Grossman, James R. *Land of Hope: Chicago, Black Southerners, and the Great Migration.* Chicago: University of Chicago Press, 1989.

Grossman, James R., Ann Durkin Keating, and Janice L. Reiff, eds. *The Encyclopedia of Chicago.* Chicago: University of Chicago Press, 2004.

Grossman, Lawrence. *The Democratic Party and the Negro: Northern and National Politics, 1868–92.* Urbana: University of Illinois Press, 1976.

Haynie, Kerry L. *African American Legislators in the American States.* New York: Columbia University Press, 2001.

Hill, Errol. "The Hyers Sisters: Pioneers in Black Musical Comedy." In *The American Stage,* edited by Ron Engle and Tice L. Miller. Cambridge: Cambridge University Press, 1993.

Holli, Melvin G., and Peter d'A. Jones. *Ethnic Chicago.* Grand Rapids, Mich.: Eerdman's, 1984.

Howard, Robert. *Mostly Good and Competent Men: Illinois Governors, 1818–1988.* Springfield: *Illinois Issues* and the Illinois State Historical Society, 1988.

Huggins, Nathan, Martin Kilson, and Daniel M. Fox, eds. *Key Issues in the Afro-American Experience.* New York: Harcourt Brace Jovanovich, 1971.

Jensen, Richard J. *The Winning of the Midwest: Social and Political Conflict, 1888–1896.* Chicago: University of Chicago Press, 1971.

Joens, David. "Ulysses S. Grant, Illinois, and the Election of 1880." *Journal of the Illinois State Historical Society* 97 (Winter 2004–5): 310–30.

Johnson, Claudius O. *Carter Henry Harrison I: Political Leader.* Chicago: University of Chicago Press, 1928.

Jones, Emil. *Know Your African-American Legislators: A Public Service Brochure.* Springfield: Illinois General Assembly Legislative Printing Unit, 1996.

Jones, James Pickett. *John A. Logan: Stalwart Republican from Illinois.* Tallahassee: University Press of Florida, 1982.

Katznelson, Ira. *Black Men, White Cities: Race, Politics, and Migration in the United States, 1900–1930, and Britain, 1948–1968.* Chicago: University of Chicago Press, 1976.

Keiser, John H. *Building for the Centuries: Illinois, 1865 to 1898.* Urbana: University of Illinois Press, 1977.

Kenney, David, and Robert Hartley. *An Uncertain Tradition: U.S. Senators from Illinois, 1818–2003.* Carbondale: Southern Illinois University Press, 2003.

Keyes, Jonathan J. "The Forgotten Fire." *Journal of the Chicago Historical Society* 26, no. 3 (Fall 1997): 52–65.

Kogan, Herman. *The First Century: The Chicago Bar Association, 1874–1974.* Chicago: Rand McNally, 1974.

Konvitz, Milton R. *A Century of Civil Rights Cases.* New York: Columbia University Press, 1961.

Kousser, J. Morgan. *The Shaping of Southern Politics: Suffrage Restriction and the Establishment of the One-Party South, 1880–1910.* New Haven, Yale University Press, 1974.

Kreiling, Albert Lee. "The Making of Racial Identities in the Black Press: A Cultural Analysis of Race Journalism in Chicago, 1878–1929." PhD diss., University of Illinois, 1973.

Lindberg, Richard C. *Chicago by Gaslight: A History of Chicago's Netherworld, 1880–1920.* Chicago: Academy Chicago, 1996.

———. *To Serve and Collect: Chicago Politics and Police Corruption from the Lager Beer Riot to the Summerdale Scandal, 1855–1960.* Carbondale: Southern Illinois University Press, 1991.

Litwack, Leon, and August Meier, eds. *Black Leaders of the Nineteenth Century.* Urbana: University of Illinois Press, 1991.

Logan, Rayford W. *The Negro in American Life and Thought.* New York: Dial , 1954.

Lowery, Charles D., and John F. Marszalek, eds. *Encyclopedia of African American Civil Rights from Emancipation to the Present.* New York: Greenwood, 1992.

Mahoney, Olivia. *Douglas/Grand Boulevard: A Chicago Neighborhood.* Chicago: Arcadia, 2001.

Martin, Waldo E. *The Mind of Frederick Douglass.* Chapel Hill: University of North Carolina Press, 1984.

McCaul, Robert L. *The Black Struggle for Public Schooling in Nineteenth-Century Illinois.* Carbondale: Southern Illinois University Press, 1987.

McMurry, Linda O. *To Keep the Waters Troubled: The Life of Ida B. Wells.* Oxford: Oxford University Press, 1998.

Meier, August. "The Negro and the Democratic Party, 1875–1915." *Phylon* 17, no. 2, (1956): 173–91.

———. *Negro Thought in America, 1880–1915: Racial Ideologies in the Age of Booker T. Washington.* Ann Arbor: University of Michigan Press, 1966.

Meier, August, and Rudwick, Elliott. *Along the Color Line: Explorations in the Black Experience*. Urbana: University of Illinois Press, 2002.

Merriner, James L. *Grafters and Goo Goos: Corruption and Reform in Chicago, 1833–2003*. Carbondale: Southern Illinois University Press, 2004.

Miller, Donald L. *City of the Century: The Epic of Chicago and the Making of America*. New York: Simon and Schuster, 1996.

Morris, Milton D. *The Politics of Black America: An Annotated Bibliography*. Carbondale: Public Affairs Research Bureau, Southern Illinois University, 1971.

Moses, John. *Illinois Historical and Statistical*. Chicago: Fergus, 1895.

Neilson, James W. *Shelby M. Cullom: Prairie State Republican*. Urbana: University of Illinois Press 1962.

Palmer, John M. *The Bench and Bar of Illinois*. Chicago: Lewis, 1899.

Penn, I. Garland. *The Afro-American Press and Its Editors*. Salem, N.H.: Ayer, 1988.

Philpott, Thomas Lee. *The Slum and the Ghetto: Neighborhood Deterioration and Middle-Class Reform, Chicago, 1880–1930*. New York: Oxford University Press, 1978.

Pierce, Bessie Louis. *A History of Chicago*. Vol. 3: *The Rise of a Modern City, 1871–1893*. Chicago: University of Chicago Press, 1957.

Plummer, Mark A. *Lincoln's Rail-Splitter: Governor Richard J. Oglesby*. Urbana: University of Illinois Press, 2001.

Portwood, Shirley J. "African-American Politics and Community in Cairo and Vicinity, 1863–1900." *Illinois History Teacher* 3, no. 2 (1996): 13–21.

Quarles, Benjamin. *Frederick Douglass*. New York: Da Capo, 1997.

Rather, Ernest R. *Chicago Negro Almanac and Reference Book*. Chicago: Chicago Negro Almanac, 1972.

Raum, Green B. *History of Illinois Republicanism*. Chicago: Rollins, 1900.

Redmond, Mary. *Mr. Speaker: Presiding Officers of the Illinois House of Representatives, 1818–1980*. Springfield: Office of the Speaker of the House, Illinois General Assembly, 1980.

Reed, Christopher Robert. *"All the World Is Here": The Black Presence at White City*. Bloomington: Indiana University Press, 2000.

———. *Black Chicago's First Century*. Vol. 1, 1833–1900. Columbia: University of Missouri Press, 2005.

Rehnquist, William H. *Centennial Crisis: The Disputed Election of 1876*. New York: Alfred A. Knopf, 2004.

Reynolds, John F., and Richard L. McCormick. "Outlawing 'Treachery': Split Tickets and Ballot Laws in New York and New Jersey, 1880–1910." *Journal of American History* 72 (1986): 835–58.

Richardson, Heather Cox. *The Death of Reconstruction: Race, Labor, and Politics in the Post–Civil War North, 1865–1901*. Cambridge, Mass.: Harvard University Press, 2001.

Schecter, Patricia A. *Ida B. Wells and American Reform, 1880–1930*. Chapel Hill: University of North Carolina Press, 2001.

Scott, R. Nathaniel. "What Price Freedom? John Jones: A Search for Negro Equality." Master's thesis, Southern Illinois University, 1971.

Simpson, Dick. *Rogues, Rebels, and Rubber Stamps: The Politics of the Chicago City Council from 1863 to the Present*. Boulder, Colo.: Westview, 2001.

Smith, Henry Justin. *Chicago: A Portrait*. New York: Century, 1931.

Smith, J. Clay. *Emancipation: The Making of the Black Lawyer, 1844–1944*. Philadelphia: University of Pennsylvania Press, 1993.

Smith, Jessie Carney, and Carrell Peterson Horton. *Historical Statistics of Black America*. New York: Gale Research, 1995.

Sorensen, Mark. "The Illinois State Capitol." In *Capitol Centennial Papers*, edited by Mark Sorensen. Springfield: Illinois Secretary of State's Office, 1982.

Spear, Allan H. *Black Chicago: The Making of a Negro Ghetto, 1890–1920*. Chicago: University of Chicago Press, 1967.

Stead, William. *If Christ Came to Chicago*. Chicago: Laird & Lee, 1894.

Styx, Sherrie. *Chicago Ward Maps, 1837–1970*. Eugene, Ore.: Styx Enterprises, 1988.

Tarr, Joel Arthur. *A Study in Boss Politics: William Lorimer of Chicago*. Urbana: University of Illinois Press, 1971.

Temple, Wayne C. "Alfred Henry Piquenard: Architect of Illinois' Sixth Capitol." In *Capitol Centennial Papers*, edited by Mark Sorensen. Springfield: Illinois Secretary of State's Office, 1982.

Thomas, Benjamin P. *Abraham Lincoln: A Biography*. New York: Modern Library, 1968.

Thornbrough, Emma Lou. *The Negro in Indiana: The Study of a Minority*. Indianapolis: Indiana Historical Bureau, 1957.———. *T. Thomas Fortune: Militant Journalist*. Chicago: University of Chicago Press, 1972.

Tingley, Donald F. *The Structuring of a State: The History of Illinois, 1899 to 1928*. Urbana: University of Illinois Press, 1980.

Travis, Dempsey J. *An Autobiography of Black Chicago*. Chicago: Urban Research Institute, 1981.

———. *An Autobiography of Black Politics*. Chicago: Urban Research Institute, 1987.

Walch, Victoria Irons. "Construction of the Capitol of Illinois, 1867–1888." Master's thesis, Northwestern University, 1979.

Wheaton, Elizabeth. *Myra Bradwell, First Woman Lawyer*. Greensboro, N.C.: Morgan Reynolds, 1997.

White, Jesse, ed. *Illinois Blue Book 2003–2004*. Springfield: Illinois Secretary of State's Office, 2004.

Willrich, Michael. *City of Courts: Socializing Justice in Progressive-Era Chicago*. New York: Cambridge University Press, 2003.

Wood, David Ward. *History of the Republican Party and Biographies of Its Supporters* [Illinois volume]. Chicago: Lincoln Engraving & Publishing, 1895.

Index

David A. Joens is the director of the Illinois State Archives and a former press secretary to the Illinois Senate Black Caucus.